Buy This Land

Chi-Dooh Li

ISBN: 978-1475060690

Cover design: Joel Markquart
Layout and editing: Peter Li
Cover photograph by Ira Lippke, used with permission from Agros
International

Scripture quotations taken from the New American Standard
Bible, Copyright © 1960, 1962, 1963, 1968, 1971, 1972, 1973, 1975, 1977,
1995 by The Lockman Foundation Used by permission.
(www.Lockman.org)

Photographs and additional information at www.BuyThisLandBook.com

To Cyd

Without whom the crazy dream could not have come true

And to Don Valencia

My co-conspirator in Agros from 1998-2007
who now dances in heaven

CONTENTS

I used to dream in my sleep, with eyes closed. Now I dream with my eyes open. It's much better to dream with your eyes open because you can do something about making those dreams come true.

Noemí López
Agros villager, San Diego de Tenango
El Salvador

He pled the cause of the afflicted and needy;
Then it was well.
Is not that what it means to know Me?
Declares the Lord.

Jeremiah 22:16

Si, pues.

An Ixil Indian response meant to indicate agreement,
but not really

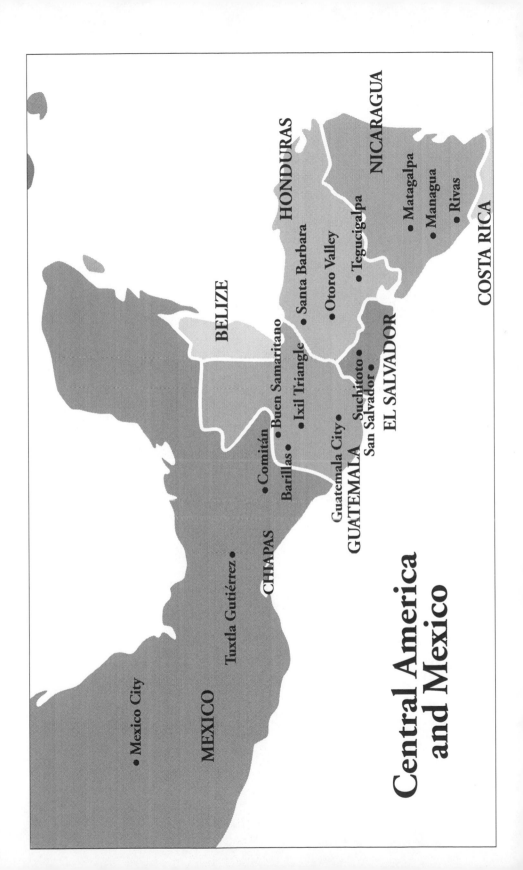

Central America and Mexico

INTRODUCTION

A Pan American Airways agent once asked me a question I couldn't answer.

I was on my way back to the U.S. from Guatemala and had just handed him my passport.

Agent: Mr. Li, this is very interesting.
Me: Why so?
Agent: Because you just handed me an American passport that says you were born in India. You're talking to me in Spanish, but you look Chinese. What are you, really? [1]

I told him I wasn't really sure, and we both had a good laugh.

That was almost 30 years ago. But today, as I sit down to write the story of Agros, I realize that brief encounter had more to say about Agros' story than I understood at the time.

There I was, a Chinese lawyer born in India with an American passport speaking Spanish, returning from a trip that

---

[1] *Agent*:   Señor Li, aquí tenemos algo muy interesante.
     Me: ¿Y porqué?
     Agent: Porque usted me ha dado un pasaporte Americano que dice que nació en la India. Ahora me está hablando en español, pero me parece que es Chino. ¿Y que es lo que es verdaderamente?

laid the foundation to buy land on behalf of Ixil Indians in Guatemala.

An unlikely story and an unlikely life.

Yet my life has seen so many unusual and improbable twists and turns. Had there been an extra turn here or one less twist there, Agros would not exist as a story to be told.

What is Agros?

From a seed of an idea first planted in 1982, it has blossomed today into a unique model of helping the poorest of the rural poor in Central America and Mexico to break the cycle of poverty. The centerpiece of the model is land ownership. Agros uses donated funds to buy land from private owners on behalf of people who otherwise would not have the means to purchase it themselves. With their harvests, they repay the cost of the land to Agros and receive titles to the property.

People who once worked as farm laborers or sharecroppers, barely able to subsist on their meager earnings, now have the opportunity to own the land they farm. In the process they regain the precious human dignity that was taken from them by generations of grinding poverty.

The statistical story makes good telling by itself:

- 42 villages in five countries
- 1,708 families in the 42 villages
- 1,600 small businesses owned by villagers
- 20 villages graduated (meaning everyone in those villages has successfully paid their land loans and received title to their land)
- 10 villages within two to three years of graduating
- 24,000 people who have directly benefitted from Agros' programs

Beyond numbers, the story gets even better.

- A whole generation of children who can now read and write, and can do math.
- Growing numbers of young people who have gone on to get university degrees, and even professional degrees.
- Many of the adults, formerly illiterate, are now able to read and write through adult literacy programs.
- Snow peas from villages in Guatemala and Nicaragua are exported and sold abroad, including at the upscale Marks and Spencer stores in the United Kingdom.
- Peppers from Nicaragua villages are exported and sold to the Tabasco Company.
- Premium coffee (shade-grown, high altitude, organic) from villages in Guatemala and Nicaragua are in high demand by roasters throughout the U.S.

Agros is also people.

In Central America and Mexico – families, widows, orphans – have been lifted out of oppressive cycles of abject poverty. They may not yet be seated with princes as envisaged by the Psalmist, but they most certainly have been raised from the dust and lifted out of the ash heaps.

In the Pacific Northwest, and increasingly in cities across the U.S., growing numbers of people have become friends of Agros villagers. Not only have they given generously in financial terms, but they have cared about the villagers, visited them, and encouraged them on their journey of hardship. Some have even worked alongside the villagers to help harvest crops, build their houses, or dig a trench to install water lines. These American friends include professionals, construction workers, students, retirees, and whole families. Their walls, desks, computer screens, and smart phones show countless photo images indicating that Agros is a huge part of their lives.

This book is my attempt to tell the highly unlikely, but undeniably grand story of Agros, and of the people who helped lay the foundation to make it what it is today. It is a story of God's tender mercies to the poor in Central America, and to the not so poor in North America. It is a story that speaks of the fulfillment of so many impossible dreams in the lives of the rural poor in Central America and Mexico.

And not least of all my own dreams.

1

BEGINNINGS

In February 1982 I was a 36-year old lawyer trying to earn a living and build a law firm in downtown Seattle. My wife Cyd and I lived on Mercer Island, an affluent island enclave in the middle of Lake Washington, connected on the west by a floating bridge to downtown Seattle, and on the east by another bridge to Bellevue. We had two children at home then – Peter (9) and Joseph (3) – and life read like a script for a typical young middle class family in suburban America. We were active at Mercer Island Covenant Church where I taught adult Sunday school classes, and Cyd taught in the children's program. We enjoyed playing tennis at a small neighborhood club and life seemed routine and unremarkable.

I had spent six years in Latin America as a young boy. Those years now seemed lost in a distant, foggy past. From time to time I wondered why God had given me a gift for languages, and particularly fluency in Spanish. It had been 20 years since I had lived in Latin America, and my work and personal life seemed to pull me away from involvement in the Spanish-speaking world. Seattle at that time was still considered a minor player in the field of international trade. Globalization had not been introduced to the language of business and commerce. There was no Internet to bring the rest of the world to our desks and phones. My Spanish was rusty and I struggled to remember ordinary vocabulary. I had more occasions to speak my native Chinese language with family, friends, and clients than Spanish.

The answer came to me, clear as a bell, one fateful afternoon, as I listened to an Argentinian preacher. He was speaking at a Mercer Island Covenant Church missions conference I did not want to attend. It was Cyd who insisted we go. We were members of MICC, and that's what members were expected to do, she said one Friday night after a long workweek – attend things like missions conferences.

Little did I know what a major turn my life would take that weekend. But before I can tell you what happened, I first have to tell you about the unusual road that got me there to begin with.

Early Years 1945 – 1950

My father, Li Chin, was a career diplomat for the Republic of China (ROC), now more commonly known as Taiwan. He was a young rising star in the Foreign Ministry at the time of my birth, and served then as the ROC's Consul General in Bombay.

Dad was a man of talents. Colleagues and strangers admired his Chinese calligraphy, and his brush-written scrolls still hang in people's homes as works of art. He had a knack for words, and how to string them together to make for interesting reading. Later in his life after he had retired in the U.S., he wrote a number of articles on life in America published by leading periodicals in Taiwan.

I am particularly grateful that he and my mother both had excellent ears – for music and for languages. The ability to discern the subtlest differences between pitch, inflections, tones, timbre, was a priceless gift passed down to me. It gave me a life-long love for great music – opera in particular, the ultimate intersection of music and language – and an ease for learning languages. It is a gift that has passed on to my children and grandchildren.

The facility for learning, understanding, and speaking languages also helped instill in me a love for different countries, cultures, and traditions. Language opened the doors for me to communicate with people at a direct level. The conversation I had in Spanish with the Pan Am airline agent in Guatemala was the kind of enriching experience that deepened my appreciation for a country and its people.

In fact, during my six-year sojourn in Latin America I found that for the expatriates I went to school with – English, Irish, German, and especially Americans – there was a very direct correlation between their ability to learn and speak Spanish and their ability to enjoy their expat experience. Kids who became fluent in the language loved being where they were; they entered into the life and culture of the country. The ones who did not or could not learn the language often resented being in a country where they had none of the familiar comforts of home.

Those six years I lived in Central and South America, from age 10 to 16, imprinted on my heart a love for the region, its people, language and culture. The marimba music of Guatemala still enchants me today. Rhythmic *merecumbés* of my teen years in Bogotá still flash through my mind, and I almost want to start dancing. I spend far too much time following *fútbol* – the real football, called soccer only in the US – and my competitive passions whip into a frenzy during the quadrennial World Cup.

But before I talk too much about Latin America and how those experiences shaped Agros years later, I have to go back even earlier to describe my more unlikely beginnings.

With unusual parents in an unusual occupation, my life took a significant turn by the time I was two. Without that turn, I would not be writing this story. The line between this present reality and what might have been is the slenderest of threads woven by a courageous child-snatching woman who refused to buckle to Chinese tradition.

I was 19 months old when my mother died at the very young age of 32. The cause of death was hypothyroids, a deadly disease then, an easily curable condition today. A little more than one year later my father remarried my stepmother Margaret, herself a young widow, and combined our two families (his three young sons and her two young daughters). I became the youngest of five siblings.

At that time my paternal grandfather, an imposing patriarch who had a brilliant legal career that culminated with serving as a Supreme Court justice in the nascent years of the Chinese Republic, played an important role. In early 1948, upon being informed that his soon-to-be-remarried son and his reconstituted family would be leaving China to take on his new post as ROC Consul General in Kuala Lumpur, Malaya (now Malaysia), Grandfather informed the family that Chi-Dooh, the baby, would not be going with the family.

He was fond of me and had plenty of help in the household, including a concubine, to care for me. My father and new stepmother had four other young children to care for, and in his alpha male judgment that would be more than a handful for a young woman like my stepmother. In the Chinese patriarchal culture of that day, Grandfather's decision was to be accepted and obeyed. No arguments or discussions were countenanced.

He had no idea what my new stepmother was made of.

She was born into a prominent Shanghai family. As a young woman she was admired for her beauty and courted persistently by legions of suitors before her first marriage and during her short widowhood. In the later years of the war with Japan she served in the Chinese underground in Shanghai, then occupied by Japanese forces that treated the Chinese population brutally. She received and sent messages via a wireless radio in the attic of her house. She then passed on messages to other underground members during strolls in the park with my stepsisters Lydia (born 1942) and Dora (1944). The messages were hidden under the girls in their pram. Other underground members would come upon Margaret, stop to dote over the lovely little baby girls, and take the notes hidden under the girls. These quick transactions often took place within plain view of vigilant Japanese soldiers.

The Japanese never uncovered her covert role during the long war that started for China in 1937. But she did lose a brother who was arrested and tortured by the Japanese for his underground activities. By the time of his release he was a shadow of a man, couldn't hold down any food given to him, and died shortly after being freed. She also lost her husband during that time, not to the Japanese, but to a deadly bacterial infection picked up after a swimming outing with friends.

This was my grandfather's new daughter-in-law. This was the woman whose ability to care for five young children in a foreign country he doubted. This was the young mother he expected would obey his edict about my staying with him without question.

Little did he know my stepmother had a plan for me – a plan she did not even disclose to my father, fearing that he would not be able to keep it secret in the face of my intimidating and authoritarian grandfather.

On July 5, 1948, the day the rest of the family was to leave Nanking for Shanghai, where they would board a ship that would take them to the Malay Peninsula, my stepmother insisted the family make a final visit to my grandfather to bid a fond farewell. With the cabs and luggage waiting at the front door, they entered the family compound, said their goodbyes, and at the last moment before exiting the house, my stepmother came to my room, whisked me up in her arms, took me out to join the family, and we were all off and gone. Instead of staying in Nanking with my grandfather, I left with the rest of my family that day.

When my incredulous grandfather discovered what had happened, he was understandably furious with his new daughter-in-law's blatant disobedience. It caused a breach of several decades between him and my stepmother.

But in that one instant my fate was forever, dramatically, changed.

Less than 18 months after my "kidnapping," all of mainland China fell under Communist rule, and the ROC government retreated to the island of Taiwan. The Bamboo Curtain went up in 1949 and was kept tightly sealed shut by a xenophobic Mao Tse-tung for 30 years. No travel was allowed into or out of China from the West. Chinese society and culture underwent intentional and traumatic upheaval, with untold and widespread physical and mental suffering especially during the periods of purges, including the crazed Red Guard era. I only have to look at what happened to my generation of cousins in China, and the enormous deprivation and suffering they endured, to understand what my life might have looked like if I had stayed in China with my grandfather.

For certain, I would not be writing this story.

The post-World War II years were a time of turmoil around the world. In Malaya, where Dad had been stationed, Communist guerrillas challenged the authority of colonial Britain. The mountains around Kuala Lumpur were lairs for the guerrillas. The British High Commissioner for Malaya sent troops to guard all diplomatic compounds. Our residence and the consular offices were in one building. A contingent of soldiers guarded the grounds, working out of a small guardhouse at the entrance to our driveway. As a young boy fascinated with soldiers and guns, I would visit the guardhouse as often as I was allowed, and played at bossing the soldiers around. They pretended to obey my commands and saluted me with a good-natured "Aye aye, Skipper."

The nickname "Skipper" stuck with me the rest of my life. It was shortened to "Skip" after I came to the U.S., where just about every name under the sun is somehow abbreviated.

The Communist takeover of China had produced a historic realignment in global geopolitics. The United Kingdom quickly granted diplomatic recognition to the new People's Republic of China (PRC), and broke off relations with the ROC. My father was informed by the British colonial government he must forthwith close the ROC consulate and leave Kuala Lumpur. Through intermediaries in the local Chinese community, the PRC government asked my father to switch his allegiance and keep the consulate open as the PRC Consulate.

A few of the consulate staff had already agreed to make the switch. When he found out about those staff people, my father took his loaded Colt revolver and ordered them out of the consulate at gunpoint. He made it clear to the PRC agents he would never go over to their side, and proceeded systematically to destroy all official documents and records at the consulate. He then invited the leaders of the local Chinese community to the consulate for a ceremonial closing of the consulate. In early January 1950, on a day long remembered by that generation of Chinese in Kuala Lumpur, he locked the consulate door behind him, lowered the ROC flag, and presented the keys and flag to the elders of the Chinese community.

The loss of mainland China to the Communists resulted in an interruption of my father's diplomatic career. The ROC government (also known as the Nationalists) retreated to Taiwan, but there was serious doubt whether they would survive a Communist attack on Taiwan.

My parents wondered where they might seek refuge for their young family of seven caught in the backwash of a major and historic geopolitical shift that radically changed the course of the world's most populous country. Diplomatically, we were *personae non gratae* in Malaya by order of the British government. Taiwan was threatened by imminent invasion by Communist Chinese troops. The Nationalist government was in disarray. Notwithstanding its own peril of extinction, the ROC government was prepared to risk all in an attempt to invade the mainland and retake the country.

President Harry Truman had declared that the U.S. would not intervene in the civil war on either side of the Taiwan Strait. Truman maintained this posture of neutrality until the outbreak of the Korean War in late June 1950. Recognizing by then that the Communist Chinese had aggressive intentions beyond mainland China, Truman ordered the U.S. Seventh Fleet to patrol the Taiwan straits to put an end to any intentions by the Communist Chinese to invade Taiwan, and also to kill any hopes of the ROC to re-cross the Straits and retake the mainland.

In those critical days for our family in late 1949 and early 1950, the enforced stability brought by the U.S. Seventh Fleet many months later was not a factor in the fateful decision my parents had to make. We were displaced persons, in the wrong place at the wrong time.

Amidst such enormous upheaval and uncertainty, help came from an unexpected source. In a personal act of great kindness, Sir Henry Gurney, the British High Commissioner for Malaya, made my father an offer on two fronts. The first was employment with the British government, helping Sir Henry on the thorny issues of the Communist guerrillas active in Malaya trying to overthrow the British colonial government. The second was permission, regardless of whether my father accepted the job offer, for our family to remain in Kuala Lumpur for as long as needed for my parents to sort out the family's very unsettled future.

Sir Henry was well aware of the terrible dilemma facing my father. The policy of his government dictated that our family depart Malaya immediately. Instead, he offered employment and the temporary refuge we needed until political events beyond our control had settled.[1]

At Sir Henry's orders, the Police Commissioner, Colonel Benjamin Shaw, rendered his personal assistance in helping us find temporary housing. Col. Shaw would eventually find us a house right next door to his own.

My father, a man deeply loyal to his own country, declined the offer of employment, and said he would, for the near future, await a summons from his government for resumption of his work in the foreign ministry. On June 25, 1950 – coincidentally the same day North Korean troops crossed the 38th parallel and invaded South Korea – my father flew to Taipei to meet with the foreign minister and find out whether there was a place for him in the reconstituted government on Taiwan. He was told that things were unsettled, and that he should wait until the foreign minister could get things worked out. He returned, deeply disappointed, to Kuala Lumpur.

At this point another unexpected kindness came from the Australian High Commissioner in Malaya, James McIntyre, offering our whole family "exemption" entry permits to live in Australia. Australia's race-conscious policies in that era under the Immigration Act 1901-1949 did not permit anyone of Chinese descent to enter the country as an immigrant. Our "exemption certificates" were good for 12 months, presumably renewable as

---

[1] Tragically, Sir Henry was assassinated by Malay Communist guerrillas in October 1951. His car was ambushed and he was shot to death. He was 51. Historical accounts of the assassination quote Mrs. Gurney as saying that her husband was shot while trying to protect her and the driver. Sir Henry's tombstone in the Cheras Christian Cemetery in Kuala Lumpur is inscribed with this passage from chapter 15 of the Gospel of John:

Greater Love Hath No Man Than This
That A Man Lay Down His Life for His Friends

well.[2] My parents took up his offer, and we shortly embarked for Australia.

Sydney 1950 – 1953

Arriving as refugees in Australia, our family faced hardships of which, being just short of age five, I was blissfully unaware. My father, a scholarly 41-year old unemployed Chinese diplomat, had no employable skills. His life up to that point required him to use his mind, his speech, and his social skills. He had never worked with his hands. He was at a loss with a leaky faucet or a broken windowpane. He hardly knew how to drive a car, since driving was always left up to chauffeurs. His young wife, still in her late 20s, herded around five energetic children ages five to thirteen. We were strangers in a foreign land, and he had no prospects for earning a living. This was a time of despair, and as I found out later, Dad wept and cried out to God when he was alone.

God answered, in the form of an angel – a man named Daniel Chen who was an ethnic Chinese businessman in Sydney. Mr. Chen stepped in like a godfather and helped us buy a modest brick house in the working class neighborhood of Homebush – today an area covered with tall buildings and remnant structures from the 2000 Olympic Games.

He also gave my father credit to obtain the inventory needed to start a small retail fabric and sewing shop. The result of that business venture was predictable: it was a complete failure. My father knew nothing about fabrics and sewing, and completely

---

[2] One of my most treasured and meaningful keepsakes from this era is a Certificate of Exemption issued by the Commonwealth of Australia dated December 6, 1951, issued to "Li Chi Dooh...age 6...Occupation: Student." This was the renewal of the original Certificate of Exemption obtained for us by James McIntyre. The renewal was good for 84 months.

lacked the disposition of a retail shopkeeper. The shop closed down, but my stepmother stepped in, took over the business, and became a traveling saleswoman. Every day she loaded up a suitcase full of fabrics and lace trimmings, stationed herself outside factories that employed a lot of women, and sold her wares to those women during their lunchtime and work breaks. My father stayed home with us children. At the end of the day my mother would call from the Homebush train station, and he would rush down to the station to greet her and carry her suitcase home.

I began my schooling in Sydney, entering kindergarten at the Homebush Primary School. My sisters and I were the only non-whites in the school. My brothers were enrolled in an all-boys school in another part of Sydney. We wore uniforms to school — a practice that eliminated, for the most part, the visible tokens of economic disparities between the children. But the racial divide could not be hidden. I was too young to understand issues of race in post-war Australia, or to make much of the fact that I was different from the other children in this respect, but I do remember to this day the racial taunts from school bullies.

One year into the Sydney experience my father was invited to a gathering of overseas Chinese in Taipei, and while there, was offered the opportunity to resume his career in the foreign ministry. He took it. In another two years, when it appeared to him that the military and political situation in Taiwan had stabilized enough, he sent for my mother, my sisters, and me to join him in Taipei. We left Sydney for Taipei in October 1953.

We left my two older brothers in Sydney to continue their secondary education. My parents' fateful decision to leave them behind was devastating to Richard, then just 15, and Bob, who was only 11 at the time. The feeling of abandonment must have penetrated to the deepest levels of their souls, no matter how my parents explained their reasons. The major consideration was to avoid the possibility of one or both of my brothers being drafted into the ROC army if they returned to Taiwan. The ROC government maintained a large standing army to defend against possible attack by the Mainland Communists, and also to keep alive the dream of recovering the Mainland. Even boys in their early teens, not yet of draft age, were prohibited from traveling abroad in order that they not evade the draft.

As rational as their thinking might have been, the enormous tragedy of the decision came to me many years later when I thought about my own children. What would Cyd and I have done under those circumstances? How would Peter, Joseph, or Kara have reacted to our leaving them behind at ages 15 and 11 in a foreign country to fend for themselves in every aspect of their lives? Consider, too, that in 1953 international long distance telephone calls were prohibitively expensive, and that the only communication possible was through written letters that took close to two weeks to travel between Sydney and Taipei.

As our ship moved away from dockside in Sydney harbor, my young heart broke as I looked from the ship's deck at my brothers waving goodbye from the shore. The streamers in our hands that connected us soon broke too, a fitting symbol of the unnatural and horrible separation that would divide our family. The image of Richard and Bob waving to us is indelibly printed in my memory and fills me to this day with sorrow.

Other than this extremely painful parting, I retain positive memories of our Australia experience. There was so much for which to be thankful: the open-handed generosity of Daniel Chen in helping us make a living; the random kindness of Australian strangers on the street who gave us directions when we were lost; and the friendly gestures of our Homebush neighbors, helping an uprooted immigrant family so out of place in so many respects.

The wholesale disruption of our lives by a civil war and our migration as refugees to a new and strange land would foreshadow my future life – intertwined with refugees elsewhere in the world whose lives were shattered even more devastatingly by civil war. Those early childhood impressions in Sydney are deeply engrained in me. The notion of what a life-changing difference strangers or friends could make by lending a hand to a family in dire straits became woven into the fabric of my life and thinking.

Taipei 1956 – 1959

The Taipei we encountered in 1956 bears no resemblance to the vibrant, pulsating city of high-rises and traffic congestion today. Automobiles were not ubiquitous. People relied on bicycles, pedicabs, and buses to get around. Drive in any direction for more than five minutes, and you were likely to come across rice paddies with water buffaloes pulling plows along semi-submerged rows.

The city had a siege mentality to it. The country was still at war with daily artillery duels between the Communist garrisons in Xiamen and Nationalist troops on Quemoy and Matsu islands. We felt under constant threat of bombing attacks from across the Straits of Taiwan. There were air battles as well. I vividly remember the headlines in newspapers proclaiming the number of Communist Chinese MiG jets shot down by our Nationalist F-84's and F-86's. Patriotic slogans were everywhere, mostly exhorting "*Fan Gung Da Lu*" – the Chinese words for "Re-take the Mainland." The sounds of air-raid sirens across the city are etched in my sonic memory bank.

Taipei had very few foreign residents or visitors. Other than U.S. military advisory or diplomatic types, no foreigners traveled to Taiwan. Tourism was non-existent. It was too dangerous. The no-holds barred entrepreneurial side of the Chinese psyche that is so evident today had not yet shown itself on an island obsessed with nation survival. Nation building would come later. Every so often you would see a crowd gather around a car parked in downtown Taipei. As often as not, it meant there were foreigners in the car – most likely American. People would stand and gawk at whoever was inside. I sometimes felt bad for the few foreigners who ventured to walk around the shopping district or the food markets. Not only would people gather in throngs around them, but some would reach out and touch their skin or their hair. There was not the slightest intention to harass the foreigners – it was simply a mixture of ignorant curiosity and wonderment to see a non-Chinese person in that era.

Our home was in a neighborhood with no paved roads. Open sewage ditches ran alongside the streets and the stench filled the air. Water came to our house sporadically, so when it did, we stored it in the bathtub of our only bathroom, and bathed by ladling out the cold water from the tub (there were no hot showers). Drinking water had to be boiled first, and even after it was boiled, it looked like it had foreign "stuff" in it. The toilet – pit style – was in a tiny adjacent space, while the kitchen was outside in a separate structure. The stove was rudimentary and burned coal. Refrigeration consisted of an icebox with a large block of ice obtained from a man who came by every few days pulling his delivery cart behind him.

At first I slept with my parents in their bed in the house's single bedroom while my sisters slept on the floor of the dining area. After a few months I graduated to my own sleeping space on a ledge in one corner of the living room. I remember trying to sleep with the sound of conversation and laughter from dinner guests who lingered late into the night. After a while we got used to the cockroaches and rats. The mosquitoes were more bothersome. We slept in enclosed mosquito netting (which could get stifling in hot weather), and at night we burned mosquito-repelling coils that emitted a distinct, but not-unpleasant aroma.

Third grade in a Chinese school with no English spoken was a major challenge. Up to then our schooling had been in English, and although we had spoken Chinese at home, we had not yet learned to read and write in Chinese. My stepmother – the one who had snatched me from my grandfather's home in China – embarked on a major and tireless effort to catch the three of us up every evening after school. My sisters and I would sit at the round dining table, each doing our homework, while my mother went from one to the other helping us learn a written language that had none of the phonetic characteristics of English or the Latin-based languages.

My experience was unlike what American children face in any of the site-specific language immersion programs popular in school districts in the U.S. today. There was no reverting to English – because absolutely no one around us spoke English. It was like being told how to swim, then being tossed in the middle of a lake and directed to swim to shore or drown. Somehow, all three of us made it to shore.

By the end of the first school year I had caught up with my classmates. I loved and excelled in brush calligraphy, perhaps because it was something in which Dad took great interest. I also took real delight in preparing the ink – getting out my inkstand, placing just the right amount of water on the three by four-inch smooth surface, taking my ink-stick and grinding the one edge gently until the water turned to thick, black, aromatic ink suitable for the brush. Too thin, and the ink ran on the thin calligraphy paper; too thick, and you just wasted your time. Besides, the ink would eventually evaporate unless you used it right away, so too much grinding meant you had less ink. It was an art in itself, getting the ink just right. Then you experienced the pleasure of running your brush through the ink, and beginning your writing exercise with ink ground to perfect consistency.

We learned the art of *"shiao-kai"* and *"da-kai"* – small characters and large characters. We were required to do pages of both for homework and in class. The teacher examined the brush writing, and circled in red the characters that were noteworthy. The satisfaction of seeing those red circles all over my submissions gave intense satisfaction to this 10-year old kid. There was one particular character *"wei"* (roughly translated "for" or "because" in English) I had mastered. It seemed like I could always count on a red circle for that character. Thus I came to excel in *da-kai* and won awards in school calligraphy contests. The winning calligraphy samples were posted prominently around the school, much like drawn or painted pictures are displayed in our U.S. schools today.

For the masters, calligraphy is a spiritual exercise as much as it is a discipline and art. It requires daily practice to maintain excellence. A lapse of a few days occasionally might not hurt, but inconsistent practice shows up on the page and is easily discernible to the trained eye. In this sense, calligraphy and classical music bear close resemblance. No matter how gifted, a musician who does not practice consistently might be able to fool most of the people in an audience most of the time, but a trained ear will immediately detect flaws in technique and execution.

Dad was a true artist of a calligrapher. Until he began descending into dementia very late in his long life, he awoke before sunrise each morning, and devoted himself to 30-60 minutes of calligraphy. Most people would love to frame and hang his daily practice calligraphy. Yet he tossed each day's output in the wastebasket. Only if asked to do calligraphy as a gift would he get out his expensive scroll paper, prepare his ink, write the characters out in pen on note paper (usually something poetic or a wise adage), then set to the task of doing the calligraphy. I marveled during the times I watched him – I don't ever remember re-do's. His first effort would be it. A masterpiece in its own right.

When Dad died in 2002 at age 93 I inherited all his calligraphy tools and paraphernalia – brushes, inkstands, ink sticks, scroll paper, and books of calligraphy samples from revered Chinese calligraphers over 2,500+ years. At various times over the years I tried to resume the discipline myself, but like so many good intentions, was never been able to maintain a consistent effort.

In early 1956 Dad informed us one night of his new overseas posting. I was old enough to understand that his then current job as director of East Asian affairs in the Foreign Ministry would probably mean an assignment somewhere in Asia. We were surprised to hear instead that he was to be the head of the mission in Guatemala, a country we did not know existed. He explained it was a small country in Central America, and told us the little he knew about it. For whatever reason, I fixated on something he said which led me to believe there would be a lot of chicken to eat in Guatemala. That, in my 10-year old mind, sounded really cool.

A few days later Dad brought home a borrowed record player and a set of Berlitz Spanish language instruction records. I clearly remember the beginning dialogue on the first record in the set:

Yo deseo.
¿Que desea usted?
Yo deseo hablar español.

Each phrase was followed by a pause to allow you to repeat what had just been said. I'm not sure how many hours we spent listening to those records, or how many of them we actually worked our way through. We would discover later, on arriving in Guatemala, that our comprehension was practically nil.

Dad left for Guatemala on his own, flying the Pan American international routes, while my mother, my sisters and I took the slow route by ship from Keelung, Taiwan, to Hong Kong. We remained in Hong Kong for about a week, going on endless shopping trips for furniture, household goods, and all the other things it took to set up a diplomatic residence in Guatemala. My mother was an extremely particular and patient shopper, which made those shopping forays a nightmarish experience for a young, restless boy. To this day I have an aversion to shopping that dates back, I believe, to those few days in Hong Kong.

We stayed with some wealthy family friends who lived on Victoria Peak with an expansive and magical view of Hong Kong harbor. The view was spectacular at night with the lights from both the shore and the hundreds of small vessels shimmering off the waters of the harbor. Imagine my excitement at dusk one early evening when I caught sight of the President Cleveland passenger liner cruising into the harbor. This was to be our home for the next two weeks as we crossed the Pacific to San Francisco, with stops in Yokohama, Kobe, and Honolulu.

Those two delicious weeks at sea were pure heaven for me. I stood on deck and watched the waves endlessly, catching glimpses of flying fish and occasional dolphins, and tossed crumbs to the seagulls that always trailed the ship. I seemed to have a built-in gyroscope that let me enjoy the entire time even in midst of storms that made the ship pitch from end to end. The only hitch during that trip was when I nearly drowned. I had been tossed unceremoniously into the ship's swimming pool, all in good fun, for the King Neptune festival, a celebration of the ship crossing the International Date Line. My tossers didn't know I couldn't swim. I was rescued after going down a couple of times and surfacing, gasping for air. I think people chalked that experience up to the normal stuff a young boy goes through in life – but it terrified me. The ship finally arrived in San Francisco, coming under the Golden Gate Bridge. The Chinese named this great city "Gold Mountain," where so many thousands of their early immigrant rail-workers began their lives in America. Now I was to set foot in the country that would become my home six years later.

From San Francisco we flew to Los Angeles, and then to Guatemala City. We dressed in our best clothes for those flights. Even at age 10 I wore a suit and tie. Flying was a very big deal back then – someone dressed in the jeans/sweatpants/shorts plus T-shirt fashion of today's travel would probably have been kicked off the flight before takeoff.

Guatemala 1956 – 1959

Guatemala in 1956 was a peaceful country ruled by dictator Col. Carlos Castillo Armas. We took a Pan American DC-6 into La Aurora airport in Guatemala City, nestled in a mountain valley at a 5,200 feet elevation. One side of the airport's sole landing strip was for civilian use, the other for military. I recall seeing P-51 Mustangs parked on the military side, the pride of the Guatemalan air force. The World War II vintage fighters remain in use today and can still be seen sometimes at the airport joined by a couple of Israeli-built cargo aircraft used during the Guatemalan civil war. The city was then clean and uncluttered, with lovely boulevards lined with trees and flowering plants of the most vividly brilliant colors everywhere.

We stepped out of the plane onto a ramp at the rear door of the aircraft. I looked across the tarmac and saw my father on the second-story balcony, an area designed to allow family and friends to greet or bid farewell with waves and shouts. A welcoming committee of sorts accompanied my father – his staff and some of the local Chinese residents.

The ROC diplomatic presence in Guatemala was in the form of a legation – headed by my father as "Minister

Plenipotentiary," a diplomatic rank no longer in use today. Back then it represented one level lower than an ambassador. We were driven to the legation in the official car, a black 1955 or 1956 Ford Fairlane with the wide whitewall tires then in fashion. I was impressed that the diplomatic license plates had an image of the Chinese flag on it.

I wish I had kept a diary and recorded my first and juvenile impressions of arriving in that strange, new land with its completely different sights, smells, and sounds. As a wide-eyed 10-year old boy, I was filled with excitement at the very idea of traveling halfway around the world to live in Central America.

The offices of the legation and our residence were in the same building, a Spanish colonial one-level structure in Zone 1, the center of town. The streets were old cobblestone and the surrounding buildings all looked to be at least 200 years old. Our building was built in the shape of a lengthy rectangle with one long side a common wall, front and back square-shaped open-air courtyards, and rooms built around the courtyards on the three other sides. The front courtyard had a fountain that became our live goldfish tank. The rooms surrounding the front courtyard were used by the legation as offices and reception room. The back half of the house was our residence. A set of stairs ascended to the roof at the rear of the building where two rooms had been built. I found out later that one of the rooms stored urns containing the ashes of deceased local Chinese residents who wanted to be buried in their ancestral hometowns in China. Since China was by now tightly shut from travel, they died hoping for the future possibility of their families returning to their places of birth to carry out the burial ritual.

I am glad I did not know about the ash-urns until we had moved to Zone 9 a year later. As it was, the structure was old enough to conjure plenty of dark corners and nooks to spook a young boy with a lively imagination. The noises from the crawl spaces above the ceilings were particularly eerie. They sometimes sounded like someone walking or moving around. We were told the noise came from rats doing their thing, but my mind, of course, only partially accepted that explanation. I was much more inclined to think of ghosts haunting the house. The Chinese culture is a story-telling culture, and a favorite genre told by adults to children when I was growing up was ghost stories. Some of these, if properly told with the right dramatic voice tones, would scare the living daylights out of you. The scariest ones were hard to forget, and at night when I tried to sleep, and the rats (or whatever) did their business above, I would bury my head under sheets and blankets to hide myself from the ghosts in my mind.

My sisters and I were promptly enrolled in the English-American School in Guatemala City. The school was recommended to my parents by a wealthy local Chinese businessman, Mr. Harry Liang, whose own children were enrolled there. He had a son, Ronny, who was my age, so it seemed a good fit.

The school was located downtown, boys and girls in separate buildings. We boys were in a large Spanish colonial style house with a central courtyard bordered by broad aisles and classrooms lined along the three sides of the U-shaped building. The first day of classes in the 6th grade, I discovered with some discomfort that the school was neither English nor American. No English was spoken. All classes were taught in Spanish. I hung close to Ronny those first few days – Ronny spoke about as much English as I spoke Spanish, which was nil. He was a friendly sort, and he had a lot of pocket money for a kid at that age. He was not a particularly good friend to me in those difficult early days; I think I was an encumbrance to him and his circle of friends.

It wasn't long before I was introduced to the world of fistfights. Some of the boys would taunt me, and even though I couldn't understand what they were saying all the time, I eventually got fed up with their teasing – "chinito" this and "chinito" that. One day during recess I erupted when the class bully, a boy named Gustavo, touched my cheek (a young macho insult). I slapped his hand away, and next thing I knew, we were at each other with fists. I remember Gustavo being a big and unusually "buff" kid – I think he was a year or two older than most of us. In the Guatemala educational system at that time, a kid could flunk an elementary grade and be made to repeat that year. Gustavo had probably flunked a couple of times by the time he was in 6th grade.

I wish I could say I beat Gustavo in that fight. I did not. I had gotten into tussles with other kids at school in Sydney and Taipei, but this was my first fight with fists, and I had no idea how to hit another person or defend myself. But before Gustavo could do too much damage to me, a teacher broke up the fight and hauled us off to headmaster Don Augusto's office. We endured a tongue-lashing from him (which I did not understand at all) and for punishment, were required to stand outside Don Augusto's office for half an hour after school, facing the courtyard, rigid and forbidden to move.

I may not have landed any blows in the fight, but after that the taunting and teasing stopped. Gustavo even made an effort to be friendly from then on.

The fight also gave me incentive to take up a bit of boxing with another friend, Juanci Lee, the son of legation staffer Enrique Lee. Juanci had two pairs of boxing gloves, and we imagined ourselves as Floyd Patterson (him) and Ingemar Johansson (me). Patterson and Johansson had a couple of great world heavyweight championship bouts during that time. Juanci was a couple of years older than me and taller too, so he had a longer reach. My one and only tactical move was to hide my face in my gloves and charge in so I could land some blows. He landed most of them, and one to my jaw just about knocked me out. When I fell to the ground I half-hoped to see tweetie-birds flying around my head the way they did in comics and cartoons of that era.

Thankfully I learned Spanish quickly and the early days were more laughable than painful. Don Augusto doubled as the geography teacher. His style of teaching was 100% lecture, and we were all required to take notes as he droned on and on. He had a way of walking up and down the aisles with a yardstick in his hand and would hit your knuckles or your thigh with the yardstick if he caught you not paying attention or whispering to your neighbor.

In those first weeks of school when I understood next to nothing of his lectures, he enjoyed pausing next to my desk to look over my shoulder to see what I was writing, which was plainly gibberish. I struggled to write down what I thought he was saying phonetically. He would get a good chuckle out of my notes and move on. I understood better when he would use the yardstick to point to countries, mountains, or bodies of water on the large map on the wall of the classroom. It allowed me to catch important place names, and I can still hear him enunciating in his deep baritone voice places like *"el mar Adriático"* or *"la isla de Japón."*

Early in our sojourn in Guatemala I discovered the world of classical music, which became a life-long passion. It began with hearing Johann Strauss waltzes over the radio. I was 11 at the time and didn't think I had ever heard anything so beautiful. The music filled the depths of my young soul with a longing I could not describe. I'm still not sure I can describe it today, so many years later, as Strauss opened the door to Bach, Beethoven, Mozart, Schubert, Verdi, Donizetti, and the vast treasury of great and enduring instrumental and vocal works.

After a year living in Zone 1 – the central area of town – we moved out to Zone 9 on Séptima Avenida, a residential district. In my mind, we had arrived in the lap of luxury. The house sat high above a beautifully terraced garden. The backyard also had a swimming pool, albeit a very small one, and I had a small bedroom to myself overlooking the front yard. Compared to my sleeping spaces in Taipei and the shared bedroom with my sisters in Zone 1, this new house and my bedroom felt positively palatial.[3]

Our move to that wonderful house also coincided with a transfer to a new school – the Colegio Americano, located in suburban Zone 10. This school had a nice campus, and best of all, a real soccer field with goal posts. The English-American School we left had students from primarily the Guatemalan middle and upper middle class; the American school had upper class Guatemalans (translate very wealthy), and expatriate kids, many of them Americans whose fathers were diplomats or businessmen.

In contrast to the English-American School, the teachers at Colegio Americano were a conglomeration of multiple nationalities, primarily Guatemalans and Americans. English was actually spoken there, and classes were taught in both Spanish and English, depending on the nationality of the teacher.

---

[3] Twenty-five years later in 1982 and 1983 when I began traveling regularly to Guatemala, I saw the house often from a distance. It looked much, much smaller than I had remembered. Early one afternoon I took advantage of a window of free time and walked three long blocks from the Camino Real Hotel, where I was staying, to our old house. The terraced front yard of the 1950s had been paved over as a driveway, and I discovered it was now used as a medical office. I asked the receptionist if I could take a look around, telling her this was where I had lived as a child. Everything was indeed much smaller than I had pictured in my mind all those years. The pool was no more – it had been paved over with concrete. I didn't ask to see the upstairs where my bedroom had overlooked the front of the house. Perhaps it was the letdown of seeing the house as it really was, a very modest residential dwelling on a rather small lot. In later years, the house became a restaurant, a rather seedy one at that. I didn't have the heart to go there to eat – it felt sacrilegious that the first dream house of my youth had been put to such pedestrian use. Today the house is no longer there, displaced by a large office/apartment building, with a McDonald's restaurant across the street. Needless to say, the area is no longer single-family residential.

It was here that I picked up my passion for *fútbol* – what Americans call soccer. The school had an active intramurals program, so I joined one of the teams. I think I was one of the last chosen in the "draft" process, since I was a rookie to the sport, where many of my classmates had played all through their childhood. One of my classmates was amazingly skilled at age 12; he could juggle the ball indefinitely standing still or on the move, using both feet, thighs, chest and head, and could shoot and pass with equal power and skill with either left or right foot. He could curl the ball inside or outside, and was a scoring machine at the striker position. His shots on goal were things of beauty – always, it seemed, low and rising toward one of the upper corners where no goalie could touch it. I was in awe of him and wondered years later whether he played professionally or even for the Guatemalan national team.

I bought my first pair of soccer shoes back then, and ignorantly picked a pair with high, hard toes, thinking this would help me kick better. As any soccer player knows today, you need the contoured, soft toes to control the ball and shoot and pass properly. In fact, I think they stopped making hard-toed soccer shoes many years ago, probably right after I bought mine.

By my second year at Colegio Americano, I had made the school team. I was so proud to wear the school jersey – a red shirt with white collar and a white diagonal sash across the chest. In the first game of the season I got lucky on a corner kick and scored a goal. Our captain/coach, a 12th grader who looked and played like a fully grown man, thought I must be far better than I knew I was and moved me up to a forward position, expecting to get more scoring from me. He was to be sorely disappointed and as the season progressed, I found myself first moved back to midfield, then to the defense, then to being a substitute. That first-game goal was the only one I scored all season.

It was also in Guatemala that I first discovered and fell in love with baseball – by way of shortwave radio. In the 1950s many radios were sold with multiple bands, including several shortwave bands. I enjoyed "surfing" through those bands, picking up transmissions from all around the world in exotic and incomprehensible languages, but as often coming upon English programs from the BBC or the Voice of America. One day I picked up the U.S. Armed Forces Radio network which broadcast major league baseball games at various times of the day, and I was riveted by the descriptions and sounds of the game. I have no memory of which teams were playing in that first game I listened to, but it didn't matter. Here was a live baseball game being broadcast from the U.S., and I was listening to it! Of course, the shortwave signal would come and fade randomly, and I remember many critical moments when the announcer's excited voice would suddenly fade into an unknown universe of static. Sometimes you couldn't tell whether you were listening to static or the roar of the crowd on a particularly big play. I had no idea then that he would become a legend in his own time, but I know I listened to Vin Scully describe Dodgers games in that smooth and inimitable way of his.

My defining baseball fan moment as a young boy was when I picked up the 1957 Milwaukee Braves – New York Yankees World Series games. I had by this time become a voracious reader of *Time* and *Life* Magazines – my dad subscribed to them – and I developed an intense interest in American politics and culture as depicted in those publications. I knew enough about the teams from my reading to form a juvenile impression that the New York Yankees were the rich bullies who always seemed to pick on the little guys like the Kansas City Athletics and steal their best players. I rooted for the underdog Braves.

In Guatemala I had my first encounter with the Christian faith. My parents thought it would be good for my sisters and me to know something about Christianity – I'm not sure why –

so they arranged for us to be instructed in the faith by the minister at the Union Church, a non-denominational Protestant church in Zone 9 attended primarily by expat Americans and other foreigners. The services were conducted in English and few Guatemalans attended. In the 1950s Guatemala was overwhelmingly Roman Catholic. I remember going to a few church services but retain no memory of anything that was said or sung in those services. Nor do I remember anything from our private sessions with the minister. In fact, he made no impression on me at all, which can either be chalked up to my total immaturity (most probably) or to his ineffective instruction.

The Union Church had a troop of Boy Scouts of America, and I signed up for scouting. I rather liked the uniform, the badges, and the U.S. Navy style caps. I was sworn in as a tenderfoot, pledging allegiance to the flag of the United States of America as a young Chinese boy living in Guatemala. The words meant nothing to me. I was a failure as a scout; in my one year I managed to get no merit badges and did not move past the tenderfoot ranking. I do retain today a long-cherished possession from that experience: an official Boy Scout pocket knife with the scouting insignia on the handle.

Within a year of our stay in Guatemala, President Carlos Castillo Armas was assassinated by one of his bodyguards on the steps of the presidential palace. Castillo had come to power through a rightist military junta in 1954 after a *coup d'état* against then leftist president Jacobo Árbenz Guzmán. The 1954 coup sowed the seeds of the long civil war between the political left and right that would tear the country apart from 1960 to 1996. After the assassination the streets of the city were filled with tension. Our Zone 1 house was not far from the presidential palace, and soldiers were everywhere. A military *junta* took over, and ruled until early 1958 when General Miguel Ydígoras Fuentes assumed sole control as president.

About a year into Ydígoras' presidency he was invited for an official luncheon at our Zone 9 residence. The lunch was scheduled for 1:00 p.m., but in typical Guatemalan custom the time meant nothing. The common joke was that the new British Ambassador, accustomed to punctuality, once arrived at a cocktail party at the scheduled hour of 7:00 p.m. only to find out that the Guatemalan host and hostess had not even begun to dress for their own party.

On the occasion of the luncheon, the president's security detail began showing up shortly after 1:00 p.m. to inspect the premises. They stationed people at strategic points around our home. Several guards were posted high on our flat rooftop. This was exciting stuff for me. By about three o'clock some of the other guests began arriving. The president finally made his appearance shortly after four o'clock. I remember nothing about the food or guests, but I do recall very clearly the moment when I was called to meet the president, and shook hands with him. I thought he actually looked a bit like the pictures I had seen in *Time* and *Life* of General Douglas MacArthur.

During our first year in Guatemala, Richard and Bob, both of whom had graduated from high school in Sydney (Richard had actually already started university), made the long trip by passenger liner from Sydney to the Guatemalan port of San José where we greeted them and brought them back to the city. It was a time of great excitement for me to be reunited with my big brothers. I had come to idolize them from a distance during the four years they were separated from the family, and now I was able to enjoy their company in person. They stayed with us about two months before continuing with their trip to the U.S. and to Seattle where both had been accepted at the University of Washington.

Their decision to apply for admission at Washington was guided by my father and turned out to be one of the great providential interventions of God in the life of our family.

As a young man Dad had been handpicked by President Chiang Kai-shek to become a member of the first class in the new National Chengchi University in Nanking (also known as the Central Political Institute), founded by President Chiang to train future government officials and diplomats. In the early 1930s Dr. George Taylor taught as a visiting professor at that university in Nanking. Taylor was a patrician-type Englishman, a professor in the East Asian department at the University of Washington. He chaired the department at UW for many years, and was a preeminent China scholar.

Twenty-some years after Dr. Taylor taught in China, when my brothers corresponded with Dad about their university education, Dad urged them to go to the UW, thinking that his professor from many years back might be able to give them a helping hand in that new environment.[4] It was my parents' dream for all of us children to go the U.S. for our university education. Richard and Bob would be the first ones to act on that dream.

My brothers made their way to Seattle to begin their studies at the University of Washington in the fall of 1956. Their letters to us describing their new life in the U.S. made for wonderful reading. I enjoyed their descriptions of college life, the friends

---

[4] My brothers tell me that Dr. Taylor took no interest in them after their arrival and attempts to contact him. I had a personal experience with George Taylor that confirmed his lack of interest. In the late 1980s I attended a China Relations Council luncheon in Seattle and by chance sat next to Dr. Taylor. Here was the man I had heard my father mention so many times when I was growing up. I struck up a conversation with him, and asked him to tell me about his experience in China during the 1930s. I also mentioned to him that my father sat under his teaching at the National Chengchi University during that time. He gave me a cold stare, shrugged his shoulders, and turned away from me without even answering me. He completely ignored me the rest of the lunch. What irony that the man responsible for my brothers and me settling in Seattle could not have cared less about his pivotal role in the life of our family. As things turned out, my living in Seattle turned out also to be pivotal for the beginnings of Agros.

they were making, and Seattle and its environs. Most interesting to me were the accounts of Husky football. What little I knew about college football came from stories in *Time* and *Life*; now I had first-hand accounts from my brothers' eyes.

About a half year into their UW adventure my brothers' letters took a drastic and puzzling turn. They wrote about having been "saved." Their two to three page letters became far lengthier, sometimes seven or eight pages filled with Bible quotations and their enthusiasm over their new-found faith in Jesus. Gone were the descriptions of college life and Husky football. It got to the point where I would scan a newly arrived letter quickly for tidbits on what I considered the interesting college stuff. Then I would put the letter down without reading the rest, which to my closed young mind was incomprehensible Bible preaching.

Bogotá 1959 – 1962

Word came to us after three years in Guatemala that Dad had been transferred from his Guatemala post and would assume the position of Minister Plenipotentiary to Colombia. I was excited by the news that we would again move to a new country. I knew from my geography classes that Colombia was a much bigger and wealthier country than Guatemala and had a far higher geopolitical standing in the hemisphere. There was no need for Berlitz records this time. My sisters and I were now fluent in Spanish, and although my parents got along as well, their Spanish lagged behind ours.

Dad again left first on his own to take up his new post, leaving us to get everything packed and moved to Bogotá. Not long after he assumed the new posting, the ROC and Colombian governments agreed to elevate their diplomatic missions in each other's countries to embassy status. Thus Dad stepped into his first ambassador role. My mother, sisters and I joined him a few weeks later flying into El Dorado airport. At 8,600 feet of elevation, Bogotá makes most arriving passengers gasp for air when first stepping outside the cabin-pressurized aircraft. Our drive into town in the official 1958 black Nash Rambler (with broad wide whitewalls) showed a beautiful city on a high mountain plateau. The architectural style was predominantly Spanish colonial, but English and continental European structures were also in evidence, giving the city a far more cosmopolitan and sophisticated look than Guatemala City.

Our first home in Bogotá was a lovely old red-brick Tudor-style house on the edge of the downtown area. Bogotá sits on the side of a mountain, and much of the city is sloped. This house was close to a park and I remember the setting was lovely. I was delighted to find I had my own bedroom on the second floor with its own private bathroom. A second door on the other side of the bathroom led to a small balcony that overlooked a small rear courtyard. I felt like a prince in a fairy tale.

Colombia in 1959 had only recently emerged from a decade of armed political warfare, aptly termed by Colombians as *La Violencia,* between the Liberal and Conservative parties. No other Latin American country had experienced this kind of unbridled, brutal violence between two major political parties, the roots of which dated back to 1899. In 1958 the conflict was resolved by the two parties agreeing to rotate the presidency every four years.

My sisters and I were enrolled in a bilingual school, Colegio Abraham Lincoln, then located in two large, old houses on *Carrera* 7a. and *Calle* 77. The school had been founded just a few years earlier by an American expatriate woman named Eleanor de Alum. She and her daughter Charlotte Alum de Samper ran the school. Mrs. Samper and her husband had about a dozen children and all of the school-aged ones were enrolled in the school. There were two educational tracks — one under the

Colombian *bachillerato* system, and the other geared to the U.S. high school system. There were overlap courses such as math, civics, biology, and physical education, taught in either English or Spanish depending on the nationality of the teacher. The teaching staff was a fascinating mix of nationalities beyond just Colombians and Americans. My physical education teacher, Señor Caparrini, was from Spain and spoke with a Castilian lisp. Lydia enrolled in the 12th grade, Dora in 10th, and I in 9th. This time there was no struggle to understand lectures and courses taught in Spanish – I switched in and out of English and Spanish during the school day and spoke mostly Chinese at home. The demographics of my schoolmates resembled that of the Colegio Americano in Guatemala City – expat foreigners, including Americans, English, and a pair of Irish twins, and upper crust Colombians, with a few middle class kids sprinkled in the mix.

At age 14 when we moved to Colombia, I found it very easy to move into the Colombian/American teen culture. There was usually a party at someone's house on the weekends, and we danced to both U.S. rock and roll and Colombian *merengues* and *merecumbés*. This was the golden age of early rock and roll – Elvis, Jerry Lee Lewis, Dion, Frankie Avalon, and Paul Anka. Chubby Checker and the twist emerged in 1960 and took the teen world by storm. By then alcohol had also made its appearance at the parties. There wasn't serious drinking going on, but I do remember my first taste of rum and Coca-Cola. Drugs were unknown in the Colombian teen culture of that era. Most of the kids were fluently bilingual (except for a few newbie expats) so conversation flowed seamlessly in both Spanish and English. Each language offered words and expressions and slang that were particularly expressive of one's intended meaning, so we didn't really think twice about switching from one to the other. In retrospect, I realize we spoke "Spanglish" not in today's pejorative sense to describe someone's very poor Spanish or English, but as a combination of both languages that made for richer verbal expressions. The Italian "*ciao*" also crept its way into our vocabulary as a trendy substitute for goodbye or *adiós*.

Many of my friends started driving by age 14, and some of them even drove their own cars to school. The official age for getting a driver's license by Colombian law was 18, but those licenses could be "bought," particularly at the police station in a small town just a few kilometers from Bogotá. By the time I was 15, Dad took me out for some driving lessons in the embassy's new Ford sedan. The stick shift was a challenge in the early sessions because of the hilly terrain in Bogotá. Once I had mastered the shifting, I made an arrangement (without my parents' knowledge) with our chauffer. Whenever he drove me anywhere during the week, he would stop a couple of blocks from the house, and I would take over. On our way back I would stop a short distance from home to let him resume his duties. If I went out on a date or to a party on weekends, I would drop him off at the nearest bus stop, he would go home, and I took over the car. The car had diplomatic plates so I was not concerned about being stopped by the police. I never got into an accident, so I never needed to contend with the thorny legal and parent problems that could have come up if I had.

Eighteen months after arriving in Bogotá we moved our residence to a beautiful home in an exclusive residential district of the city. You knew it was a ritzy neighborhood when you found the American ambassador's residence a block away. Their driveway and adjacent grounds alone were at least twice the size of our whole lot. The Ambassador then was Fulton "Tony" Freeman, a State Department veteran who happened to speak perfect Mandarin Chinese, learned years earlier from postings as a junior officer in the U.S. Embassy in Nanking, China, in the 1940s. Because he spoke fluent Mandarin, Freeman and my parents got along famously. He had a daughter my age, and we met a few times at diplomatic and other parties. She went to a different school so we did not see each other that often. Our friendship was more a passing acquaintance. But my parents were always inordinately curious about whether I had spent any time with her at our weekend parties. I think they sometimes bantered about us getting together in an arranged marriage old-China style. In 1964 Freeman went on to become U.S. Ambassador to Mexico. A *Time* magazine article at the time described his tenure in Colombia in glowing terms and commented that he was "one of the most energetic and effective U.S. diplomats on the job in Latin America." Freeman was the prototype professional diplomat, unlike the growing number of political appointees today who, as rank amateurs, are given major ambassadorial postings by presidents paying off political debts.

During our time in Bogotá I took my first piano lessons from a Russian émigré named Tatiana Espinoza. She was short in stature and had small hands with stubby, short fingers. But my, how those stubby fingers flew over the keyboard. The sounds she produced were magical. Consistent with classical Russian piano pedagogy, as I have come to understand in later years, she stressed the fundamentals – scales, arpeggios, hand and finger position, supple wrist. I can vividly recall her spot-checking my wrists with an upward chop of her hand to see if they were too stiff. I so wanted to play fun stuff, but she kept me on an endless diet of Bach, Clementi, and Kuhlau.

By the time I finished 10th grade both Lydia and Dora had left home, each having gone to the U.S. for college; Lydia to Vassar and Dora to Tufts. As each of my sisters embarked for the U.S. they traveled through Seattle to spend time with Richard and Bob. I noticed in my sisters' letters home the same pattern that occurred with my brothers. Early letters were full of interesting details about their new life in the U.S., but later the letters got much longer and were full of Bible preaching after each, in turn, converted to Christianity. I wondered at the time whether this would happen to me when it was my turn to go to college in the U.S. but resolved that I would be different from my brothers and sisters. No way, I thought. They might go for this Jesus stuff, but not me.

Midway through my 10th grade year Mrs. Samper, who was the principal at that time, called me into the office and made a surprising offer: if I was willing to go to summer school at the end of 10th grade, she would allow me to skip the 11th grade and go straight into 12th grade at the beginning of the next school year. This meant graduating a year earlier than normal and entering college at age 16. My classmates Paul Jiménez, Clemencia Vásquez, Rafael Samper and Ricardo Child were also in on the deal. I loved the idea and was excited at the thought of going to college earlier in the U.S. like my brothers and sisters. So our little group gave up our summer that year and went to school every day, essentially being tutored by Mrs. Samper to get in a year's 11th grade courses in three months.

My last year of high school in Bogotá was truly enjoyable. Our class of around 18 seniors was close-knit; there were too few of us to form cliques. Three of us summer school buddies, Dickie Child, Paul Jiménez and I made the school basketball team. We played mostly on outdoor courts – there were few schools in Bogotá with indoor gyms. Our school fight song was as corny as they came, so we adopted Dion's *Runaround Sue* as our unofficial team song. Our level of play might have beaten a few junior high school teams from very small towns in the U.S. We had one guy who had lived in the U.S. and really knew how to dribble and shoot a classic jump shot. The rest of us did what came naturally without any coaching. I was also editor of the school paper, and wrote pretentious editorials about world peace and justice that make me cringe when I think of them today. Thankfully I remember very little of what I wrote back then. I'm even more thankful the Internet was not around then so none of that juvenile writing can come back to haunt me today.

I was then old enough to go around the city on my own, taking buses everywhere. I enjoyed attending *fútbol* matches at

Estadio El Campín to watch my favorite team, the Millonarios, and watching bullfights in the Plaza de Toros. There I saw a *mano a mano* duel between the legendary Spanish matadors Luis Miguel Dominguín and Antonio Ordóñez. These duels were chronicled in Ernest Hemingway's *The Dangerous Summer*. My Spanish was good enough now to fool people into thinking that I was Colombian when I answered our home or Embassy phone. The highest compliment I was paid was when people called me "*rolo*," a Colombian slang term meaning someone born in Bogotá.

I was fortunate to have learned the art of "wearing native clothes," an idiomatic expression used in some Latin countries for a foreigner's ability to blend in by speaking the local language or understanding and appreciating local culture and customs. Not all my expatriate friends were so fortunate. In fact, one experience in particular showed me how difficult it is for an American to overcome historical enmities and prejudices.

At basketball practice one afternoon an American teammate exploded in tears and rage. Another teammate, a Colombian, had taunted him with the term "*gringo*" and various other put-downs about his being American. My American friend screamed that in five years of living in Bogotá, he had learned to speak the language flawlessly, tried his utmost to live and think like a Colombian, and was the last person in the world to act "gringo." The barbs from our Colombian teammate pushed him over the edge, and all his pent-up frustration in being treated as a "gringo" teenager in Colombia burst out in conflagration.

Any American who has lived abroad for a length of time, particularly as a young person interacting daily with nationals, will empathize with my friend's feelings. It seems that anywhere in the world there is no more favored target of insult than an American. A generation later it hasn't gotten much better.

A number of us went through the U.S. college application process – taking the SAT's one Saturday at Colegio Nueva

Granada, and writing to schools to ask for admissions packets. It was exciting to open the thick manila envelopes that came in the mail and look through the materials each school sent. I had by this time a hopeless case of the big-fish-in-tiny-pond syndrome, thinking I was really hot stuff. So I applied to Harvard, Princeton, and University of Pennsylvania, determined to be an Ivy Leaguer. Rejection notices came fairly quickly from Harvard and Princeton. The envelope from Penn was much thicker than the slim ones that brought the polite "We congratulate you on your achievements...but we regret to inform you" letters. Penn wanted me. At age 16, I was Philadelphia-bound and terribly excited.

2

BACKDROP

The young man who boarded the Avianca Boeing 707 in Bogotá bound for Idlewild International Airport (now JFK) in New York City on June 20, 1962, was full of himself. I don't know where the arrogance came from, but it was as powerful a case of self-deception as there can be. The memory of him is painful to me.

I remember feeling that the other passengers on the plane were lucky I was on board – it meant this flight would surely not crash. The passenger list that day included the newly elected Colombian president, Guillermo León Valencia, in the first class cabin. I thought the Colombian nation should be grateful that I was also on the flight. Flying was a very big deal back then, and even coach passengers had ample leg room and fancy folders in the seat pocket with little amenities and a menu describing the culinary delights to be served on the flight. I asked the stewardess to take my folder to President Valencia, and she soon brought it back with his sweeping autograph across the front.

We arrived in New York City around 8:30 p.m., and as the aircraft circled the city to make its final landing approach, I was astonished that there was still bright daylight outside. I had never lived in a northern latitude where the summer solstice meant such long days and short nights. It didn't occur to me as I set foot on the ground that this country would become my home, a country I would grow to love deeply. My ROC diplomatic passport with its student visa issued by the U.S. Embassy in Bogotá said I was a foreigner entering the country, but I had no idea this foreigner would embrace what he found here and build a full and fulfilling life with the unending opportunities offered.

Brother Bob and sisters Lydia and Dora were at the airport to greet me. We were all to spend that summer together on Staten Island in a home graciously loaned to us by Bob's dear friends, the Hoshiwaras. Doc & Yuri were gone with their children on a medical mission trip over the summer. The sights and sounds of the trip from Idlewild to Staten Island, including the salt air smells of the Staten Island Ferry ride that clear and warm summer evening, are still imprinted in my memory. Coming to the U.S. had seemed such a distant hope in my younger years. Now it had happened.

As soon as we arrived at the Hoshiwara home and I had changed from my suit and tie to casual clothes, my siblings gathered around the upright piano in the living room and asked me to accompany a singing of *Amazing Grace*. This notwithstanding Lydia was a much finer pianist than I was. Anyone who plays the piano and has spent time in church will be familiar with the particular cadence and common chord structures in many hymns. I had never sung or heard this or any other hymn before and my sight-reading skills were not well developed. So I stumbled through the simple but totally unfamiliar notes and rhythm of John Newton's great hymn.

That first night in Staten Island, Bob, Lydia and Dora mounted the first assault on their little brother. The effort was gentle, but unmistakably firm. I was just as firm, and stubbornly held to my arrogant 16-year old intellectual prowess that precluded religion and faith.

But over the course of the hot, humid New York City summer, my self-vaunted intellectual defenses against the historical and personal Jesus of Nazareth dissolved like a tray of ice cubes left in the sun. I began to acquire the beginnings of understanding on who he was, and what he taught. In the dark of the Hoshiwara kids' bedroom one late evening, I told my brothers (Richard had joined us in Staten Island for a couple of weeks) and sisters that I believed in this Jesus.

In Shanghai my stepmother had rescued me from a China that would become a 30-year totalitarian, xenophobic nightmare in which the human spirit would be suppressed in ways previously unknown to the most despotic autocrats in history. In Staten Island my brothers and sisters showed me a new world that freed the human spirit and a glimpse into a new life full of paradoxes – that to live, we must die; to be first, we must be last; a life where we love our enemies, and where the poor shall inherit the earth.

My parents came to New York City late that summer, and with Richard having arrived earlier, all seven of us were together for the first time in six years. One afternoon during that time my mother took me down to the basement of the Hoshiwara home, sat me down next to the dehumidifier, and informed me for the first time that she was not my real mother, but my stepmother. I had no idea up to this time, and it came as quite a shock. She said that Dora and I were both too young to remember or understand what happened when her first husband had died, my mother had died, and she and Dad had remarried to join the two families. She and Dad had agreed not to inform us until we were older. Richard, Bob and Lydia were sworn to secrecy, and to their credit, I have no memory of them ever even coming close to hinting that there was something unusual about our family makeup. Dora had been told during that first year we were in Colombia. As I thought back I remembered one afternoon at our home in Bogotá when my mother, Dora and Lydia were ensconced in my sisters' bedroom for what seemed like an entire afternoon with the door closed, and I heard Dora crying like her heart was broken. I also remember that after they emerged from the room, Dora, with eyes still filled with tears, came to my room and gave me a huge hug, without telling me why. I told my mother that afternoon in Staten Island that nothing had changed for me, since I had no memory of my real mother, and she was the only mother I knew.

That summer in Staten Island I also discovered what would become a lifelong delight. Each day I walked to the corner grocery store to buy a few food items for us, and picked up a copy of the *New York Times*. I was a confirmed newspaper reader by that time, devouring from cover to cover both Bogotá dailies, *El Tiempo* and *El Espectador*, during my three years in Colombia. I promptly fell in love with the *Times*, but what really got me were the crossword puzzles in the back pages of the paper. They were hard, but I managed to get a few words. That was the beginning of my addiction to *NYT* crossword puzzles – an addiction that has stayed with me to this day (although I now limit myself to the Saturday and Sunday puzzles).

In the fall Bob drove me to Philadelphia to begin my life as a college student. During signups for my freshman classes at the Palestra gym, I saw the frosh basketball team scrimmaging out on the court and discovered one of my dorm floor mates played center on the team. At 6'8" he was the tallest human I had ever met. I also watched as a shorter guy with thick eyeglasses sank jump shot after jump shot from all distances and angles while tightly guarded. That may have been the moment when I first awakened to the existence of other very much larger ponds in the world, and that my little pond back in Bogotá was so small it was invisible. I was astounded how much bigger the fish were in my new pond.

I declared architecture as my major. I wanted to study political science and history, but my parents in typical Chinese fashion asked, "Where will your rice come from?" All – as in 100% – of Chinese students coming to the U.S. in that era, particularly the men, studied science or engineering. Richard did civil engineering, Bob electrical engineering. Lydia majored in math, Dora in occupational therapy. In my parents' minds, these were all fields of study that would lead to good jobs and careers in the U.S. What could one possibly do with a degree in political science or history?

It did not take me long to discover that my fast-track high school education in Colombia that sent me brimming with confidence to Philadelphia at age 16 had prepared me not at all for Ivy League academics. Within a week of classes in calculus and physics – requirements for the architecture major – I felt like a first century tourist who happens to wander into the sandy arena of a Roman coliseum, is mistaken for a gladiator, given a sword and shield, and told to fight for honor and glory.

I was slaughtered.

All that phony arrogance built up in me was pulverized. I was overwhelmed. European history, freshman English, and intermediate French were manageable, even enjoyable. But that first semester at Penn I don't think I even understood the most basic concepts of calculus and struggled to do the mathematical calculations required in physics. My Colegio Abraham Lincoln A's in algebra and trigonometry might as well have been bright gold star stickers given to kindergarten kids for learning how to color within the lines and cut paper shapes.

The pressure on a young person in the Chinese culture to excel in academics is not something well understood in the western culture. That pressure is magnified exponentially if a young woman or man is gifted with the coveted privilege of going to the U.S. for college study. My parents were not unique in dreaming of sending their children to the U.S. for university. It was then, and still is, a common aspiration among Chinese parents, and I suspect parents around the world. So it might have been worse for me to fail academically than to contract leprosy. I began to wonder if I would be the disgrace of the family, an utter failure. Would I flunk out of Penn? What would happen with my student visa if I flunked out? Would I be sent home to Bogotá after just one semester of school in the U.S.?

But other than the severe academic shock to my system that first semester at Penn was actually enjoyable. I settled into a routine and began my discovery of new life in the U.S. – a life I had dreamed about ever since my brothers went to Seattle and the University of Washington. Penn was at this time a mostly-men affair. A small number of women were enrolled in their own separate college, in separate physical facilities. It was true segregation, by sex. The freshman class (all men) ate dinner together in the dining hall. We were served by upperclassmen, and because it was a formal affair, had to wear a coat and tie. We were on our own for breakfast and lunch, so to save money I did not eat breakfast. For lunch, my "usual" was two hamburgers and a Coke for 50 cents at the White Castle lunch counter where I learned the meaning of a "greasy spoon" eatery first hand. The hamburgers were a thin patty of gristly ground beef in a bun at 20 cents each. The ketchup I lathered over the burger gave it its only discernible taste. The Coke cost 10 cents. There were no trimmings and I could not afford the extra dime for fries. Food was grilled across the counter by unhappy looking cooks and served by indifferent waiters who came close to tossing your plate in front of you. I got used to being hungry during the day.

I tried out for the freshman soccer team, which consisted entirely of foreign students from all around the world and a couple of Americans who had grown up abroad. I enjoyed bantering in Spanish with the Latin American students on the team who were a little surprised this Chinese guy could speak like them. That was the era when no one played soccer in the U.S. In pickup games with Americans who had not played before, anyone – even me – with skills in the fundamentals of trapping, juggling, dribbling, and kicking the ball, could act like the one-eyed man in the valley of the blind. I participated in a few frosh team practices before calculus and physics blew a hole in my magic-carpet ride and made me realize I needed to spend every spare minute of time trying to comprehend what seemed to come so easily to others in those classes.

The first Christmas break at Penn was a long one. Most of the students left midweek immediately after their last class or test. I had bought a Greyhound bus ticket for New York City to join Bob in his Brooklyn apartment for the holidays (Bob by then was working on his Ph.D. in microphysics at Brooklyn Polytechnic Institute), but I first had to spend two days and nights in an empty dorm on an empty campus. It snowed during that time, and even though I delighted in the snow and its mesmerizing beauty, I was overcome by a feeling of intense, despondent loneliness made worse by the doubts crowding my mind. I wondered what had gone wrong with my grand dream of glorious success in America.

I told no one about my academic troubles, and my letters home gave no hint of my struggles. The next semester I repeated calculus and passed with the help of a student tutor. I felt far more comfortable about academics that second semester and even got a part time job as a file clerk in one of the university offices. For that I obtained my social security card and registered my first earnings in the U.S.

I managed to pull myself out of academic probation by the end of the year, but my hopes for getting a scholarship for the next year were smashed. Dad had promised one year of financial support; I was on my own and had to pay my way after that. The $3,000 cost for tuition, room and board per year – common to all Ivy League schools and at the top of the range for universities in the early 1960s – was beyond my reach. Student loans were non-existent in that era.

On May 10, 1963 I boarded a Greyhound bus for a cross-country trip to Seattle. The plan was to spend the summer with Richard and return to Penn in the fall. The 72-hour ride, with stops in small towns along the way for meals, was a memorable and delightful experience. I saw up-close the vastness of this country, the unending golden fields of grain in the Midwest, the awesome majesty of the Rockies, the endless plateau of eastern Montana, and the lush greenness of the Pacific Northwest. It seemed that the further west we went, the friendlier the people became. East coast curt/rude became Midwest polite/warm before finally morphing into west coast outright friendly. I was amazed when arriving in Seattle that perfect strangers at the Greyhound station would look me in the eyes and say "Hi."

During that three-day trek across America I read Louis Nizer's *My Life in Court*. As much as I was absorbed in Mr. Nizer's description of his colorful career, it never once occurred to me that the law might someday become my own professional calling.

We had another full family reunion in the summer of 1963 in Seattle to celebrate Richard's marriage to Elisa Hwang. He was by now designing water and sewer systems for municipalities as a civil engineer. Elisa had just graduated from Seattle Pacific College (now University). During the course of the summer it became apparent that my expectation of returning to Penn in the fall was wishful thinking, and Richard and Elisa both urged that I consider transferring to SPC. I visited the campus, applied, and was accepted for the 1963-64 school year. The school even gave me a small foreign student scholarship. The academic year cost at SPC was $1,500, half what it cost at Penn. With Richard's help I did some calculations and figured that between the scholarship, part time work during the school year, and full time work in the summers, I might be able to squeeze by and pay my own way. In my deluded mind I thought after a year I might still be able to make my way back to Penn.

By the time the fall quarter began, I could hardly wait to shed my major in architecture. I declared as a political science major at SPC. I didn't care whether the rice would be hard to come by in the future; I wanted to study something in which I had real interest.

Switching to Seattle Pacific proved to be a huge turning point in my life. I was gradually pulled into the life and culture of a small liberal arts campus. Friendships came easily, it seemed, and the small class sizes allowed interaction with faculty who would become great mentors and friends. By the end of that first academic year, I had run for and won election to a student-body officer position for the next school year, and any thoughts of returning to Penn faded away.

As I had hoped, turning to the study of politics, government, history, philosophy and economics was a complete and welcome change from the science and math that made up so much of the curriculum of an architecture major. I had found an academic home and thrived in it. My academic record improved by leaps and bounds, and by the time of graduation in 1966 I was headed to graduate school at George Washington University in Washington, D.C. with a full fellowship to study international politics. I dreamed of getting a Ph.D. some day, and teaching at the university level.

Seattle Pacific proved a blessing in other ways as well. There I met a young woman from Sunnyside, Washington, whose deep blue eyes and sparkling personality captured my heart. It began in an American Literature class in the spring quarter of my senior year. Cyd was a junior at the time, and always seemed to arrive late to class. The only seat open just happened to be next to mine. How is it that such great things start with such innocuous beginnings?

Cyd had grown up poor – very poor – in the Yakima Valley of Eastern Washington. If opposites attract, then she and I were Exhibit A of the most extreme case of opposites in just about every way possible. Consider our backgrounds – I grew up around the world, privileged, living in different cultures, and learning to speak different languages. As cosmopolitan as my parents were, we children were imbued with Chinese cultural values particularly with regard to family and ethics. Cyd was the product of the great American melting pot, with German and other strains in her bloodline.[1] Her family home in Sunnyside was a converted garage. Her father had built it as the first structure in a multi-room house, but he became seriously ill and never got beyond the garage. Cyd had never traveled outside the U.S., and her knowledge of Chinese people was confined to the one family who ran a Chinese restaurant in Sunnyside.

Those were just cultural and family background differences. Start getting into personality traits, and the checklist would show us as polar opposites in just about every category. Love is blind, indeed.

Four more years in academia ensued. A year's study at GWU in Washington, D.C., brought serendipitous connections with two giants of politics and law. I managed to get a part-time, lowly clerical position in the office of Sen. Warren Magnuson. I loved getting sent on errands. I never knew who I would encounter in those hallowed hallways of the Capitol or the Senate Office Building. One time I walked into an impromptu press conference being held in the rotunda by GOP Sen. Everett Dirksen, the minority leader. The senator was casually seated on the base of a statue, surrounded by reporters asking questions. His deep, gravelly voice resonated throughout the building even though he was speaking in an ordinary conversational tone. I often walked past Arizona Sen. Carl Hayden, whose office was in close proximity to Magnuson's, shuffling along slowly in the Senate Office Building. He was 90 years old at the time, and was two years short of retiring from the Senate after serving seven terms.

---

[1] Early on in our relationship Cyd told me she was part-Cherokee Indian, and grew up in Mobile, Alabama. I believed her until I met her mother for the first time and asked what it was like raising a family in Mobile, Alabama. I realized then my leg had been pulled. Cyd later confessed she would throw out all kinds of misleading information to guys with whom she thought there would be no future at all.

I enjoyed graduate studies, especially the classes taught by adjunct faculty from the State Department and the Pentagon. These people knew what they were talking about, were on the front lines of international events as they happened and were reported in the *Washington Post* and *New York Times*. My international law classes were especially lively – the instructor was a lawyer in the State Department who had laid out the legal foundation for the blockade of Cuba during the 1962 confrontation with the Soviet Union and the military intervention in the Dominican Republic in 1965. My class on the Chinese Communist Party was taught by a brilliant China hand on loan to the Defense Department from the Hoover Institution at Stanford University.

Yet, political science as an academic discipline had taken a significant turn I did not appreciate. In the decade of the sixties it seemed that social scientists envied their natural science brethren who could measure, evaluate, and predict with some degree of certainty. Social scientists wanted to be real scientists, only they were dealing with human nature, not with science and the physical world. My least enjoyable classes were in statistics and quantitative analysis – new curricula that had invaded the field of political science.

I lamented having to study statistics, or anything to do with math. I strongly rebelled against the notion that human beings could become predictable in their decisions and conduct. What mathematical or statistical formula could predict whether Nikita Khrushchev would deploy nuclear missiles against the U.S.? How much measuring and analysis before we could look into the crystal ball and see that Mao Tse-Tung would send Chinese troops across the Straits to invade Taiwan?

One night in the fall semester I met a friend for coffee after an evening class. He was also from Washington State, held the same fellowship as I, and we had mostly the same classes. My friend came into the coffee shop with an enormous stack of strange-looking books under his arm. To my inquiries, he responded that those were his law books. Contracts. Torts. Property. I found he had concurrently enrolled at Georgetown Law School and was doing two full-time academic programs at the same time.

I leafed through his law books and discovered an enormously appealing world I had not known. As I glanced through the pages I saw that this was a world where judges and lawyers applied reason and logic to resolve real-life issues between people, between companies, between governments. This was a world that balanced public versus private interest, a world in which the rule of law, not the rule of might, became the arbiter of disputes.

That night I went back to my dorm room and decided to switch from international politics to law. I called Cyd on the phone – our relationship had gotten quite serious by then – and told her she might some day be married to a lawyer, not a political science professor. I resolved to apply for admission to the University of Washington law school. The next day I wrote the UW to ask for application forms, and within 90 days my new course – surprising and unforeseen – had been set. The UW Law School accepted me and offered a scholarship. I was heading back to Seattle.

Even my trip home to Seattle took an unusual twist. During my final weeks in D.C., Senator Magnuson's press secretary told me he had given my name to U.S. Supreme Court Justice William O. Douglas as someone who might be able to drive the Justice's car back to Washington State for him. He told me to call the Justice's secretary to make the arrangements, including a personal meeting with Douglas so he could see who would be entrusted with his car.

About a week later I walked into the U.S. Supreme Court building, asked for directions to Justice Douglas' office, and then proceeded to spend a half hour with the man who was already a legend by that time. Justice Douglas spent summers in Goose Prairie, WA, and each spring asked a young man or woman working for "Maggie" to drive his car back for him. He and his new young (age 22) wife Cathie would fly out to the state later when the Supreme Court term was adjourned.

After asking me a few questions about myself, the justice handed me the keys to his 1964 Dodge Dart, his Texaco credit card, and a letter on his official embossed stationary signed by himself as proof that I had his personal authorization to drive his car. Surprisingly, during the three-day cross country drive I was never challenged over use of the card bearing the name of William O. Douglas.

In August 1967 Cyd and I married in a very small ceremony held on the Seattle Pacific campus. A month later she began a new job teaching English at Blaine Junior High, and I began my law school studies. Considering the stress of a new teaching job and first-year law school studies, and how fundamentally different we were as people, it was a miracle we stayed together. I am thankful we did, because during the last quarter of my three years of law school I encountered a challenge that would play a huge part in defining the person I have become.

The Bar Challenge 1970

In the spring of 1970 during my last quarter of law school, all the soon-to-graduate students congregated in the basement dining room of the old Condon Hall to fill out forms and get fingerprinted. This was the process of applying for admission to the bar. I joined my classmates and went through the exercise. In the back of my mind I knew this might not turn out the way it would for everyone else. I was at this time not a U.S. citizen. I was still a ROC citizen and had been granted U.S. permanent resident status based on my marriage to Cyd. I knew from reading state law and the Washington Supreme Court rules that admission to the Washington state bar had a four-fold requirement: (1) graduation from an accredited law school, (2) passing the bar exam, (3) good moral character, and (4) U.S. citizenship. The bar exam was scheduled in July that summer, and that would be the last hurdle for everyone else in my class. I wondered what would happen to my application.

I found out within a week. A letter from the Washington State Bar Association informed me that because I was not a U.S. citizen I would not be eligible for bar admission; nor would I be permitted to take the bar exam in July. I immediately wrote back to the Board of Governors of the Bar Association and requested that they at least grant me an exemption to take the bar exam with my classmates. I would not be eligible to undergo naturalization until October 1972 and was willing to wait until then to be admitted to the bar. But I wanted very much to take the bar exam in July, knowing that there is no better time to take it than right after finishing law school when three years of intense schooling are still fresh on the mind.

I was not surprised, but was certainly disappointed, when a letter from the Bar Association came a few days later to inform me that the Board of Governors had denied my request.

In our constitutional law classes we had studied the Equal Protection Clause of the U.S. Constitution, and its application to residents in this country, whether they were citizens or not. As a U.S. resident, even though not a citizen, I was subject to being drafted for service in the armed forces – a real issue at the time because of the Vietnam War. A year earlier I had reported to the Selective Service offices to undergo my draft physical. I could be required to fight for the country and die for the country, but I could not even take the Washington bar exam because I was not a citizen? I felt the injustice acutely. I also thought of the intransigence of the Bar Association's Board of Governors: what great public interest were they protecting by not allowing me to take the bar exam with the rest of Class of 1970 graduates? The more I thought of this, the more it ate at me, and I could hardly sleep at night.

I resolved to do something about it. I was convinced this was an injustice. After researching equal protection case law, I became convinced the citizen requirement for bar admission was a violation of the state and federal constitutions.

I met with Law School Dean Luvern Rieke, told him what I was up against, and asked if he would consider giving me academic credit for an independent research project that would involve filing a lawsuit in the state Supreme Court to seek admission to the bar on the grounds that the citizenship requirement for bar admission was unconstitutional. I gave him a brief synopsis of the research I had done and how I planned to go about it. Dean Rieke, a wonderful man and excellent teacher and scholar, hardly gave it a second thought. He agreed with a big smile on his face and gave me great encouragement to pursue the case. He brought in professor William Andersen, who was then associate dean of the law school, told him what I had proposed, told him he had agreed, and suggested that the two of them act as my supervisors and advisors for this project.

The case I contemplated filing was unusual, to say the least. A lawsuit is generally started by filing an action in the lower Superior Court. After that court has decided a case it might work its way up the appeal process and eventually reach the state Supreme Court. But my case was an original action in the Supreme Court. My theory was that the subject of bar admission was a matter of original jurisdiction in the Supreme Court, and need not and could not be decided by a lower court. It was also highly unusual that I was filing the case *pro se*, meaning I was representing myself as my own counsel. Yet not only was I not admitted to the bar, I hadn't even graduated from law school. There was no way Cyd and I, between her teaching job and my law clerk work, could afford to hire a lawyer or law firm to take on this case for me. Besides, my blood was hot and I was eager to take on the Bar Association personally without the help of any lawyers or law firms. I had something to prove. They may not have thought I was fit for admission to the bar or even fit to take the bar exam, but I was out to show them U.S. citizenship had nothing to do with one's competence or ability to be a good lawyer.

I went to my boss and mentor, Carl Jonson, and laid out my plans. (Since the summer after my first year of law school I had been clerking at his downtown law firm, full time in summers, part time during the school year.) I asked him if he would give me permission to use the firm's resources – typewriters, copy machines, pleading paper – for my project. He readily agreed.

In May 1970, I drove to Olympia and filed my petition with the clerk of the Supreme Court, asking the court to strike down the citizenship requirement for bar admission as unconstitutional. In the alternative, if the court did not agree with my argument about the unconstitutionality of the requirement, I asked that the court grant a waiver to allow me to take the bar exam that July. I served a copy of the petition on the Washington State Bar Association knowing that they were my adversaries in this proceeding. Within a few days I received notice that the Bar Association indeed was opposing my petition and had hired the prestigious Seattle firm of Guttormsen, Scholfield, Willits & Ager to represent the Board of Governors. The pleadings from that firm were signed by Jack Scholfield and John Hamill. Scholfield would later become a friend and occasional tennis partner.

In my mind, my petition to have the U.S. citizenship requirement declared unconstitutional amounted to shooting for the moon; I had very little expectation I could win that argument. Courts were extremely reluctant, I knew, to rule statutory requirements unconstitutional. They gave great deference to the legislative branch, and would prefer to find any other way to grant relief, if relief was justified, than to rule something unconstitutional. Truth be told, I would have been delighted if the court would simply grant me the waiver to allow me to take the bar exam. Asking for the waiver was more akin to jumping up and reaching as high as my arm could go to pluck the ripe peach off a high branch of a tree. Difficult, but not impossible.

Not more than 10 days after I filed my petition, a letter came from the Supreme Court, informing me that the court had (1) granted me a waiver to take the July bar exam, and (2) set the case of *In re Chi-Dooh Li* for hearing on the merits, *en banc*, in September 1970. The term *en banc* meant all nine justices would hear the case in September and not just a smaller panel of the court.

I was ecstatic. I think I jumped up and down and whooped and hollered for at least five minutes. Not only had the court given me the peach I sought high up in the tree, but they were even going to give me a chance to shoot for the moon. I had gotten what I most wanted – to take the bar exam in July with my classmates. On top of that I would have the incredible privilege of arguing my own case to the nine justices in September – without ever having been admitted to the bar.

After graduation in June I settled down to the full time task of studying for the bar exam. I joined my classmates in a bar review course taught by local lawyers every weekday evening, and some Saturday mornings, at Condon Hall. On the fateful day we all headed to the Seattle Center where the three-day exam was conducted. There must have been about 600-700 of us in one of those great halls. After each session we gathered for a break outside, talked about the questions, and discovered how people answered them. That was nerve-wracking because someone inevitably came up with an answer or explanation you hadn't thought of, and you wondered if you had just managed to blow the whole question.

I actually didn't feel too insecure – until the last session of the third day. During that session the questions included several areas of law I had not devoted much time to; I felt like I was making up the answers. I left the final session feeling miserable. I thought what a disgrace it would be if I flunked the very bar exam the Supreme Court had allowed me to take.

My case was set for hearing in mid-September. The week before the hearing I received a telephone call from a friend who said he had just gotten word that the bar exam results were out. The individual notification letters were sent to home addresses, but we might be able to find out if we walked to the Bar Association offices in downtown Seattle during our lunch break. So with two friends, we walked to the Bar office and asked the receptionist if she could get someone to tell us the results. She picked up the phone and told us to have a seat.

About five minutes later out walked Miss Alice O'Leary Ralls, executive director of the State Bar Association. She was a stern looking woman in her 50s, and she had on her most intimidating demeanor. She had a clipboard in hand, and after each of my friends gave their names, she looked through the list and informed them they had passed. Then she turned around to walk out of the reception area. I called out to her and asked if I had passed; without even looking back or consulting the clipboard, she said in an icy tone, "You passed too, Mr. Li."

Alice Ralls did not like me. I knew that because each time I served pleadings or briefs on the Bar Association, she was the one who would receive the papers. And she made it very clear she thought I was a most impertinent and arrogant young man. Miss Ralls had her personal reasons for disliking me and what I was attempting to do with my lawsuit, quite apart from her role as chief executive officer of the Bar Association. She had attended the University of Washington law school as a Canadian citizen, and after graduation had been prevented from taking the bar exam or being admitted to the bar by the same U.S. citizenship requirement. Unlike me, she waited until she became a naturalized citizen to take the bar exam and get admitted. I think in her mind I was like the rude person who pushes his way to the front of a long line when others had dutifully waited for hours for their proper turn.

The timing of the bar results coming out was providential. The following Monday I made my appearance before the Supreme Court. As the petitioner I was the first to present my case. When the justices all filed in and took their seats, my case was called, and I got up from my seat, went to the podium, and began in the traditional way:

> May it please the court, my name is Chi-Dooh Li, and I am the petitioner...

I had gotten no further than "petitioner" when Justice Hugh Rosellini, peering at me intently from the elevated and long bench where the justices were seated, interrupted me and asked, "Mr. Li, did you pass the bar exam?"

I think it was one of the most memorable moments in my life, when I was able to answer, "Mr. Justice Rosellini, I am thankful to report that I did pass the bar exam." He rejoined, "Then you may proceed, Mr. Li."

It was very obvious then, and in discussions with fellow lawyers later, that had I answered "no" to the question, the court would have immediately declared the case moot, and dismissed my petition. In other words, "Don't bother to come back until you've passed the bar exam so we have a real case before us." As it was, the issue now presented itself in sharp focus for the court: I had satisfied the requirements of graduation from an accredited law school, good moral character, and passed the bar exam. The only requirement I could not meet was U.S. citizenship. The court could now squarely consider that question.

The rest of that oral argument before the Supreme Court is a blur to me. I cannot remember anything else I said or anything the Bar Association lawyer argued to the court. I drove back to Seattle in a daze wondering if this had been a real experience or something I had dreamed. It seemed so improbable that at age 24 I had just argued my own case to the state Supreme Court.

I went back to the routine of work and life. Carl Jonson had hired me full time even though I was not admitted to the bar. I did much research and writing, and ghosted many briefs and letters for him.

In late December 1970, a little over three months after the oral arguments in the Supreme Court, I received a phone call from my dear friend and fellow SPC graduate and law school classmate Bob Gunter. After graduating from law school Bob was hired as law clerk to Justice Walter McGovern of the state Supreme Court, a prestigious position. Justice McGovern had sat in on my oral argument, and Bob was the only person I knew in the court room that day as he sat on a bench reserved for court clerks and staff.

Knowing he would probably have the inside scoop on whether or how the court had decided on my case, I was eager to hear what Bob had to say. Here, word for word, is what he said that had such a profound impact on me; I can hear Bob in my mind as if I had just heard him yesterday:

Skip, I have good news and bad news for you. (Pause)
The bad news is that I cannot tell you the good news.

Jubilation!

I knew I had won my case. I knew the court had ruled in my favor. Bob had told me nothing, yet he had told me everything. As a clerk to one of the Justices, Bob was sworn to keep confidential the deliberations and decisions of the court before they were announced publicly. Of course he couldn't tell me the good news! But that was all I needed to hear; Bob could not have gotten the message across to me any clearer.

About one week after Bob Gunter's good news/bad news phone call the Supreme Court's decision was made public and reported in newspapers. The decision had not yet been published, so I drove to Olympia once again to pick up a copy from Court Clerk Reginald Shriver, who had extended kindnesses to me on more than one occasion during the process. I pored over the majority opinion in the 7-1 decision, and the lengthy dissent filed by Justice Frank Hale. The court indeed avoided the constitutional issue. Instead, it found that matters of bar admission were the sole jurisdiction of the Supreme Court, and therefore the legislature had no business setting requirements for bar admission. In effect the court declared the statute on bar admission requirements to have no effect, something like Bob Dylan's *Blowin' in the Wind*.

As to its own court rule on bar admission requirements which mirrored the statute, the court amended the rule to remove the U.S. citizenship requirement. That amendment would be effective March 10, 1971 – the date on which I would be eligible to be sworn in to the bar. The last paragraph in the majority opinion read like the sweetest music I had ever heard:

> As petitioner now meets all qualifications for admission to practice, he will, upon taking the oath of office and payment of the requisite fees, be admitted to the bar.

Justice Hale's impassioned dissent spoke to the importance of lawyers' roles as officers of the court and that citizenship was a proper requirement to serve in that capacity. He pointed out that I was not being denied bar admission forever – I had only to wait another period of time, and upon naturalization, could be admitted to the bar.

The court's opinion was published eventually in the state Supreme Court reporter, and earned a permanent citation as *In re Chi-Dooh Li*, 79 Wn.2d 561, 488 P.2d 259 (1971). For a few years after its publication I received letters and phone calls from other non-citizens who had decided to move to the State of Washington because of my case, and they expressed their thanks to me for my personal quest that opened the profession's door to them as well. In 1974 the United States Supreme Court considered a case similar to mine, squarely confronted the constitutional question, and threw out the citizenship requirement for bar admission as a violation of the Equal Protection Clause of the United States Constitution. This experience proved to be a great watershed in my life. Its impact on me was profound in so many ways. In retrospect, winning the right to practice my chosen profession 18 months earlier than otherwise allowed may have been the least significant of all.

It instilled in me a profound appreciation for this country in which I was now a permanent resident. Where else on earth might an absolute nobody like me, with no connections, no wealth, no accomplishments to his name, have addressed a petition to the nine members of a high court, have them listen to his arguments, and be granted a ruling in his favor? Is there any other country where the rule of law is so deeply engrained that even a foreigner can invoke rights under that law to have a legislative enactment nullified and a Supreme Court rule changed, all within a period of nine months from beginning to end?

In some countries, including my native China, I might have been shot or imprisoned for even speaking up to challenge the system. In too many other countries what I sought to accomplish would have required massive bribes paid to the right people. This was something much more significant than the drivers' licenses with falsified ages bought by my high school friends in Bogotá from a nearby small town police chief in Colombia.

What are the chances I could have succeeded in even the bedrock democratic nations in Western Europe? How would the infamous French bureaucracy, for example, have tolerated my challenge? Would the intricate British legal system have recognized a valid claim in my argument, or would I have been required to resort to an act of Parliament?

I had discovered first hand before my legal career had even begun that in the U.S., the image of Justice blindfolded, dispensing judgment without regard to social status, money, or power, was more than a symbol. It was reality.

In my undergraduate and graduate political science, history, and philosophy classes I had studied the underpinnings and structures of governments around the world, democratic and totalitarian. I had read about and written papers on the strengths and weaknesses of the constitutional system of government set up by those courageous and wise men whose collective genius produced the great principles by which this country is governed. Now I had personally taken a deep draft and tasted an incomparable sweetness from that great chalice of rights and liberties prepared by the founders.

The experience taught me something that helped fuel my determination 12 years later to help the rural poor in Central America buy their own farmland. I had learned in this encounter that one man, faced with a law or a social system that is fundamentally unjust, can indeed set into motion actions that bring about change – significant change sufficient to redress even historic injustices.

Had it not been for *In re Chi-Dooh Li* I doubt whether I would have had the mindset to consider taking on the consequences of 400 years of oppression, and the institutional forces built and entrenched over that time that condemned great masses of people to lives of abject poverty stripped of human dignity.

I can look back and see how this God I now worshipped was completely rebuilding my persona and character. He had shattered to smithereens, through failure at Penn, the arrogance of the 16-year old who had set foot on U.S. soil thinking the world was his oyster. He had also opened my eyes to the gigantic dimensions of this pond I now swam in. The large and regal fish I had pictured myself was a complete delusion. I was then, and had always been, a tiny minnow.

I believe God used the bar admission fight to introduce me to a new kind of confidence and a new awareness to possibilities that might have otherwise been dismissed as improbabilities. He had handled me like a sculptor does a work in process. Dissatisfied with how the early version of me was turning out, He had destroyed it with hammer blows and was now chiseling away on a new piece of stone. "Create in me a new heart," the song goes. In my case it wasn't just heart; it was also mind, soul, and strength.

Governor's Legal Counsel 1973 – 1977

I was sworn in as a lawyer on March 10, 1971, in the Thurston County Courthouse by Superior Court judge Hewitt Henry. I had taken a short leave from my law firm in Seattle at the time and was working as a caucus attorney for the Republicans in the state House of Representatives. (My being hired to serve in that role was another unlikely development, considering I was not even admitted to the bar as the legislative session began January 11, 1971.)

By the time of my swearing-in ceremony the legislative session was in full swing, and I was immersed in reviewing bills, drafting floor amendments, communicating with state agencies, the Governor's office, and the Attorney General's office regarding proposed legislation.

The 1971 caucus experience led to an invitation to reprise the role in the 1972 legislative session. During this second stint with the House GOP caucus I had increased contacts with staffers in the Governor's Office. These contacts resulted in a telephone call in the summer of 1973 from Ruth Yoneyama Woo telling me that the Governor's legal counsel position would soon be vacant and encouraging me to apply for the job. Ruthie Woo was the receptionist in the Governor's Office but that job title belied her true role. She had a network of political friends and contacts across the state that was second to none. A consummate behind-the-scenes organizer, she was a tremendously effective political liaison within the Dan Evans moderate branch of the state Republican Party. She had a special interest in advancing people of Asian descent since there were few of us involved in the political or legal world during that era.

To my utter surprise, after one interview with Richard Hemstad, the incumbent legal counsel, and Jim Dolliver, then the Governor's chief of staff, and a later interview that afternoon with Gov. Dan Evans himself, I was hired for the job. During the interview with Dan Evans, I practically fell out of my chair when he asked me "Well, Skip, when can you start?" I stammered a reply that I did not know I had been hired.

Thus at age 27, barely three years out of law school and admitted to the bar a little over two years earlier, I took on the legal counsel position – a dream job in any young lawyer's book. My job description as the Governor's in-house lawyer included producing the Governor's executive request legislation and shepherding it through both Houses, reviewing and assembling comments on all bills passed by the legislature for the Governor to sign or veto, and in the event of a veto, to write the Governor's veto message. I was also the chief clemency officer in the Governor's office handling all requests for gubernatorial pardons and commutations.

When I arrived for my first day on the job in late August 1973, I walked through the doors of a turbulent political world full of contradictions: high principle and easy expediency, uncompromised integrity and slimy corruption, thoughtful policy and spur-of-moment lawmaking. For the next three-plus years I was immersed in what I had studied as an undergraduate and discovered first-hand what a great misnomer the term political science was. Dan Evans, a three-term governor nicknamed "Straight-Arrow" and admired for his statesmanship, was far less a scientist than a consummate political artist. An engineer by profession, his leadership combined a brilliant and open mind, an easy manner, a profound knowledge of history, and a stubborn disregard of what his critics thought of him. Working closely with Evans and watching him in action gave me the finest schooling and on-the-job training I could have hoped for, not just in politics, but in human relationships where we dealt with people of every stripe and background.

One last experience during my early career was also of particular relevance to the Agros story. I witnessed first-hand and even experienced personally how one person or a small group of like-minded individuals can make a difference in the lives of many, many other people.

In April 1975, in the wake of the fall of Saigon to the Viet Cong and North Vietnamese armies, waves of Vietnamese refugees escaped in vessels large and small to scattered points across Southeast Asia and the Philippines. The U.S. government, acknowledging its responsibility to help, prepared to accept thousands of these "boat people" as they came to be known. The State Department issued a call to state governments asking for help in resettling the refugees in their states. On arrival, these refugees would be processed and settled first at Camp Pendleton, the Marine base near San Diego.

The initial response across the country was not encouraging. Some prominent politicians replied that their states did not want refugees. The loudest protest came from California's Governor, Jerry Brown, who insisted his state's welfare system could not afford adding thousands of refugees to its rolls and who did not want refugees taking jobs away from Californians. Among others, Senator Ted Kennedy echoed Brown's shrill voice and said his state of Massachusetts could not possibly take on such an additional welfare and economic burden.

Washington's Secretary of State Bruce Chapman was disturbed by these highly negative reactions. How could we not help people who were fleeing the fallout of a war that the U.S. had lost in their country? He recruited Ralph Munro, then the Governor's assistant on education issues, and me to talk to Gov. Evans about speaking up against the developing tide of anti-refugee politicians.

The three of us managed to get an appointment 30 minutes ahead of the Governor's regular Monday morning nine o'clock press conference. We talked about the anti-refugee sentiment growing across the country and how Gov. Brown had even tried to prevent special charter flights carrying refugees across the Pacific from landing at Travis Air Force Base near Sacramento. We urged the Governor to speak up and take the opposite view from Brown and Kennedy and welcome refugees to Washington State. We were well aware of Evans' self-described contrarian nature, particularly when it came to politicians who like to grab headlines.

Gov. Evans was not a morning person and sometimes arrived early to the office in a rather grumpy mood. He sat there listening to us with a blank face, asked a few questions, and even grunted a couple of times. When press secretary Jay Fredericksen came in to remind him it was time for his press conference, he got up out of his seat without saying what he would do, if anything.

We followed him into the large conference room adjoining his office where the newspaper, radio and TV reporters and cameras were waiting. Evans stepped up to the podium, led off with a five-minute extemporaneous talk summarizing the anti-refugee attitudes that were rising up across the country, and informed the press that Washington State would not join the naysayers. In fact, on behalf of the state, he welcomed the Vietnamese refugees to make their home here and said he would send his assistant Ralph Munro to Camp Pendleton bearing a personal letter from him extending a warm welcome from the people of Washington State.

Bruce, Ralph and I were stunned. Evans spoke to the press that morning as if this had been a decision well thought through and planned. Perhaps he had already pondered taking this course even before the three of us met with him that morning. Maybe his grunts were his reaction to our thinking this was our idea when he had been thinking it all along.

During my three and one-half years working with the governor I do not remember another time when my chest burst with pride the way it did that morning in late April 1975. Dan Evans was the first governor in the country to declare publicly that refugees were welcome in his state. His bold action quickly reversed the tide   other governors and states followed suit. His were not just words. Action followed quickly. The Governor ordered the state Department of Emergency Services to coordinate public and private help to the refugees who would resettle in the state. Churches everywhere in the state responded just as spontaneously, it seemed, and the flow of refugees into Washington soon began.

To this day, the Vietnamese refugee community in Washington state honors the memory of Gov. Evans' welcome and Ralph Munro's visit to Camp Pendleton. Many young boys born of Vietnamese refugee parents have been named Daniel in tribute to the significance of Evans' decision in their lives. The Governor's wholehearted welcome was the deciding influence for many refugee families to make their way to the Pacific

Northwest. Today, Washington has the highest Southeast Asian refugee population proportionate to its population.

Within five years from that memorable morning meeting with the Governor and the subsequent press conference, I embarked on another refugee adventure – one that became the final training exercise before taking on the cause of other war-torn refugees far, far away from the turmoil of Southeast Asia and in the mountainous regions of Central America.

3

REHEARSAL

"Do you know where L'Abri is?"

The woman who asked me this question in October 1978 sat in the passenger seat of a car that had roared up a narrow two-lane Swiss mountain highway and pulled into the only patch of gravel shoulder within sight. My family and I had just reached that same spot on foot, ready to cross the highway to pick up the trail down to the next village, Huémoz.

In 1978 I was trying to build a law practice and make a living to support a young family. I had finished my stint with Governor Evans, and in January 1977 returned to Seattle to start my own law firm. During our time in Olympia Cyd and I had a significant spiritual encounter that saved our marriage. Our lives up to that point had been diverging, and we had come to the brink of divorce. We recommitted to one another and resolved to rebuild our marriage. Part of our rebuilding process was to spend the month of October 1978 in the Swiss Alps at a community known as L'Abri located in the tiny village of Huémoz about 17 kilometers southeast of Montreux.

Cyd, son Peter (age five), a young family friend Sharon, and I were midway through our 30-day stay in that little village, living and studying among people from the four corners of the earth drawn to L'Abri, French for "The Shelter." Huémoz is one of many tiny villages along a road that winds up the mountain to upscale ski resorts such as Villars and Chesières, all in the Canton of Vaud. Cars speeding on their way up or down the mountain take all of five seconds to drive through Huémoz. No signs point to L'Abri, and the village looks no different from any of the dozens of other small Alpine hamlets inhabited by hardy Swiss dairy farmers, small shop owners, and a mix of permanent and seasonal residents.

L'Abri was home to Francis and Edith Schaeffer and some of their extended family. In the 1950s, unsettled by doctrinal schisms in the Presbyterian Church in which he served as a pastor, Francis Schaeffer and his family packed up all their belongings and moved to Switzerland to follow a vague sense of calling to live and work in Europe. By the time our family made our way there in 1978 Schaeffer had authored a series of intellectually challenging books that appealed to skeptics of the Christian faith, and people who would not settle for easy answers to tough questions surrounding faith and belief in God.[1]

Atheists, agnostics, and a broad spectrum of Christians, Buddhists, and Muslims, primarily young college and post-college types, found their way, some intentionally, some not so, to Huémoz to probe the limits of their belief and unbelief. After a stay of anywhere from a few weeks to a year, few came off the mountain without having had their foundational constructs significantly shaken and recast.

Cyd, who had grown up in an anti-intellectual church environment, had gone through a period of questioning her faith during our time in Olympia. A friend pointed her to Schaeffer's *Genesis in Space and Time*. I recall her telling me that for the first time in her life she had found someone who had actually thought through some of the tough philosophical and faith issues she struggled with. Her spiritual and intellectual catharsis was a turning point in both our lives and led us a few years later to our pilgrimage (of sorts) to Huémoz.

---

[1] *The God Who is There* (1968), *Genesis in Space and Time* (1972), *He is There and He is not Silent* (1972).

Taking off for 40 days didn't make much sense when running a law practice, but the pull of everything we knew about L'Abri was a strong one. It turned out to be everything Cyd and I hoped for and much more. We lived in a chalet rented from a retired couple who resided in Lausanne. For a closet hermit like myself, Chalet Le Roc, built on a steep mountainside at 2,600 feet elevation in the Swiss Alps, served as a perfect temporary hermitage. It was as if we had stepped off a bullet train rushing through life to embark on a one-horse carriage that took us on a leisurely and meandering ride through the Swiss countryside with plenty of restful stops. The change of pace was stunning and immensely restorative.

I rose at the crack of dawn each morning while everyone else still slept, went to my study downstairs, and began my morning studies – reading from the Bible, and working my way through Alfred Edersheim's magnum opus *The Life and Times of Jesus the Messiah*. From my desk I looked straight across to the magnificent Les Diablerets mountain range. The early mornings were extraordinarily peaceful, their serenity interrupted by the occasional and soothing sound of cowbells around the necks of the small herds grazing in nearby pastures.

The sounds of Cyd, Peter and Sharon awakening were my cue to put the reading aside and take a stroll down to the village *boulangerie* to pick up a baguette and croissants for breakfast. Freshly baked breads with butter and jam, cereal and coffee topped with the fresh cream that had risen to the surface of the milk left overnight on the window ledge (collected from the village dairy the evening before and still warm from just having been offered up by the farmer's cows) – these were the elements of a breakfast made in *Vaudois* heaven.

Our daily routine included homeschooling for Peter, Sharon working on her pre-arranged school assignments in the mornings, and a brisk 45-minute afternoon hike along alpine meadows, grazing cattle, and small farms to Villars, the next village up the mountain. Villars was a tourist attraction and chic winter ski resort to others, but for us it was the place to buy a few groceries for the next day's meals, browse through a store or two, and pick up a copy of the International Herald Tribune, our only connection to the world outside our idyllic mountainside retreat.

It was providential that Art and Leona DeFehr, intent on visiting L'Abri, had stopped along that mountain highway on a beautiful, crispy-clear October day to ask us where it was. Why they thought we might know its whereabouts is a question without an answer, but we converged on the one spot on the roadway where they could pull off at exactly the same moment. Five seconds earlier or later, and if we had lingered just a bit longer or shorter at any of our Villars stops, we would have missed the DeFehrs. I have pondered from time to time how fate might have taken us in a completely different direction but for that chance meeting.

We not only directed the DeFehrs to Huémoz, but invited them to stay with us in our chalet for their two days at L'Abri. Art DeFehr, a businessman from Winnipeg, Canada, had just spent two weeks inspecting the Cambodian and Laotian refugee camps in Thailand. He and Leona were decompressing from that experience by traveling through Europe.

During their time with us, Art wrote long reports to the United Nations High Commissioner for Refugees (UNHCR) in Thailand and the International Committee of the Red Cross (ICRC) on conditions and problems at the Thai refugee camps along the Cambodian border. He also recommended solutions. I was singularly impressed that he was doing all this on his own time and at his own expense without any official status. He was a concerned private citizen who felt he could make a difference for refugees not just in Thailand, but in other trouble spots of the world. The son of Russian immigrants to Canada, with a Harvard MBA and a brilliant analytical mind, he put that mind to work on behalf of the poor and oppressed. His Mennonite faith undergirded his actions, helping refugees from war who had lost everything. He didn't need anyone to invite him or sanction his work. He just did it.[2]

Those two days with Art DeFehr opened up a new way of thinking and a new world of possibilities to me. It was a world where one person really could make a difference. Perhaps breathing the clear Swiss alpine air had something to do with it. Or maybe it was recalling my own bar admission quest. But I left Huémoz rested, physically and emotionally, with a heart full of hopes and aspirations for grasping something as yet undefined – something clearly out of reach.

Just 15 months later the opportunity came for me to fly solo into uncharted terrain and to follow Art DeFehr's example. The Cambodian refugee camps in Thailand beckoned, and I went, uninvited and unsponsored.

Thai Refugee Camps 1980

In October 1978 when we met the DeFehrs serendipitously on that mountain road in the Swiss Alps, the refugee camps in Thailand were already filled with over 100,000 Cambodians who had fled the sadistic brutality of the Khmer Rouge. Just two months after our highway encounter, Vietnamese troops invaded Cambodia and, in short order, deposed the Khmer Rouge and installed their own puppet Cambodian government. This produced a wave of new refugees pouring across the Thai border, including Khmer Rouge fighters and sympathizers. Another large population also sought haven in Thailand – Cambodians of Chinese descent. As a largely educated and business-oriented

---

[2] Art DeFehr's private efforts on behalf of SE Asian refugees gained enough respect in international circles that he was later appointed U.N. High Commissioner for Refugees in Somalia 1982-1983.

ethnic group, Chinese Cambodians had already suffered horrible persecution under the Khmer Rouge. Now the Vietnamese occupation made life even worse for them. The historic enmity between Vietnam and China had flared up to border skirmishes between the two armies, fueled by China's concern that Vietnam's invasion of Cambodia was concrete evidence of even greater Vietnamese ambitions throughout Southeast Asia. To be ethnic Chinese in Cambodia now meant you were persecuted by both the Khmer Rouge and the Vietnamese.

By 1979 tens of thousands of ethnic Chinese Cambodians had sought refuge in Thailand. The Thai government grew increasingly concerned that the swelling refugee population along its borders would far exceed the international community's ability to resettle them in third countries. Thai officials could foresee the day when the remaining un-resettled refugees would become a huge economic, political, and social problem for Thailand. Thus the Thai army began rounding up thousands of refugees at a time from the camps and forcibly repatriating them, at gunpoint, into Cambodia. Stories abounded of ethnic Chinese refugees in the thousands caught between the Thai and Vietnamese armies, wandering through the border jungles eking out meals of insects and tree bark, and looking for an opportunity to cross into Thailand again. And again.

In 1979 some good friends, George and Sonia Haas, traveled to Thailand under the auspices of Food for the Hungry, one of the many non-governmental organizations (NGO) working in Thai refugee camps at the time. They spent almost two weeks in the emergency feeding centers at several refugee camps. George and Sonia were fellow members of Mercer Island Covenant Church, and we were in a small community group together. They came home from their trip telling heartbreaking stories of what they had seen and experienced. One evening at a meeting of our group, they brought an aerogram letter that had just arrived from Thailand. It was written in Chinese. Sonia was

Chinese-American and spoke Cantonese but could not read Chinese. Knowing I could, they asked me to translate.

The letter was written by one person representing three ethnic Chinese families, all of whom had been befriended by George and Sonia during their time in the refugee camps. They pleaded for help from the Haas's to get them sponsored and resettled into third countries. They told of holding out no hope for resettlement unless there was outside help, and that every day they lived in fear of being forced back into Cambodia at gunpoint.

More letters arrived from these three families, each more urgent than the last in pleading for help. Each time our group met, I would translate the most recent letter. Soon the group began considering what we might do to help. In my mind, it became very clear what I must do. With the recollection of Art DeFehr's forays into the Thai refugee camps fresh in my mind, I discussed it with Cyd and she gave me the green light to go to Thailand and see what I could do about helping the families. The friends in our group were supportive and even contributed toward my travel expenses.

In preparation for my trip I contacted Maury Hausher, a friend who worked as an administrative assistant to Congressman Joel Pritchard who represented Washington State's First Congressional District. I had met Pritchard while working for Gov. Evans in Olympia. Evans and Pritchard were longtime personal and political friends. Maury was able to determine from inquiries to the State Department that there was an unmovable barrier between our three families and resettlement in the U.S. or anywhere else. Thailand had stopped granting refugee status to any refugees arriving in Thailand after a cutoff date in late 1978. The Thai government declared any arrivals after the cutoff date to be "illegal immigrants" subject to deportation en masse. This meant a great majority of the several hundred thousand refugees in the camps would have no chance at resettlement. Until a person or family was given refugee status by Thailand, there was no way to activate on their behalf the international resettlement process, run through UNHCR and ICRC. And Thailand was making no exceptions. That meant our three families and most of the ethnic Chinese who escaped Cambodia after the Vietnamese invaded the country were out of luck.

Maury did more than just get information from the State Department. He also managed to contact the U.S. Embassy in Bangkok and asked the Embassy to help me in whatever way it could. I also got some help from another quarter – my former legal secretary, Hope Phillips, who was a family friend of the Abramowitz family. Morton Abramowitz was serving as U.S. Ambassador to Thailand. Hope's mother wrote to her friend Sheppie Abramowitz, wife of the Ambassador, to let her know I was coming to Bangkok.

Providentially, on January 20, 1980, about three weeks before my scheduled trip to Thailand, a lengthy Sydney Schanberg story entitled *The Death and Life of Dith Pran* was published in the *New York Times* Sunday Magazine. This was the deeply moving story of Schanberg's escape from Phnom Penh, aided by his Cambodian stringer Dith Pran, on the fateful day in 1975 when the Khmer Rouge marched into the capital city. Schanberg, a *New York Times* journalist, unsuccessfully tried to get Dith Pran into the U.S. Embassy grounds with him. The two lost contact, and Schanberg spent over four agonizing years searching for any sign of whether Dith Pran had survived the Cambodian holocaust. On October 3, 1979, Schanberg finally got word that Dith Pran had escaped into Thailand. His written account of their friendship, their work together, their parting in 1975, and finally their reunion in 1979, made for one of the most compelling real life stories I had ever read. The story subsequently was made into the 1984 Academy-award winning and powerfully moving film *Killing Fields*.

More importantly for my quest, Dith Pran's story gave me something I had searched for in vain up to that time: a precedent – highly publicized, at that – for making an exception to the rule. Pran came out of Cambodia well past the cutoff date for refugee classification, but was promptly resettled into the U.S. after his escape. This meant that everyone – the Thai army and government, the UNHCR, the ICRC, and the U.S. Embassy – had allowed an exception to the rule for Pran. Otherwise, Dith Pran would have stayed in the refugee camps in Thailand, joining several hundred thousand others who woke up every morning wondering if this would be the day when the Thai army would force them back to Cambodia yet again.

My research disclosed that there were roughly 30,000 ethnic Chinese refugees in the camps. I prepared a "brief" on their plight, arguing that of all the Khmer refugees in the Thai camps, the ethnic Chinese were most at peril if repatriated to Cambodia. Whether Cambodia was ruled by the Khmer Rouge or the Vietnamese, the Chinese had already suffered and would continue to suffer severe persecution. The ethnic Chinese population in Cambodia had been decimated by the Khmer Rouge; the remaining among them had no future in Cambodia and should be granted refugee status to be resettled in third countries. The typical profile of the ethnic Chinese refugees, with a higher-than-normal education level and a record of success in business, made them more likely to succeed once resettled. This made it more likely that third countries would welcome them as refugees.

On February 15, 1980, I took the long trans-Pacific journey to Bangkok, Thailand. I had 10 days. Prior to departure I talked to Fred Gregory of World Concern, a veteran Southeast Asia traveler doing relief and development work, to get some ideas on what to expect in Bangkok. He not only provided helpful guidance, but said he would be traveling to Thailand a few days before my trip and welcomed me to join him in sharing a hotel room to save on lodging expense.

The patent absurdity of what I hoped to accomplish in Thailand was not lost on me. I had no official status of any kind. Maury Hausher's inquiries on my behalf had resulted in an appointment at the U.S. Embassy on the Monday after my arrival in Bangkok. Otherwise, I was on my own, heading into a geopolitical maelstrom involving not only Cambodia, Vietnam, and Thailand, but 900-pound gorillas lurking in the shadows – China (backers of the Khmer Rouge), the Soviet Union (Vietnam's big brother), and the U.S. (trying to regain its footing in Southeast Asia after a graceless fall). Not only had the Vietnam War torn apart America's national fabric, but in the aftermath of the U.S. defeat and withdrawal, it was as if a giant, boiling cauldron of violence had been upset, and millions of innocents in the region were scalded badly.

By now I had settled on a strategy. I would make inquiries of all the government and international agencies with any authority or involvement in the refugee camps and argue the case for the 30,000 ethnic Chinese Cambodians to be granted refugee status. I would also plead the case of the three specific families, and ask for their reclassification as refugees – even if the other ethnic Chinese were not reclassified.

On Sunday evening after my arrival, Fred Gregory took me to a gathering of expatriates at the apartment of one of his colleagues, Reg Reimer of World Relief. There were relief and development workers of various nationalities there, and most interestingly, *New York Times* Bangkok correspondent Henry Kamm. I had regularly kept up on Kamm's pieces in the *Times* in advance of my trip, and now felt like a gold miner who had hit a mother lode. I quizzed him about refugee issues and who might be helpful within the Thai government, the Thai army, the UNHCR, and ICRC. In particular, I peppered him with questions on what he knew about Dith Pran, his escape into

Thailand, and the quick resettlement to the U.S. Thankfully, Kamm was very accommodating and did not seem to mind my steady stream of questions.

The next morning I showed up for my appointment at the U.S. Embassy and was ushered into the office of the *chargé d'affaires*, a subordinate of the Ambassador's. He explained that Ambassador Abramowitz was back in Washington, D.C. on consultations. The man had been briefed on my background and interest, and not long into the conversation, told me that the reclassification of the Cambodian refugees for resettlement purposes was entirely a matter of Thai government policy and that the U.S. could do nothing without a change in the Thai position.

I asked if the U.S. government could exert pressure on the Thai government to change their policy for humanitarian reasons, explaining to him the perilous position of the ethnic Chinese Cambodians. He said there was absolutely no chance of that, they could not make exceptions, and they did not expect the Thai government would make any exceptions either.

That was my cue.

He had set himself up by making such an unqualified statement. I asked him about Dith Pran, and whether that was not a very public example of an exception to the rule and the willingness of the Thai government to grant exceptions in extraordinary cases. I added that the U.S. government had obviously made an exception for Dith Pran, too, in making the request to the Thai government and all other concerned agencies. He had no response for me. He simply shook his head, and I could detect a hint of a smile that I interpreted as a nonverbal "*touché.*" His silence spoke volumes.

It seemed I had gotten nowhere with the *chargé d'affaires*, and yet I had achieved my purpose. Before the meeting, I had needed to find out whether there were other factors in the Dith Pran case that I did not know about, whether there were classified reasons why Dith Pran got out of the Thai camps, or other reasons why Dith Pran's case did not prove an exception to the rule. Answers to any of those questions would have slammed the door in my face. But through his silence, I now saw that the Dith Pran case left the door ajar for me to attempt my entry.

As I got up to leave, he informed me that Mrs. Abramowitz had invited me to lunch at the Embassy later in the week.

That whole week I spent knocking on doors, showing up at government and agency offices without appointment, without portfolio, simply as a private U.S. citizen. The Thai Interior Ministry, the Thai army, UNHCR, ICRC – I spent hours waiting in reception areas for someone to talk to me, then would be gone in the space of 10-15 minutes after finally having someone see me. No one really wanted to talk to me, and no one wanted to hear what I had to say. One Thai army major assigned to get rid of me did ask me a difficult question: "Mr. Li, you ask for reclassification of the Chinese Cambodians to give them refugee status. And you say that if that is not possible, you still want those three families to be reclassified and resettled. There are thousands of families who came out of Cambodia before your three families, who are hoping for reclassification and resettlement. Why should we move your three families to the front of the line? How can you justify that?" I had no answer for the major. Indeed, there was no compelling reason for the three families to move ahead of thousands of others who despaired, hoped, and prayed for a new life in a third country. I did not even know these families personally. They were friends of friends, and very recently acquainted, at that. Not much of an argument there.

Thinking about it in my hotel room that night, doubts invaded my mind. The major's question weighed on my conscience. Pleading the case of 30,000 was right, for sure. Pleading the case of the three families even when others had waited in the camps many months longer – was this right, even if none of the other 30,000 were reclassified? Wasn't that asking for arbitrary and special treatment? I called Cyd that night, confessed my doubts, and asked her to poll the members of the group on whether I should give up the case of the three families. I told her I would call again early the next morning, and I hoped she would have some helpful counsel for me from the group.

The next morning Cyd was ready for my call. She said that in addition to talking to other members of the group, she had called our pastor, Bud Palmberg. Bud asked her to tell me that in his view, you do everything you can, for the many or for the few. We knew these families through George and Sonia Haas, and there was nothing wrong with doing everything we could to help them. I should not back off my efforts for the three families. Bud talked to Cyd about how God doesn't help people in numerical order, and in Exodus told Moses:

> I will have mercy on whom I have mercy, and compassion on whom I have compassion.[3]

She said that all in the group agreed that I should not back down on helping the three families in addition to arguing for all the ethnic Chinese.

I discovered at that moment the strength of working within a community of people. I did not have the capacity on my own to work through the moral and ethical considerations to answer the Thai army major's question. The counsel of others gave me peace and renewed my determination to do everything I could.

Midweek I went to the U.S. Ambassador's residence with my lunch invitation. There were three guests, including myself, sharing a simple lunch of sandwiches and salad with Sheppie Abramowitz. Mrs. Abramowitz quizzed me on why I came to Thailand, and spoke of her friendship with the Hope Phillips family. Hearing that I would be returning to the U.S. through

---

[3] Exodus 33:19

Hong Kong, she told me she would arrange a meeting for me with her friend, the U.S. Consul General there. She thought he might be sympathetic to my cause.

Later that week, I tagged along with Fred Gregory to visit Khao-I-Dang and Sakeo, two of the camps set up to house the Cambodia refugees fleeing from their country. Both camps were on the eastern border of Thailand. Khao-I-Dang was also where the three families were housed.

I was unprepared for what I saw: thousands of people, many emaciated from years of deprivation and starvation wandering the jungles in western Cambodia to escape the Khmer Rouge. An extraordinary number of them had lost teeth from lack of oral hygiene, malnutrition, and from chewing on roots and bark. Many had crossed over into Thailand, then been driven back across the border into Cambodia by the Thai army. Feeding stations, some manned by westerners working with humanitarian NGOs, were constantly crowded with people waiting for their allotment of food. The Sakeo camp was particularly grim. Its population consisted entirely of Khmer Rouge fighters and their families. The men had countenances seemingly devoid of human emotion. They looked on us visitors with suspicion, and their inhuman stares sent chills down my spine.

To my great disappointment, I discovered that our three families were not at Khao-I-Dang. They, along with other ethnic Chinese refugees, had been recently moved to Mairut, a camp on the southern coast of Thailand. I took the removal of ethnic Chinese refugees as a good sign – that the people in charge of the camps, including the international agencies, recognized the difficulties for the ethnic Chinese being mixed with the general population in the camps, particularly since there was a strong Khmer Rouge presence.

Fred left Thailand after we returned from the visit to the camps. He had been a good friend to me during his stay, helping me at every turn. He even paid for the room in full up to the end of his stay; I only needed to pick up the tab for the remaining days of my own stay.

Two days after visiting the border camps, I made my own way by bus to Mairut. The bus left Bangkok around noon, made stops all along the way, and finally arrived in Mairut late afternoon by which time it was too late for me to show up at the camp. The bus stopped at a local hotel where I got a room for the night. Compared to this hotel, the most dilapidated and seedy hotel room in the U.S. would have felt like a Ritz Carlton suite. After dinner when I returned to my room, I noticed bugs and insects crawling everywhere, particularly on the walls. Each leg of the bed sat in a tin can filled with water to keep insects from crawling up into the bed. I took the extra precaution, before going to sleep that night, of pulling the bed about two feet away from the wall so there wouldn't be bugs coming off the wall either.

The next morning I showed up at the Mairut camp gate with credentials from World Relief arranged for me by Reg Reimer. I was admitted without problem and soon located an English-speaking relief worker in the camp office who I asked about the three families. She spoke to someone in the office to find the families and to let them know they had a visitor. Within five minutes I saw people running toward the office – members of our three families. I told them, speaking in Mandarin Chinese, that I was a close friend of George and Sonia Haas. I found that most of them spoke the Cantonese dialect, but a couple of the men did speak Mandarin as well. They took me to the cluster of tents where they lived, and I met other family members and young children. Not surprisingly, they were terribly excited, and eagerly asked about George and Sonia, and just as anxiously asked if anything could be done for them to be reclassified as refugees and resettled. I told them we were doing everything we could, but that so far none of the Thai or international authorities had given any positive indications. I did not want to raise unreasonable expectations in their minds, knowing the near impossibility of the task at hand.

I spent about two hours with them, during which time they told me their individual stories. They had all been in the Cambodian middle class – one man was an acupuncturist, another a cook, and the third a machinist. They had been uprooted from their homes in Phnom Penh and driven into the countryside at gunpoint by the Khmer Rouge almost five years earlier and had to live by their wits to stay together and survive. Four years ago they joined the mass exodus toward the Thai border, crossed into Thailand, and were driven back by the Thai army into Cambodia. They struggled for survival along the border, and crossed again into Thailand when the Thai troops backed away. The process repeated itself; this was their fourth crossing into Thailand, and eight months had passed without being driven back. They were hopeful of staying this time, but the anxiety of not knowing whether the Thai army might turn them back to Cambodia again was an extreme stress factor in their lives.

When the time came to leave, I bid them farewell, telling them I had to catch the noon bus back to Bangkok. There were tears in their eyes as I left them behind at the camp gates. I left with a huge lump in my throat and was holding back tears myself. I had no idea whether I would ever see these people again.

I left Bangkok wondering if my 10 days in Thailand had done any good at all. I felt a bit like Don Quixote tilting with windmills and came to understand first-hand what it felt like to engage in what appeared to be a ridiculously quixotic quest.

My last stop was Hong Kong where between visits to clients I met with Sheppie Abramowitz's friend, the U.S. Consul General. His office was in charge of processing those refugees from Thailand who had been cleared by UNHCR and ICRC for resettlement in the U.S. Hong Kong was the intermediate stop for refugees on their way to the U.S. A final stamp of approval from the Consulate on their asylum application meant new travel papers with the coveted immigrant visa for the U.S. Thus the U.S. Consulate office in Hong Kong represented the last hurdle before the refugees could board flights to the U.S. where they would eventually join their church or family sponsors who awaited them in cities across the country.

The answer to my plea for the ethnic Chinese and for the three families, not surprisingly, did not differ from the official position I had heard from the State Department through Maury Hausher and from all the officials I met in Bangkok during the prior week. "Absolutely no," he said, because the Thai government would not grant them refugee status, and the U.S.'s hands were tied until the Thai government changed its position. As with all the others, I then raised the Dith Pran case with him. He said he did not think that case would mean anything for anyone else; it was a special case with special circumstances.

On my return to Seattle, other than telling the group and friends about the families in Mairut and the experiences of the trip, I had no good news to report about any of the objectives I had set out to achieve. I called Maury Hauser, who had heard from the State Department about my visit with the *chargé d'affaires* in Bangkok and about my meeting with the consul general in Hong Kong. Each of those individuals had reported my requests, and the State Department let Pritchard's office know they had done what they could to accommodate the Congressman's constituent. They gave no indication of any change in policy.

By this time Senator Magnuson's office had also begun to intervene on behalf of the three families, and I was able to get help from the Senator's office through contacts made during graduate school days. Maggie's staff even persuaded Senator Henry Jackson's office to join the bandwagon.

The first indication of a crack in the policy so firmly set in stone came five months after my return from Thailand. At the end of July 1980 Maury Hausher told me over the phone that the State Department's director of Thailand Affairs, Paul Cleveland, called him to say that a change in policy was afoot – our three families might be eligible for resettlement in the near future. However, a lot had to happen before anything could be confirmed.

We greeted the news with great joy. Any celebrating, however, would be premature. Days of waiting turned into weeks, then into months. It was not until mid-October that the crack became a full breach in the dike – not only had our three families been reclassified, but all the ethnic Chinese refugees as well, and every one of them was eligible for resettlement in third countries.

By that time Maury informed me that even Congressman Stephen Solarz, then chairman of the Asian and Pacific Affairs Subcommittee of the House Foreign Affairs Committee, was pressing for the State Department to expand its categories of refugee visas to allow the Sino-Khmers to be resettled in the U.S. Solarz argued that the ethnic Chinese in Vietnam had been resettled in the U.S. within six months of the fall of Saigon. The ethnic Chinese who escaped from Cambodia, in contrast, had been in the Thai camps for five to six years. Persistent cables from Ambassador Abramowitz in Thailand also urged the higher-ups in the State Department to reclassify and accept resettlement of ethnic Chinese refugees from Cambodia.

On October 15, 1980, Maury Hausher called to say that Joel Pritchard had just been informed by the State Department that the process of reclassification and resettlement of the Sino-Khmers, including our three families, was proceeding "full steam ahead."

We soon began receiving letters from our three families indicating they had been transferred to different locations in preparation for resettlement. They told us the cook had decided to resettle in France where he had distant relatives who could help his family. The acupuncturist had friends who had earlier resettled in Salem, Oregon, and decided to head in that direction. Acupuncture was not a legal practice in Washington State at that time, but was legal in Oregon. By settling in Salem, he would be able to make a living to support his family. The machinist – Hy-Soung Kaing, his wife Sim, and their little baby boy Yong-Se, born in the refugee camp – had no family connections or friends elsewhere. They were headed for Seattle, sponsored by our group of families and Mercer Island Covenant Church.

Bureaucratic wheels turn slowly. It was not until late May 1981 that I received a call from World Relief, the NGO that assisted refugees in the resettlement process, telling me the two families headed for the U.S. had arrived in San Francisco, and would be traveling to Seattle on a Northwest Airlines flight on June 1.

On that date, at least two dozen of us, members of our community group and other church friends, greeted the Kaing family upon their arrival at Seattle-Tacoma International Airport. What a profoundly joyful reunion that was. They had come halfway across the world to begin a new life, leaving behind the nightmare existence of Khmer Rouge savagery, border crossings and repatriations, starvation and deprivation. Over the next weeks and months, our group of friends helped them find housing, furnishings, and jobs, and then shuttled them to medical and dental appointments.

No explanations were ever given to me on why the policy had been changed. I have no idea whether the ground had already been shifting when I undertook my quest to pester every official in Bangkok who would see me. Did my puny efforts provide a catalytic spark for a chain reaction that moved governments, armies, and international agencies? It does not really matter. Far more important to the story of Agros is that I now had a first-hand experience taking on a task far greater than common sense dictated could ever be achieved. Just two years after the Swiss alpine sojourn and the providential encounter with the DeFehrs on that mountain highway, a small family of three souls living in Bellevue, Washington, were living proof that faith can indeed move mountains – if we're crazy enough to believe it.

4

CLARION CALL

In February, 1982, Mercer Island Covenant Church had invited Juan Carlos Ortíz, a dynamic preacher from Argentina, to be the principal speaker at a three-day missions conference designed to expand the congregation's perspective on work being done around the world. He was scheduled to speak four times – Friday night, Saturday afternoon, then Sunday morning and evening.

During that opening session on Friday evening Juan Carlos spoke from the kingdom parables taught by Jesus to his disciples. He was a spellbinding orator, and brought unique insights to otherwise familiar material. Though I was tired from a long and hard week of work, I was captivated by Juan Carlos' presentation. On Saturday afternoon I needed no coaxing from Cyd to go to the second session. I went expectantly, anticipating a fresh perspective on the parable in Matthew 13:45-46: "Again, the kingdom of heaven is like a merchant seeking fine pearls, and upon finding one pearl of great value, he went and sold all that he had and bought it." I was utterly unprepared for what turned out to be not just a great talk, but a clarion call that changed my life.

Juan Carlos plunged into the parable in his unique, Spanish-accented speaking style. He spoke with few notes and blended humor with *gravitas*. In particular I recall the imagined dialogue he carried on between the merchant and the owner of the pearl of great price, and how the merchant, in payment, had to give up everything – possessions, money, even his family – to buy that pearl. If you have ever listened to comedian Bill Cosby do the imagined conversation between God and Noah about building an ark, Juan Carlos' one-man dialogue over the pearl of great price had the same kind of humorous elements to it.[1]

Midway through this captivating sermon, Juan Carlos spoke about giving to the poor as part of the price God asks of us in order to buy the great pearl of the parable. He lampooned our modern Christian notions of giving to the church, particularly when our gifts are used to make church facilities more pleasing and comfortable for ourselves:

> Most of the time the offering is for us. We say, 'Let's bring an offering to the Lord so we can put in air conditioning.' The Lord doesn't need any air conditioning! 'Let's bring an offering to the Lord so we can put in new carpet.' He doesn't need new carpet! Most of the money we bring is for us, for our comfort. Here's what God says about giving: 'Whatever you give to these poor little ones, you're giving it to me.' Even if it is a glass of cold water. We can help the needy, we can give to the poor.

Then Juan Carlos took the detour that changed my life. He even stepped from behind the podium at this point, and stood next to it with his right arm resting on its side. Call it a sidebar, call it a rabbit trail. He spoke of having watched a presidential press conference on the news that morning in which President Reagan announced a $300 million arms assistance package to the

---

[1] For many years I was not aware that this sermon was taped. One day, some 18 years after that MICC missions conference, my good friend Ken Lottis surprised me by presenting to me an audio tape of Juan Carlos' message that Saturday. He said he had been looking through the audio catalog at the church and had come across it. Knowing how much it meant to me, he had made a copy for me. I was overjoyed to listen to it and found my recollection of that day's message faulty in some respects, but accurate in its essentials.

Central American countries fighting Communist insurgencies. He lamented how that would be such a waste – with that kind of money, you could buy all the land in Central America and give it to the poor, and you wouldn't have to fight the Communists. He talked about how we Christians could come up with the $300 million just by selling our church buildings. Then he added:

> So, if we would give money to the Lord to help the poor, we would be bringing the kingdom of God to earth. As Jesus said, 'Seek first the Kingdom of God and his righteousness.' But we spend the money on comfortable ventures; we change the carpet when we have a stain. We say now that organ is too old; we'll get a bigger one. Those offerings are not for Jesus. They're for us.

At this point it was as if he woke up to the fact he had really wandered from his message. He got back behind the podium, and finished the detour with these words:

> Well, let's continue with our parable. This was just a parenthesis.

Just a *parenthesis?*

His parenthesis hit me like a fully charged electric shock. I was stunned. My mind was scrambling to find its bearings. I listened to the rest of his message, but heard very little. My mind was on its own rabbit trail now.

In my law practice I had been doing a great deal of work in securities law. This included helping clients who syndicated groups of investors in limited partnerships to buy large tracts of undeveloped land in the path of growth. The business plan projected that the land, in key locations, would increase in value with urban or suburban expansion, and would eventually be bought at much higher prices by developers, or by state and local governments for highways, roads, and public infrastructure development.

I asked myself, could we not syndicate groups of donors to raise funds to buy large tracts of agricultural land? Couldn't the land in turn be sold at cost to the poor on credit terms that would be affordable? I had just read a few weeks earlier a front page lead story in the Wall Street Journal on the failure of U.S. government-funded land reform in El Salvador due to the Salvadoran government's incompetence and corruption. The poor had their hopes and expectations raised, only to have them smashed to bits. Things were made worse, not better. In fact, failed land reform was one of the Marxist battle cries in the bloody civil war raging in El Salvador at that time.

As I sat there pondering what Juan Carlos had said, I asked myself why we always waited for governments to help the poor through land reform. Wasn't helping the poor a clear calling by God to his people? Why couldn't we take God seriously and help the poor buy land ourselves; why wait for governments to do it?

That night at home I wrote a concept paper on private land reform. I thought of different ways to get land into the hands of the poor. Just giving the land to them was not an option. It seemed that people, however poor they were, needed the dignity of knowing that their well-being was earned through hard work, and not handed to them on a platter. I thought of forming a nonprofit to buy land and then lease it to poor farmers. But then I thought better. I realized that even though we might give them far better terms than other landlords, they would still operate under the cloud of not owning the land. When title to the land is in someone else's hands, a farmer will always suffer from the anxiety of losing his living to others. For generations, too many tenant farmers had learned to expect their *dueño* to mistreat them or take advantage of them. Why should they trust North

American *dueños*, no matter that these owners had charitable intent?

It all boiled down to this essential fact: farmers anywhere in the world would far prefer to own their land than to lease it. The motivation to work hard for one's family will always be diluted by the insecurity of not owning one's own farmland. Ownership was the key. The poor must be able to own the land. There must be a way to let them get on the land, work hard, and repay the price through their harvests.

We might never raise $300 million, and that amount might never be enough to buy up all the land in Central America. But we could start with one parcel of land in one region of one country. We could help one group of people. If that worked, we could go on to buy more land in other regions and help more groups of people.

What more logical place to start, I thought, than Guatemala? I had lived there as a young boy and spoke the language. Perhaps by now, some childhood friends would be in positions of influence to help. Travel would be relatively painless; one could leave Seattle in the morning and be in Guatemala by that same evening. The country was only a couple of time zones away.

I knew there was a bloody civil war in Guatemala, just as there was in El Salvador. I also knew the causes of the civil war were similar – oppression, injustice, and total imbalance in the distribution of wealth and availability of opportunity for the poor. Land tenure would be high on the list of reasons why the Marxist guerrillas gained adherents among the rural poor. While I had no self-proclaimed messianic calling to defeat international Communism, I did feel an unmistakable summons to help the poor.

The experience of flying solo in Thailand and having had a small hand in the resettlement of tens of thousands of ethnic Chinese refugees from Cambodia gave me the nerve to consider taking on the issue of land tenure in Central America. Besides, I had seen Art DeFehr as one lone businessman from Winnipeg, Canada, take on the enormous issue of refugees displaced by civil warfare in Southeast Asia and East Africa.

I could hardly sleep that night. Sunday morning at church I collared my friend Dick Nelson – Juan Carlos was staying at the Nelsons' home during the missions conference – and asked him if I could go talk to Juan Carlos about the idea he had tossed out in the Saturday session. After the morning service Dick came to me and said Juan Carlos had agreed to meet with me at the Nelsons' home after the evening service. I thanked Dick profusely. The rest of the day couldn't pass quickly enough. Cyd and I attended both Sunday morning and evening services, but I remember nothing of what Juan Carlos said in either of those sessions, I was so completely absorbed in thinking about the private land reform idea.

That night Cyd and I went to Dick and Meri's home on the south end of Mercer Island. To say I was eager and excited would be an understatement. After we arrived and Dick had let him know we were there, Juan Carlos came out to greet us in the Nelsons' front living room. He was already dressed in pajamas and a dressing gown. His eyes looked glazed over. I realized this man was in a state of absolute exhaustion. He had thrown himself into four one-hour messages and had nothing left in the gas tank.

In my excitement I began to blurt out my ideas, built around his little rabbit trail exhortation on buying land for the poor. Within four to five minutes of my spiel, he interrupted me:

Skip, if you feel the call from God to do this, please do it. My calling is to be a preacher, and that is what I am, and that is all I know how to do.

He hardly seemed to remember his little parenthesis, and the thoughts that had so moved me were left somewhere on one of the many side trails in his trek through the kingdom parables. He struggled to stay awake and listen to me. Even in his exhaustion he made it very clear to me he had no interest in pursuing the subject of buying land privately for the poor. I cannot say I was surprised, but I did feel a distinct sense of disappointment. How I would have loved to support Juan Carlos Ortíz in a new venture to buy land for the poor! His total lack of interest meant I'd have to find someone else to pick up the idea, or go it alone.[2]

My first option after striking out with Juan Carlos was Art Beals, president of World Concern, an international relief and development agency based in Seattle. World Concern had cut its disaster relief teeth in Guatemala during the aftermath of the devastating 1976 earthquake there. That effort had put the organization on the map, so Guatemala held a special place in Art's thinking. I served on an advisory committee for World Concern at the time and attended occasional meetings where Art and staff would brief us on work they were doing around the world. Art was an inspirational guy, full of ideas and enthusiasm. He was excited when I laid out the idea and immediately began thinking aloud of Guatemala connections who might help carry out the scheme. He agreed we should take an exploratory trip there, and we settled on a date six months from that time, in October. I would have liked to do it sooner, but Art's travel schedule was fully booked until then. We agreed that he and his

---

[2] Years later, in June 1999, Juan Carlos Ortíz returned to Mercer Island Covenant Church as the principal speaker at the 50th year anniversary of MICC. The Agros board arranged to meet Juan Carlos at MICC for an hour before the beginning of the anniversary program. At that meeting I told Juan Carlos how I had heard him speak in February 1982 and how his then throwaway comment on buying land in Central America had sparked the whole idea of Agros. I told him what Agros had become in the intervening years with the villages and the poor who now owned their own land. Tears streamed down his face as he listened. "I had no idea," he responded after hearing the story.

office would do the advance work with people to meet and involve in Guatemala.

I felt great at that point. Art loved the idea, and I now had an international NGO interested in taking it on. I would have been content to stay in the background and let Art and World Concern take over the whole thing while I concentrated on building my law firm and caring for my young family.

Any sense of self-satisfaction over those encouraging developments came to an abrupt end somewhere toward the end of August 1982. Art called me to say that on the very strong advice of his Latin America director, he had decided to cancel his trip to Guatemala in October. When the director heard what Art had agreed to do with me, she called him from Costa Rica. She told him that it was far too dangerous to travel to Guatemala at that time. She had heard from NGO colleagues in Costa Rica that Guatemala was under martial law, meetings involving three or more people were banned, and guerrillas were in Guatemala City battling the army in the streets.

Dismay preceded anger. In one phone call from Costa Rica, my hopes seemed dashed. Costa Rica! A country of beautiful resorts and beaches. It is what I would call a "transition" country – not wholly Central American – a place where Americans feel safe. You don't hear about guerrillas or kidnappings in Costa Rica. You're in Central America, but you're not in Central America. Costa Rica is a favored destination for American tourists and retirees. In the early 1980s, it was also a haven for a good many American NGOs who felt the other Central American countries were too dangerous for their personnel.

To top it all off, Art also informed me that no arrangements or contacts had been made for the trip on his end. I did not blame Art; his professional staff was sending him a warning he could not ignore.

I was in a state of shock after the phone call. All I had hoped for in a partnership with World Concern was gone. I had already booked my flight to Guatemala for October 8, and I knew there was not enough time to ask another organization to take the baton Art had just handed back to me.

My shock turned into profound discouragement. First Juan Carlos Ortíz expressed zero interest in being involved. Then Art Beals pulled out of the scheduled October trip to Guatemala. I was told that martial law had been imposed in Guatemala, that there were firefights between guerrillas and the army in the streets. No contacts had been made in Guatemala. The possible now seemed improbable.

Should I cancel my own flight reservations and forget about the whole idea? It felt as if a wide-open door had slammed in my face just as I stepped on the threshold. As my heated emotions cooled down a few notches, I began to consider earnestly whether I should continue.

Memories of my time two years earlier in Thailand came to me. I recalled the same feelings of frustration and despair; how I had encountered one closed door after another; how I was told repeatedly there was no possibility that my petition on behalf of the ethnic Chinese refugees could be considered, much less granted.

I eventually got over the negative emotions. So be it, I thought. If I had to go on my own without World Concern, I'd move ahead until I came to a dead end and could not move any further. One phone call from Costa Rica did not mean the idea of buying land for the poor was not worth pursuing. I started to think of friends and acquaintances from years past in Guatemala who might be able to help.

I pondered who might have connections in Guatemala and thought of Kent Hotaling, a friend who worked with Doug Coe in Washington D.C. Doug was a unique man with amazing contacts in practically every country around the world. Perhaps Kent would know of some Coe contacts in Guatemala.

Kent's response surprised me. "Skip, your best contact for Guatemala is in your own back yard in Seattle – Richard Barrueto."

Richard Barrueto? "I thought he was Italian," I replied.

I had known Richard for several years, had come across him at a downtown breakfast group, and also worked with him on a nonprofit board. It turned out that Richard, a businessman in Seattle, grew up in Guatemala and still traveled there every year.

I called Richard, found him at home, and asked him if I could come over to talk to him about some ideas I had. He invited me over right away. When I arrived he was testing his new high-end Danish stereo system on which he was playing Tchaikovsky's 1812 Overture at full blast. When he finally turned down the volume, I told him about the private land reform idea that was stirring in my head. He had a good laugh when I told him I had thought he was Italian. We began speaking in Spanish, and out of his mouth came a beautiful, refined Castilian Spanish.

The son of a prominent Protestant pastor, he was born and raised in Guatemala. He had come to the United States when he was 16 to go to school and had stayed. Early in his career he worked as a scientist at Boeing on the manned space program. One of his colleagues had been the great science fiction writer Isaac Asimov. After he left Boeing he bought a small distribution business that he still ran at that time. He traveled back to Guatemala just about every year to visit his family and close friends.

I shared with him my own childhood background in Guatemala, laid out my thinking about private land reform, and told him I had a plane ticket for Guatemala in early October. He volunteered to contact a very close childhood friend of his, Walter Schieber. Walter, he said, was the business manager for the Lutheran Church – Missouri Synod – in Central America and the Caribbean. He recommended Walter as an excellent contact and a trustworthy man who understood the situation in Guatemala and who could advise me on how to proceed.

In 1982 universal e-mail and low cost international calls were figments of techie geek imaginations. The fastest way to communicate with someone outside the U.S. was by fax. So Richard faxed a letter to Walter Schieber, and Walter responded that he would be delighted to meet me when I flew to Guatemala.

The connection with Richard Barrueto and through him, Walter Schieber, was a dose of encouragement for me at a critical time. Looking back, I can see that Walter's integrity and trustworthiness meant more than any role he actually played in the development of the Agros idea. My hopes also were raised by another strange and highly unlikely door that would soon open for me.

About a month before my October 1982 trip, still searching for more points of contact in Guatemala, I read about a professional colleague who was then working for President Reagan. Herb Ellingwood had been legal counsel to Ronald Reagan during his two terms as governor of California. Herb was now on the legal counsel staff at the White House. I had met Herb during meetings of chief extradition officers across the country when I was legal counsel to Gov. Dan Evans. Working in the White House, Herb's network of international contacts, I thought, must be quite extensive.

My telephone call to Herb triggered a sequence of events that has still not ended. After listening to me tell him what I was up to – the upcoming trip to Guatemala, and my need for contacts who might help – Herb told me that a group called Gospel Outreach in Eureka, California, was involved with a church in Guatemala City. He said that the Guatemalan president, Efraín Ríos Montt, was a member of that church. He suggested the head of Gospel Outreach, Jim Durkin, might be able to help me get some connections and contacts in Guatemala.

Websites and Google being non-existent then, I called directory information for Eureka to get a phone number for Gospel Outreach. Thus ensued a cold call to Jim Durkin from a Chinese lawyer in Seattle who claimed to have gotten his name through Herb Ellingwood in the White House asking for names of people in Guatemala. Predictably, his response was very guarded and cool.

This unlikely course took an even stranger turn when a client from New Zealand came to consult with me on legal matters in late September 1982. Doug Maskell was a businessman from Christchurch who was spending some time in the U.S. with his daughter and son-in-law. As we chatted, he found out I was traveling to Guatemala, which led to questions on why I would do that, which led further to my telling him about my search for contacts there who might be helpful, and how one trail had gone cold on me in Eureka, California.

Eureka? Doug said he knew someone in Eureka by the name of Jim Durkin who has great connections in Guatemala.

Jim Durkin? "You know Jim Durkin," I asked him.

"Sure," he responded, "and I'd be happy to give him a call."

Shortly after that fortuitous meeting with Doug Maskell, I received a phone call from Jim Durkin, and his tone was completely changed. He asked me for my flight number, arrival time, and where I was staying in Guatemala City. He also told me that he would arrange for someone to contact me at my hotel after my arrival.

The unlikely and improbable adventure was set to begin.

5

GUATEMALA

Few international airlines flew into Guatemala in 1982. Not many people traveled there since the civil war that engulfed the country for 36 years, from 1960 to 1996, was probably at its most violent peak from late 1981 to early 1982.

When I first traveled to Guatemala as a young boy in 1956, the country was poor, but peaceful – not often the case in Guatemalan history. In 1520 the Spanish armies, led by Hernán Cortés, used brutal violence to conquer the indigenous tribes, and planted seeds of corruption and violence in the country's culture. Even after Guatemala won independence from Spain in 1821, the country was never more than one greedy power-grab away from political violence.

Historians now trace the roots of the 36-year civil war to 1954, when the left-leaning government of Jacobo Árbenz Guzmán was overthrown in a coup that looked suspiciously like it was engineered by the CIA. Árbenz's policies, which until then had consisted of a rather mild series of reform measures, began to favor labor and the poor in a way that appeared to the CIA to lead straight toward Communism. And at the time, Cold War saber rattling between the U.S. and the Soviet Union meant that Uncle Sam would not tolerate a Central American government that even hinted at favoring Communist ideology.

The hard-right turn carried out by the two successive military dictatorships of Col. Carlos Castillo Armas and Gen. Miguel Ydígoras Fuentes from 1954 - 1963 was bitter bile in the mouths of those who had so recently tasted the fruits of leftward change. In 1960 a leftist group of officers in the Guatemalan army began an insurgency campaign, aided by the newly successful Cuban revolutionary Fidel Castro. For the next 36 years the civil war became a surrogate battleground with the U.S. on one side, and the USSR on the other. The Soviet pipeline shipped weapons to Cuba for transshipment to southern Mexico and then to the guerrillas in the mountainous regions of the Guatemalan highlands. The indigenous people, poor and oppressed since the Spanish colonial times, had the least to gain from the war but suffered the most. Caught in a middle ground that did not allow neutrality, they were coerced and brutalized by both sides of the conflict.[1]

Not long before I began making plans to travel to Guatemala City, the guerrillas had fought their way out of the mountainous regions and were threatening major urban areas. Battles were fought even in the outskirts of Guatemala City.

The routes for someone traveling from Seattle went either through Los Angeles, Houston or Miami to connect with Pan American, United, or Continental to Guatemala City. I chose the Los Angeles route in order to have a quick reunion with my parents who lived there at the time. My sister Lydia brought them to the airport, and during our short rendezvous my parents handed me six or seven small gifts and letters for me to hand over to their long-time friends in Guatemala City. My mother also gave me a rather stern lecture about what seemed to her a rather reckless venture into a country wracked by war and violence.

When the cabin door was closed and the Pan Am Boeing 727 jet moved onto the tarmac for takeoff, I found I was one of an underwhelming total of 10 passengers on that flight. At least

---

[1] The best and most evenly balanced account of how the civil war trapped indigenous Guatemalans between two deadly pincers is David Stoll's *Between Two Armies in the Ixil Towns of Guatemala* (1994).

that was how many I counted in the coach section. Maybe there were one or two passengers in first class.

It certainly made for a comfortable trip, stretched across three seats, with no one in the row in front or behind me. The plane had a full complement of crew so the ratio of flight attendants to passengers was excellent. Back then international flights came with an elaborate dinner service in coach class as well, and we passengers felt like we had booked ourselves into an all-you-can-eat restaurant, as we were offered multiple drinks and appetizers and even a full second meal if the first go-around did not fill our stomachs.

Our flight arrived at around eight o'clock in the evening. La Aurora airport was not as I remembered it from the 1950s. It had obviously been renovated years earlier. But the lighting in the halls and open spaces was dark and dingy as our small group of passengers made our way through immigration and customs checkpoints. Grim-faced soldiers in camouflage fatigues and carrying submachine guns were plentiful. I noticed their fingers touching the triggers of their guns. Ours was the only flight arriving at that hour, and we were probably the last flight arriving that night. I felt anything but a warm return welcome into this country I had left as a 13-year old in 1959.

The scene that greeted a foreigner arriving in this strange country at night and walking out through the airport doors was quite intimidating. I was grateful I spoke the language, which made things a little easier. I noticed the other passengers had local people picking them up. I was the only one to hail a taxi to go to my hotel.

As we drove the rather short distance from the airport to the Camino Real Hotel in Zone 9, I noticed that other than a few soldiers on patrol, the streets were empty of people on this Friday evening. I started to wonder whether I had been foolish to make the trip and if what Art Beals had been told about the situation in Guatemala City was true. Approaching the Camino Real, I found my anxiety level shot up when I saw a large group of people milling around the entrance to the hotel. I feared we had come upon a riot or disturbance of some kind. But as the taxi came up to the hotel I heard the unmistakable throbbing beat of disco music, and when I got out of the car I realized I was standing in a crowd of teenagers gathered for a party at the hotel. They filled the lobby and had spilled out into the hotel driveway. They were dancing, talking, and acting like teenagers partying anywhere on a Friday night in Seattle.

This was martial law?

I soon found out — no great surprise — that outsiders, including people in Costa Rica, greatly exaggerated what was happening in Guatemala City. In fact, there was no martial law imposed, there were no firefights between army troops and guerrillas in the streets, and the teen party I had walked into was a weekly Friday night occurrence at the hotel.

The Ríos Montt government had successfully turned the tide in the guerrilla war. The rebels did in fact conduct raids in Guatemala City in 1981, but now they were on the retreat, and for much of the country some normalcy had returned to daily life.

A phone message from Walter Schieber awaited me when I checked in. It was a warm invitation to join him and his wife Heidi for the day on Saturday at their lakeside retreat on Amatitlán, a beautiful lake not far from the capital.

That night as I lay in bed, I thought of the range of emotions and experiences of just one day. The unknown was now opening up and the adventure had begun. Ahead was a blank slate and I had no idea what would be written on it in the days, and perhaps years, ahead.

The next day I called Enrique Lee, the long-time Chinese-Guatemalan staffer who had worked under my father when Dad headed the mission in Guatemala. Enrique still worked at the Embassy and said that not only was his family excited to see me again, but that he had arranged for me to attend the Double Ten reception the next day – to be held in the ballroom at my hotel, no less.[2]

I spent the rest of the day in delightful conversation with Walter and Heidi Schieber in Amatitlán, hearing stories about childhood times with Richard Barrueto and exploring the idea of private land reform. Walter's story was fascinating. Born in Guatemala of German immigrant parents, as a child he and his family and others of German descent were deported during World War II to Germany. There, he was separated from his family and lived on the streets scrounging for food before he was eventually reunited with them months later. After the war his family returned to Guatemala to pick up the pieces and rebuild their lives.

A cautious and conservative man by nature, Walter expressed complete willingness to help, but wasn't quite sure how doing land reform privately might work, nor was he certain of its feasibility. To him the prolonged civil war had drained the country of its lifeblood, and the peaceful postwar years of the 1950s seemed a distant memory. He was not optimistic for the future of his country.

We returned to the city late that afternoon. I had a phone message at the Camino Real from Bob Means saying he had been asked by Jim Durkin to contact me. He invited me to attend an evening service at the Verbo Church located just two blocks away from my hotel. We could meet then and make plans to meet others.

That night I walked the short distance to the Verbo Church and found not a building, but a very large tent that seated at least 700-800 people. A band was playing, and the place was about

---

[2] October 10 is the National Day of the Republic of China, and is celebrated by Chinese diplomatic missions around the world with a lavish reception for local dignitaries and the foreign diplomatic corps.

half-filled with people singing worship songs. I asked for and was led to Bob Means. He had worked with Jim Durkin in Eureka and was sent by Jim to help coordinate relief assistance to the thousands of indigenous refugees fleeing from the civil war.

Bob told me some of the elders of the church had proposed meeting me at my hotel room Sunday afternoon to hear what I had to say about private land reform. Those arrangements made, I stayed at the Verbo service to listen to the speakers, Ray and Helen Elliott. I had no idea this middle-aged, plain-looking couple would turn out to play such pivotal roles in the development of Agros.

The Elliotts shared the stage and told their story – how they came to Guatemala as young Wycliffe translators[3] and were assigned to live in Nebaj in the highlands region known as the Ixil Triangle. They related their inspirational and personal saga of how they lived among the Ixil Indians and the difficulties encountered before they developed enough trust with the people to engage in the kind of conversations that eventually allowed them to learn the Ixil language (and the Nebaj dialect) little by little.

I was drawn to the Elliotts by their intelligence, courage, perseverance, and humility. Theirs was a remarkable story. A little over two months later, Ray and Helen were featured in a cover story in *Time* Magazine (December 27, 1982) on the *New Missionary*. The *Time* piece focused on how a new breed of missionary went beyond traditional bounds of "preaching the gospel" to reach people in remote lands and tell them about a loving God. The story Ray and Helen told that night at Verbo was written up in the *Time* article.[4] I approached Ray and Helen

---

[3] Wycliffe Bible Translators – a nondenominational organization that trains linguists to translate the Bible into every known language of the world.

[4] Here is a key excerpt from the *Time* Magazine piece:

When Ray Elliott, 50, and his wife Helen, 56, came to Guatemala in 1953, Protestants were a scorned and despised minority.... The young couple, who had been high-school sweethearts in Independence, Kansas,

after they spoke, and our conversation led not only to an appointment two days later to talk about private land reform, but it also marked the beginning of a cherished friendship. They invited me to join them the next morning at the Union Church, which was their own regular place of worship.

---

settled with their three children into a two-room dirt-floor sharecropper's cabin.... The Elliotts faced stony opposition for two years. Then, one day, there was an explosion in a storehouse for firecrackers, which the Ixil tribesmen used to get the attention of gods to whom they offered sacrifices. Two boys were horribly burned. By the time Helen arrived on the scene, neighbors had already plastered the burns with a mixture of lime, wood ash and motor oil.

Helen, who had had no medical training, gave the boys morphine and antibiotic injections, picked off the goo and seared flesh, wrapped the victims in sheets sterilized in a pressure cooker, and forced them to drink eggnog through straws (all the water was contaminated). When Helen returned after putting her own children to bed, she discovered that a witch doctor had ripped off the bandages and was rubbing hot pepper on the wounds, invoking Christian saints and Mayan deities, all the while drinking rum. In a scene reminiscent of Elijah confronting the prophets of Baal, Helen told the parents that they must choose between her treatment and the witch doctor's.

The parents chose Helen. As the boys hovered near death, she prayed as never before. "This was a chance for people to experience the living Gospel," she recalls. But, she adds, "My family's lives were at stake." The boys survived and Helen was so besieged by the sick that she soon became the village's practical nurse, delivering hundreds of babies, suturing hundreds of wounds. The Ixils began to accept the Elliotts as prophets of a loving god.

The crisis also produced a breakthrough in Ray's torturous translation struggle. An Indian woman, marveling at Helen's treatment of the boys, used a word they had never heard: shum, which means giving without receiving anything in return. This was the word Ray needed to translate "love" into Ixil.

Operating from a house trailer in Guatemala City, the Elliotts now work to get shipments of roofing, food, blankets, clean water and medical supplies for their village. Every few days the Elliotts board a cargo flight to Nebaj, where 10,000 refugees, many burned out of their homes, huddle in camps. The planes land, amid bursts of guerrilla fire, and are immediately surrounded by the Elliotts' Ixil friends. Helen's eyes mist over. "Nebaj is the home of our children," she says. "Now most of the people understand the word of God because of Ray's work."

Sunday morning I stepped into the Union Church where I had my first encounter with the Christian faith as a young boy during my three years in Guatemala, 1956-59. The place had not changed much, and memories of my times as a boy scout in the Church-sponsored troop, meeting weekly in the church social hall came rushing back. This church was one of many dozens of nondenominational congregations across the world ministering to English-speaking expatriates, diplomats, and locals. The church bulletin that morning of October 10, 1982, opened with this exhortation:

On entering this Sanctuary let a mood of quiet and reverence on the part of every worshipper separate the world within and beyond from the world without.

I confess I had a hard time making the recommended separation. My mind was anything but quiet and reverent, being filled with the sensory stimulations of returning, 23 years later, to a country I had left as a 13-year old boy. I have no memory of that morning's sermon preached by a visiting minister from Chicago.

After church I invited the Elliotts to a brunch at the Camino Real. I could tell the lavish spread of meats, seafood, fruits, breads, pastries and desserts was quite a treat for them. It was a treat for me as well – the Sunday buffet rivaled any I had experienced in the U.S. – although I carefully avoided the salads and other uncooked vegetables. Over the meal I peppered them with questions about the country and people. They were gracious teachers. They told me more about the Verbo Church and gave me the names of two other American expats who might be helpful: Harris Whitbeck and Carroll Behrhorst. Whitbeck was a businessman and Behrhorst a physician who had done some groundbreaking work on public health among the Indian peoples in Chichicastenango. I even got a recommendation on a good Spanish-English dictionary to help my reentry into the Spanish language.

Later that afternoon at the appointed time there was a knock on my hotel room door. I opened it to six of the Verbo elders, one of whom was Alfred Kaltschmitt. I had not expected such a large contingent and realized the Doug Maskell/Jim Durkin connection had produced quite a response. My room had only two chairs so most of them ended up sitting on the two double beds in the room. I was seated in one chair in a corner of the room. I noticed that Alfred grabbed the other chair and planted himself in the opposite corner of the room, farthest from me.

Most of them sat with grim faces, politely listening, but saying very little. Grimmest-faced of all was Alfred in the far corner. If ever there was a suspicious and wary nature in his part-German ancestry, it was on heightened display during that meeting. His inner radar was sending strong signals in my direction, scanning to detect any "bogie" communications coming from me.

Why should they not be suspicious and wary? Here was a Chinese-American lawyer from Seattle, Washington, sitting in a hotel room in Guatemala City in a time when few Americans traveled to Guatemala, talking to a group of church elders about tackling one of the region's most intransigent and troublesome social and economic issues for the past 400 years. The concentration of land ownership with the wealthy, and the miserable poverty of the rural farm laborers who could never aspire to own and farm their own land, was a principal rallying cry of the Marxist guerrillas. The subject of land reform (*reforma agraria* in Spanish) was an explosive political topic that would bring out primeval instincts in people. Speak the words "land reform" in the wrong audience and you risked alienating your listeners and raising their blood pressure.

During the late 1970s and early 1980s, while the civil wars in El Salvador and Guatemala raged hottest, there was no neutral ground on the issue of land reform. If you spoke out in favor of land reform a whole segment of the population would automatically consider you a Marxist who would willingly upset the entire social and economic order of the country. For anyone who believed the existing land tenure system was in need of change, you made sure to keep your views to yourself or to your close family and friends. It was foolish to speak openly about the subject. On the other hand, if you defended the status quo, a whole other segment of the population would write you off as a right-wing zealot; you were either one of the wealthy few, or someone at a lower rung trying to kiss up to the rich and powerful elite in the country.

A law school classmate, Mark Pearlman, had been gunned down in a San Salvador hotel in January 1980 because he was too outspoken on the issue of land reform. Mark was on the job in El Salvador working for the AFL/CIO sponsored land reform project. The news accounts I read indicated that Mark was not shy in advocating the cause. He paid a terrible price for so doing.

That afternoon in my hotel room the Verbo elders heard me out. They acknowledged that the private land redistribution concept I spoke of might be a worthwhile effort, but they made no commitment to help or be involved. Not having heard any great negatives from them or anyone else so far on this trip, I told them I would be back in the near future and would look forward to meeting with some of them on a second trip. They told me to contact Alfred Kaltschmitt if I did come back, saying that he was the elder in the church who coordinated some of their work in the rural areas. By their comments, I sensed they had serious doubts whether I really would return as I promised.

That evening I walked down from my room at the Camino Real Hotel to join the Chinese Ambassador's Double Ten reception in progress downstairs. The first person I recognized was Enrique Lee. It was a warm reunion with Enrique, his wife Consuelo, and his son (my former sparring partner) Juanci. I also met the Ambassador and his wife, followed by all the other friends of my parents I had not seen in 23 years.[5] We all were much older, of course, but I think my transformation from a skinny 13-year old boy to a full-grown 36-year old lawyer in the U.S. was the more dramatic change. All of the people on my parents' gift list were there. Couple by couple I took them up to my room to hand them their present. My mother had considerately bought small-sized gifts that could easily fit into a coat pocket or purse.

In the course of two full days I had accomplished all I had hoped to do and more. In those 48 hours I had met key people, trustworthy and committed types – Ray and Helen Elliott, Walter Schieber – who would be instrumental in the early years of building the foundations for Agros in Guatemala. They were a great source of encouragement and offered to help in any way they could. I had no idea Alfred Kaltschmitt would come to play the most important role of all in Guatemala. For all I knew, from the meeting in my hotel room that afternoon, he did not believe a word I had said, and further doubted the sincerity of my motives. I had even carried out the gift-giving mission entrusted to me by my parents. It felt like a two-day magic carpet ride.

Monday morning I went to the Pan Am desk at my hotel and asked to move up my return date. Because of the dearth of travelers from the U.S., there were no daily flights. One flight had left early that morning. The next was on Wednesday October 13. The rest of that day and the following day I spent mostly with the Schiebers and Elliotts.

---

[5] Photos of the Double Ten reception appeared in full-page coverage of the function in the October 15, 1982 issue of the Prensa Libre – the leading daily newspaper in Guatemala. One of the pictures shows me in conversation with two other guests.

Walter was a rare commodity in a culture of corruption and graft. I knew he could be trusted to handle money matters if and when we started to work in Guatemala.

With Ray and Helen Elliott, I first discovered their love for Chinese food and their favorite Chinese restaurant located in Zone 9. Then over the next several hours of conversation, I discovered the depth of their wisdom. They had worked first-hand with the poorest of the rural poor in the Ixil region for years. Their insights into the indigenous people of the Ixil Triangle and the Ixcán region came to undergird much of Agros' working philosophy and methodology in future years.

To my animated advocacy of the notion of private land reform, Ray brought up a choice tidbit he learned in the early years of exploring the Ixil language. Knowing I was a lawyer by profession, he told me how the Ixil Indians understood the Spanish word "*justicia*":

What happens to a man when he goes to court and they take his land away from him.

This is not a definition of justice you will find in Webster's Dictionary. But it articulated clearly and concisely the collective and bitter experience of the Ixil people since the Spanish first set foot in the region over 400 years earlier.

But the experience that clinched my growing sensitivity to the vulnerability of the indigenous poor happened at the artisan's market the afternoon before my return flight home. I had picked out some woven placemats from a small Indian woman, and settled on a bargained price of 25 quetzals. I handed her two Q20 bills in payment. As she proceeded to give me change and quetzals began to pile up in my hand, it quickly dawned on me that this woman could not count. She had given me back at least Q25 out of my Q40 and was still putting bills in my hand. Had I allowed her to continue I might have received more than the

Q40 I had handed her. I stopped her, counted out the proper change, and gave the rest back to her, assuring her that this was all I was entitled to get back. She gave me a smile and thanked me. As I walked away my heart broke for that woman – and for the countless others in her situation. Illiterate, and hardly able to speak Spanish, she was an easy target for being cheated out of her livelihood.

Recollections of the intense experiences and conversations of the past five days crowded my mind as I sat on the early Wednesday morning flight back to the U.S. As the plane took off from La Aurora airport and began its steep ascent, I looked out at the city and the surrounding mountains. I was overcome by a powerful emotional reaction – a strange mixture of love and compassion for this country I had once lived in as a young boy, and a strong sense that I was wandering into the unknown at multiple levels. Tears streamed down my face; I was unaccustomed to crying, and did not fully understand why I cried uncontrollably sitting in the plane at that moment. On later trips there were occasional tears too, and I recall that some of those tears were shed over the plight of the poor Indian people I encountered. That morning in October 1982 I wondered where this would lead. So many questions came to me during the flight home. I had only an unmistakable feeling that this was just the beginning of an adventure unlike any I had experienced before.

My reports to Cyd, Art Beals, and Richard Barrueto on my return were full of enthusiasm. I felt there was an open door to the idea of private land redistribution – redistribution being a euphemism I began to use for "reform." I committed to a second trip in December and sent faxes to Alfred Kaltschmitt, the Elliotts, and Walter Schieber about the dates.

Art Beals, who I believe regretted not going on that first trip, suggested that Fred Gregory, one of his key men at World Concern, join me. I knew Fred well from the Thailand trip in

1980 when we visited together the Khmer refugee camps and was delighted he would come on this second Guatemala trip. Cyd agreed to come with me as well in order to see for herself what had me so stirred up. Her mother would care for our two young boys while we were gone. In Cyd's mind, the task of supporting a family seemed hard enough; she wondered what this new idea meant for us.

We flew to Guatemala on December 6, 1982, on another mostly empty Pan Am flight and checked in at the Camino Real. The next morning Cyd and I walked to the Verbo Church office, and to my great surprise, we were greeted by a much friendlier Alfred Kaltschmitt. His first words were "Skip, you came back." I thought that was certainly stating the obvious. But I learned over the next several trips the full meaning of those words.

Efraín Ríos Montt, the new president of Guatemala, had created a stir within U.S. evangelical Christian circles. They thought of him as one of their own. A growing number of church and business leaders made their way to Guatemala to meet this president, have their pictures taken with him, tour the development projects involving particularly the rural poor in the Ixil Triangle, and leave for home promising to come back with help for the rural development efforts. Once back home their newsletters and publicity pieces trumpeted their trips, always prominently displaying the photos of the pastor or business person in close conversation with the Guatemalan president. Tragically, almost no one returned to Guatemala. And rarely were promises of financial or other aid honored.[6]

No wonder Alfred was suspicious of me – and my promise to come back. His skepticism was rooted in experience. As a special

---

[6] These broken promises, exacerbated by self-serving and self-aggrandizing written and publicized reports of development projects and consultations with the Guatemalan president, did not make for a proud chapter in 1980s American evangelical church history.

representative of the president on rural development issues, he had learned the hard way that promises made by American visitors meant nothing.

Encounter with USAID

We had just begun to talk in Alfred's office when he answered a phone call. I remember his side of the conversation going something like this:

> Hey, Harris, how are you doing? Glad you called. Remember I was telling you about the guy from Seattle who was here a couple of months ago? Skip Li? Yeah, the guy who was talking about buying land. He's back, and his wife is here too. (Silence while he listens). You want us over there right now? Skip too? OK, we're on our way.

Harris Whitbeck was an unusual man. He was American by birth, a graduate of Auburn University, but had lived in Guatemala most of his life. He was thoroughly American and thoroughly Guatemalan. He spoke both English and Spanish with native ability. How he got pulled into the tight circle of Verbo Church evangelical Christian advisors to Ríos Montt, I never found out. He was a Union Church man himself – a mainline Protestant. Among other duties, Harris acted as the principal liaison to the flow of Americans who were visiting Guatemala at the time, and all who wanted time with the president. Twenty years later, Harris was himself a presidential candidate.

Harris had called Alfred to let him know there was a group visiting from the U.S. he wanted Alfred to meet, and on finding out I was there, said that I might be interested in meeting this group as well. Within 20 minutes Alfred, Cyd and I walked into a large conference room in the presidential palace.

Around an enormous, long conference table were seated about a dozen men. Except for Harris, who was on one side of the long table by himself, the others were all seated on the other side. Harris welcomed us and had us sit next to him on his side of the table. He introduced us, and then explained that I was a lawyer from Seattle interested in land reform issues in Guatemala. He then asked the other men to introduce themselves. One by one, they revealed that they were mostly a team of U.S. Agency for International Development (USAID) personnel and academicians on a land reform fact-finding trip to Guatemala. Also at the meeting were a couple of U.S. Embassy staff people.

At Harris' request, one of the men used a large flip chart to diagram what was brewing within U.S. government circles, and how they planned to help the government of Guatemala (GOG in bureaucratic jargon/acronym) institute a new land reform program. Here were the bullet points Cyd and I both remember clearly, starting at the top of the chart:

- USAID feasibility study on GOG land reform program (conducted by the visiting team) finalized and to be submitted sometime in fiscal year 1984 (U.S. government fiscal years begin October 1, so this meant some time between October 1983 to September 1984) to congressional leadership;
- GOG land reform package to be incorporated in omnibus foreign aid package some time in fiscal year 1985;
- Appropriations and Foreign Relations Committees in the U.S. Senate and House approve financial package for GOG land reform;

- GOG land reform assistance package, including appropriation of needed funds, approved by Congress and POTUS (President of the United States) sometime in fiscal year 1986;
- Funds are transmitted as a foreign assistance grant to GOG, to be monitored by USAID;
- GOG remits funds to Guatemalan Central Bank (GCB);
- GCB remits funds to Guatemalan national banks (GNB);
- GNB remit funds to regional branches of GNB;
- Regional branches remit funds to local banks;
- Local banks receive and approve loan applications by landless local farmers to buy land.
- Farmers buy land, plant and harvest crops, and repay loans to bank.

By the time the explanation was completed, the chart was filled with cryptic notes, acronyms, numbers, and arrows between bullet points. In essence, their goal was to establish a credit system for small farmers much like the system that the Farmers Home Administration (FHA) operated during that era in the U.S. They intended to make credit available to the rural poor to buy land. The problem, according to one of the leaders of the team, was that there was no market in which farmland was bought and sold. This funding program would be designed to establish such a market.

The USAID team then quizzed me on what I was doing in Guatemala and my interest in land reform. I told them that my concept was private land redistribution – buy large tracts of land in rural Guatemala with private funds raised through donations to a U.S. tax-exempt non-profit organization, and then help the poor farmers in Guatemala buy that land from us through harvests from the land, so that eventually, those farmers could take title to the land. I went to the flip chart, took the black marker pen from the USAID man, and drew a long, curved arrow from the top bullet point to the bottom bullet point. I explained that it would be a two-step process: at the top of the chart, we would raise the money privately through the 501(c)(3) organization, then at the bottom of the chart, we would buy the land privately with those funds and get the poor farmers on the land. My one long arrow meant no intermediary governments, government agencies, banks, and bureaucrats.

They nodded their heads and showed some interest in the concept. But I could tell it hadn't sunk in. Their minds were constrained to think that land reform could only be done by governments. It was inconceivable to them that private efforts could accomplish such redistribution. I wanted to ask them, but of course did not, how much funding appropriated by the U.S. Congress would really get into the hands of the rural farmers for their designated purpose. Every one of their intermediary steps represented an opportunity not only for bureaucratic waste, but outright corruption and graft. A full pipeline of hundreds of millions of dollars at the top of their chart might, at best, result in a weak trickle of pennies at the bottom.

U.S. Government-financed land reform had turned into a tragic failure just a few years earlier in El Salvador. Per the plan, the Salvadoran government expropriated land from private landowners and parceled out the land to poor farmers. But instead of receiving compensation for their land with the U.S. funds designated for land reform, the landowners were paid with El Salvador government bonds. The cash had disappeared, either used for other purposes, or stolen outright by officials and bankers through varied schemes of corruption.

Most of the landowners who had their lands taken by government edict were farmers themselves. Like large or small farmers around the world, they were bound to the agricultural cash flow cycle: money was spent throughout the year, but income came only when the crops were harvested and sold. The cycle required farmers to borrow the capital required each year to plow, plant, tend, harvest, and market the crops. Then they would wait, hoping and praying that their crops would survive drought and disease, so that the harvest and sale of those crops would bring enough income to repay the bank loans and leave a profit for their own living. The next year, the cycle repeated itself.

In El Salvador many of the landowners who had their land expropriated were already into that cycle and had borrowed money for the season. Those bank loans were not only secured by the farmland and crops, but also by the owners' houses, many in nearby towns and cities. The loans could and should have been repaid with cash compensation from the earmarked land reform funds given by the U.S. to the El Salvador government. But the bonds they received instead, issued by a government on the verge of collapse from fighting an intense civil war were, for all practical purposes, worthless. Now the landowners were in default on their agricultural loans, and the banks refused to take the bonds in payment. And since the banks could not foreclose on the expropriated property now held by land reform beneficiaries, they sought to foreclose on other properties and assets, including the homes of the expropriated landowners. The landowners found themselves on the verge of losing everything they had. The more powerful and wealthy among them resented losing their land, and feeling cheated by their own government out of rightful payment, hired private armies to repossess by force their expropriated land. The whole tragic mess was a massive powder keg waiting inevitably to explode.

And it did explode – from a powerful mix of outraged landowners whose livelihoods were threatened by bank foreclosures and land reform beneficiaries evicted from their newly possessed farms at gunpoint, their short-lived hopes for a new life cruelly dashed to pieces. The Marxist guerrillas had only to point to the failed land reform program to justify their violent means. An atrociously corrupt and inept government turned bright new hopes and expectations of economic and social justice into a violent cesspool of outrage and despair.

To their credit, the USAID team sitting in that conference room doing their fact-finding in Guatemala was contemplating a different scheme than the one that had failed so disastrously in El Salvador. They, too, must have read the Wall Street Journal's detailed account a year earlier of the Salvadoran debacle, and understood that the failure of land reform had become a major contributing cause to the brutal Salvadoran civil war. The USAID program they charted for Guatemala would be different; it would provide loans to the landless poor to buy the land from the owners. Credit the USAID team too for actually moving away from the government expropriation model of land reform.

But the critical component of any successful government-sponsored land reform equation, based either on the expropriation model of El Salvador or the loan program contemplated for Guatemala, was the ability of the ruling government to carry it out. In order to succeed, the government must run efficiently and honestly. In 1982, the obvious flaw in the equation was that the governments of El Salvador and Guatemala were both notoriously inefficient. Corruption was rampant in both countries. It may have mattered that Efraín Ríos Montt was making a much-publicized effort to clean up corruption in his government, constantly preaching the theme *"No robo, no abuso, no mentiro"* from his bully pulpit. (I don't steal, I don't abuse, I don't lie). Perhaps the U.S. government saw in Ríos Montt a ruler who actually could pull off a land reform program. They would never have the chance to try; Ríos Montt was deposed in a coup eight months later.

That night Cyd and I had dinner with Adolfo Lau, older brother of Alberto, my best friend and fellow baseball enthusiast during the time I lived in Guatemala. Adolfo and Alberto had both become prominent architects, but Alberto had moved with his family to the U.S. because of the civil war. Adolfo had sent his family to the U.S., but he himself still worked and lived in Guatemala. During our dinner I related the day's experience with the USAID team, and he laughed out loud after hearing the story. He asked me, "Skip, do you know what we call USAID here in Guatemala?"

"No," I answered.

"We call them *Misión Imposible*!"

We had a good laugh at the cynical reference to the popular TV show from the 1960s and early 70s. The premise of all Mission Impossible TV episodes and movies was that a team of special agents would tackle improbable if not impossible missions with extreme efficiency, cleverness, daring, and panache. I don't think even the most naïve USAID official would ever accept the *Misión Imposible* description as complimentary. It was a devastating commentary on the U.S. government's methodology to assist poor and developing countries in that era: throw crate-loads of money and personnel at the problem of poverty and injustice and hope that it would all work out. The results were rarely clever, efficient, or daring, and certainly never had any trace of panache. The Guatemalan view of USAID, as cynical as it was, nevertheless represented the ordinary person's assessment of how enormous sums of money were wasted by the U.S. government in those days.

If Cyd and I had not laughed with Adolfo, we might all have cried over the bureaucratic myopia and muddled thinking in the U.S. government's foreign aid program, which during that era poured hundreds of millions of dollars down a sewer drain with no discernible return. Juan Carlos Ortíz may have been simplistic in his thinking, but he was absolutely on target in this respect: with that kind of money, you could have bought enough land in Central America to give to the poor, and you would have taken from the Marxist revolutionaries their reason for existence.

Si, Pues

During the rest of this trip I introduced Cyd to the Schiebers and Elliotts, and showed her some of the Guatemala City of my youth. We even made it to the Union Church for Sunday worship. We spent an evening with the Enrique Lee family at their home in Zone 1; the smells, the sights triggered a flood of memories. Juanci was there with his wife, and we had fun recollecting the great Patterson-Johansson bouts we staged in the long hallways of that home. Fred Gregory joined us for some of this activity, while doing World Concern business at other times.

It became settled that each time I returned to Guatemala I would spend a day or evening with the Elliotts, either in Guatemala City or in their working base in Nebaj. So much of the Agros ethos in working with the indigenous peoples of Guatemala today is rooted in the early tutoring from Ray and Helen.

Among other things, I learned that the indigenous peoples of Guatemala exceeded 60% of the population, and that the twenty-plus tribal groups were divided by their own unique linguistic and cultural differences. Many of the indigenous men spoke Spanish, but poorly; most of the women did not speak Spanish at all. Notwithstanding their numerical majority in the population, the indigenous peoples were powerless, and at the bottom of Guatemalan political, economic and social structures. Their status resembled that of indentured serfs. They related to *ladinos*, the white or non-indigenous peoples, almost as slaves would relate to masters. When an indigenous man spoke to a *ladino*, he would hold his hat in both hands in front, eyes looking down to the ground. He did not initiate any conversation and spoke only when spoken to. He was inured through countless generations not to speak his mind, but would answer a *ladino's* question according to what he thought the person asking wanted to hear.

A common two-word response I often heard, slowly enunciated by a poor rural Indian man: "*Sí, pues.*" This translates very roughly to "well, yes." It was a way he could agree with you in order not to express disagreement, or in any way give the appearance of contradicting what you might think. But it also carried with it a subtle indication that you really did not and could not know what your respondent might be thinking, because he would never tell you what he really thought. The Elliott children were so struck by the frequency of the "*Sí, pues*" response that they used the term to name one of the family dogs.[7]

The 400 years that had passed since the times of the Spanish *conquistadores* were filled with cruelty and oppression for the indigenous peoples. First the Spaniards came in with their blunderbusses and swords, enslaved the resident populations, and extracted all the gold they could possibly find. Then the Spanish crown made enormous land grants to royal favorites in complete disregard of the indigenous peoples who had lived on the land as a birthright since time immemorial.

In more modern days what little remaining land the indigenous people owned was often taken from them systematically by *ladinos* manipulating the legal system and sometimes by outright theft. To survive and feed their families, the people either worked for large landowners at meager wages, or looked for migrant seasonal work in the coastal regions. I

---

[7] Ray and Helen had eight children. During one visit to their home I saw a family portrait including their unusually good-looking grown children and asked the trite question to Ray of who their children got their good looks from. Without a moment's hesitation, Ray said with a twinkle in his eyes, "From me, of course. Helen still has hers." Helen was very pleased with that answer, even though I'm sure she had heard it many times before.

began to understand that the land registration system in Guatemalan law could bewilder even an educated person; how much more difficult was it, then, for the largely illiterate indigenous peoples to protect their legal title to land?

During lunch one day at the hotel Cyd pointed out the window to an elderly man who had stopped across the street with the big cart he was pulling. It was the kind of heavily built cart better pulled by an ox. He sat on the edge of the cart, pulled out a tuber of some kind, and ate his lunch while we ate ours. Our lunch came from the usual sumptuous buffet put on by the Camino Real. That single tuber or turnip was all the lunch this man had. He finished it, rested about five minutes, then, bent under the weight of the cart, went on his way.

Anyone traveling from the U.S. to a developing country cannot help but notice the juxtaposition of wealth and poverty that jars the mind and senses: the pitiful slums a short distance from upper class gated communities; luxury autos stopped at a traffic light surrounded by street vendors, as well as small children, pleading for a sale that might bring a few pennies income; beggars missing limbs waiting on the sidewalks outside modern air-conditioned shopping malls for the occasional coin from a shopper; the sight of an oxcart-pulling man who stops to eat his meager lunch while we sit with plates full from the cornucopia of meats, fish, vegetables, pastas, fruits, and sweets in the hotel restaurant.

These experiences can shake up and scramble our tidy worldviews. We might choose to suppress the images from our minds and go on with our lives with no change. Or we might allow our souls to be stirred at the very core, and our thinking and our lives cannot remain the same. Cyd was moved beyond words and had a hard time finishing her lunch.

On another occasion I took her to the *mercado de artesanías* (artisans market) where I had, on the previous trip, encountered the Indian woman vendor who could not count. Dozens of stalls in long aisles provided untold choices of "*típico*" items – wood carvings, silverworks, artwork, tablecloths, napkins, blankets, and clothing. As we finished buying a few items and went into the parking lot, a group of child vendors converged on us, offering their small hand-made goods of all kinds. One child in particular pleaded with Cyd to buy a small bird made of a pipe cleaner and dyed feathers. I had warned Cyd not to buy anything. In my experience, if you bought from one, all the other children would plead with you to buy from them as well. She was torn – I could tell with one look. I stepped up our pace to get to the car waiting for us, and we avoided having to buy anything from those children.

But the experience shook her and she never forgot it. She has re-lived that scene over and over since then and wished she had bought that pipe-cleaner bird from that little child. She thought how the pennies could have meant a meal for the child's family. So what if we had been besieged by the other children? Couldn't we have bought some from them too? How much would it have taken? Pocket change – that's what it would have cost us.

I have learned over the years that Cyd's instinct for generosity far exceeds mine. She grew up poor but has a gift for holding loosely to money; not in a spendthrift way or for any personal needs or desires, but always when it comes to helping others in need.

I was not proud of the defense mechanism I employed that day to resist buying anything from those children. I had rationalized it, knowing how persistent the children were, and how, even at a very young age, they can pick out the most likely buyer from a group of people standing on a street corner, and plead incessantly with that person to buy something from them.

Every trip I took after that, Cyd would tell me to buy something from the little children. I did, a few times. But more often than not, my defense mechanisms clicked into place and I came home empty-handed.

In the course of one week that December 1982, with the whole notion of helping the rural poor to buy land still nothing more than a vague idea with not a touch of tangible reality, Cyd told me, upon our return home, that she had seen enough. That is, she was ready to be fully supportive of whatever it might take to pursue this dream. She went as far as to declare that she would be ready to move to Guatemala if that was required. She had seen the country, met its people, and had her heart broken by the hopeless plight of the poor. She had never claimed to be a person of vision and could not begin to imagine how this dream might be fulfilled. But she gave me her full agreement and, moreover, granted me full freedom to do whatever I thought needed to be done, using whatever modest resources we had.

Our children were young at the time. Brian, our adopted son, was beginning a career as a television news cameraman, and was self supporting. But Peter was nine and Joseph only three at the time. My daughter Kara would not arrive until 1984. We had no savings. My downtown law practice, now in its sixth year, provided a living for us, but there was no surplus. We lived in a modest home on Mercer Island. But Cyd was determined that we would find a way to answer this calling upon our lives.

I think our friends wondered what had come over us. They were mostly supportive, but the whole scheme sounded so far-fetched, I would not blame them if they had thought I had gone off my rocker. I wondered myself what I was getting us into. Most friends wished me well. Some wondered why I needed to go to Guatemala to help the poor. Weren't there poor people right here in Seattle who needed help? A few well-intentioned friends actually challenged me on this point, saying that perhaps I was wrongly entertaining romantic notions of working with the poor in Central America when there was so much I could do to help the poor in our own city. I could only answer that I was trying to respond to what felt distinctly like a divine nudge and would continue to walk through whatever doors opened in front of me. I knew there might come a time when those doors shut tight, and my efforts would feel like an enormous exercise in futility. I would stop at that point, but not before then. I was never someone who heard God's voice speaking to me, but the sense of calling was distinct and powerful. The only way I could test whether it was authentic or a product of my errant imagination was to move forward step by step.

My mother also had a hard time understanding what seemed to her like a compulsive fancy in me. She was dismayed that after two trips in three months I intended to continue traveling to Guatemala. I think she hoped those trips would have cleared my system of some strange obsession. To be fair to her, frequent travel to Guatemala seemed a reckless thing to do in 1982. Television news and the newspapers regularly reported on the civil war, dwelling on alleged massacres of the civilian population in the rural areas. U.S. State Department advisory notices repeatedly warned American citizens to avoid travel to Guatemala. She looked at me askance when I talked of scheduling yet another trip early the next year, and her voice took on a distinct note of disapproval. My father never told me what he thought about it. He sat quietly while my mother quizzed me from every angle on the subject. I like to think he was secretly pleased that I was doing something so out of the ordinary, particularly since I was returning to a country where he had served as a Chinese diplomat.

Encouraging Developments Early 1983

Not all reactions were skeptical. The U.S. mail brought some great encouragement at the end of the year. I received a $5,000 check from World Concern, a donation to help fund a feasibility study on private land redistribution in Guatemala. The December trip apparently made a positive impression on Fred

Gregory. Art Beals wanted World Concern involved as a partner on the land project in Guatemala and not just with financial assistance. Art instructed Ann Sorley, his Latin America director, to contact me to see how World Concern could be of help, particularly on the relief end in providing clothing, blankets, and other items of practical need to the Ixil refugees in Nebaj. Art also asked Ann to travel to Guatemala to get a first hand view of the situation and the needs. The irony was not lost on me that just a few months earlier Ann had advised Art not to travel to Guatemala with me because of the dangers arising out of the civil war.

The developments by mid-January 1983 greatly encouraged me. In the two trips to Guatemala during the past three months it seemed we were driving down streets with lights turning green at every intersection. Good people who cared about the poor were excited by the idea and prepared to help. Now I had a relief and development agency based in my own backyard of Seattle prepared to be a partner in the venture, and spending its money to get a feasibility study going.

I returned to Guatemala January 31, 1983, this time with Richard Barrueto accompanying me. Alfred and I convened a committee to advise and give direction to us. Our first meeting took place on February 1, 1983, attended by Ray and Helen Elliott, Walter Schieber, and Dr. Carroll Behrhorst.

Behrhorst had a fascinating background. A Tennessee expatriate and medical doctor, Behrhorst had arrived in Guatemala 22 years earlier as a Lutheran medical missionary. Eventually he established a clinic in Chimaltenango, which became internationally known as a well thought-out and culturally sensitive model of health care for the indigenous poor. He lectured widely at medical schools in the U.S. on the subject of health care in the developing world. He was a pioneer – not just treating disease, but identifying and dealing with the causes of disease, many of which he traced to rural poverty. When we first met and he found out why I was in Guatemala, he looked me squarely in the eyes and told me something I have never forgotten:

> Mr. Li, in my many years dealing with the rural poor, I have found that there is a direct link between land ownership and good health. The peasant who does not own his own land will eat less, drink more polluted water, and be much more susceptible to disease.

Everything I have experienced in the intervening years has confirmed what he told me.

At that first meeting of our ad hoc committee I was deeply impressed by and grateful for the thoughtful discussion I heard. The many years of experience accumulated between the Elliotts and Behrhorst who worked directly with the rural poor, showed in their comments and analysis. What stood out in my mind in particular was their expert knowledge on the plight of the indigenous peoples. If the rural poor were on the bottom rung of the Guatemalan socio-economic ladder, the indigenous poor in the rural areas had no place on the ladder at all.

The group decided that a feasibility study should concentrate on a pilot project in the Ixil Triangle area of Quiché, even though this was the area where the civil war raged the hottest and might pose the most physical dangers to us if we worked there. We also agreed that our work should benefit the landless poor regardless of their religious belief.

It made sense to start in the Ixil area. It did not take much to persuade a poor indigenous person that he or she was getting the shortest possible end of the Guatemalan economic stick. The more difficult task for our land project would be to convince the Ixil people that the stick existed at all, and that the possibility for them to grasp it fully was not a cruel delusion. To them, it seemed like neither they nor their forbears had ever laid a hand on it.

The discussion on helping the poor without regard to religious belief exposed yet another layer of complexity under the strata of political exclusion, ethnic discrimination, social and economic deprivation, and historical injustice. In the rural areas of Guatemala, the problem of religious strife was a serious one. This was particularly the case between Roman Catholics and *"evangélicos,"* a term whose meaning in Latin America encompassed more than the North American idea of evangelical Christians. *Evangélicos* were converts to Christianity in other than the Roman Catholic tradition.

Anecdotes abounded on persecution of *evangélicos* by Catholics in the rural regions. Whole families were shunned and lost work; physical attacks were not unknown. In many rural communities to this day, Catholicism is a syncretistic mix of Catholic and indigenous pagan beliefs in which alcohol, shamans, and wax figures of indigenous idols are all tossed in the pot. The church in the town square of Chichicastenango, with its wax figure of Jesus encased in a glass sarcophagus, is a vivid example. While many Catholic churches in Guatemala hold orthodox Christian beliefs, the best way I can describe the syncretistic rural church such as the one in Chichicastenango is a pre-Reformation Catholic church that worships an unresurrected Jesus.

First Trip to Ixil Triangle

During that trip in early 1983 I had my first look at the Ixil Triangle. Harris Whitbeck, Alfred Kaltschmitt and I went with a group of 10 or so prominent business and church people from Dallas, including a reporter and cameraman from a Dallas TV station. Harris and Alfred wanted to show them the extent of the need. They hoped the visit would motivate the Dallas contingent to open their pocketbooks, and perhaps motivate others in the U.S. to do so as well. I was invited to come along for the ride. A reporter for BBC Worldwide Radio also joined us.

The group rode on a bus from Guatemala City to the military base in Huehuetenango. Harris and Alfred both came along, with Harris as the tour guide. At the base we were ushered into a large conference room and joined by the colonel who commanded the contingent there. The colonel, dressed in full army camouflage with sidearm, cut an impressive figure. He briefed us on the state of the civil war, and particularly spoke of *"fúsiles y frijóles"* – the guns and beans program carried out on orders from President Ríos Montt. The Ixil people had been on the twin horns of a terrible dilemma in this civil war: if they sided with the government, the guerrillas came into their communities and killed them. If they sided with the guerrillas or were even suspected of giving food or assistance to the guerrillas, the government troops killed them and burned their homes. The idea was to give the people rifles to defend themselves against guerrilla demands and threats, with training to organize the people into *"patrullas civiles"* – civilian patrols. At the same time, the army also provided food – corn and beans – in exchange for the men, when not engaged on patrols, to build much-needed roads and infrastructure in the Ixil region.

The colonel spoke of how the western press had focused on the human rights abuses perpetrated by the Guatemalan army, and how there was little understanding or mention of abuses carried out by the guerrillas. He showed us flyers left in rural villages by guerrilla fighters passing through. Some of these were encased in small plastic envelopes resembling "baggies" to protect the messages from the rain and moisture. The messages all had the same content: the "People's Revolutionary Army," as the guerrillas called themselves, had determined that certain individuals in a particular village or hamlet were guilty of aiding and abetting the Guatemalan army. These people were to be executed if found by the guerrillas. Then their full names were listed.

These were death lists. Moreover, the unstated warning to others was crystal clear: cooperate with the government, and your name will show up on the list as well. The colonel handed out samples and I kept one (which I still have in my files). They were grim reminders that in a war like this, there is no room for neutrals. You take one side or the other. If you try to sit in the middle, you are likely to get shot at by both sides. It helped to put into context the many stories I heard in later years from Agros villagers about how they hid themselves from both sides in the war in the mountains and survived on eating roots, insects and occasional small animals.

The guns and beans program had proven successful so far. The army had regained control of the Ixil Triangle, a far cry from earlier times when army troops did not venture from their bases except to carry out search and destroy missions against the guerrillas. The colonel explained it this way: the rifles given to the people were old weapons of World War II vintage, and the men were minimally trained to shoot and patrol. He likened the guerrillas to a bully who believes he can invade your home with impunity and demand that you give him money and food. As long as you have no means of fighting back, he will return again and again. But if the bully knows you own a gun, no matter how antiquated, and are prepared to use it, will he still come?

The colonel also showed us a cache of U.S. army M-1 rifles used in the Vietnam War that had been captured from the guerrillas. He claimed that these and other weapons were supplied to the guerrillas by the Soviet Union (who had obtained the weapons from the Communist Vietnam government), via their surrogate Cuba.

After the colonel's briefing, we boarded an Israeli-made Arava-201 military transport, just like the ones parked on the military side of La Aurora airport in the capital, and flew the short distance over the Cuchumatánes mountain range down to the airfield at Nebaj, elevation 2,000 meters. We were then taken in two military helicopters to a "beans for work" site high in the mountains where about 30 Ixil men were building a road to their own nearby village.[8] The men had their civil patrol rifles stacked nearby as they worked, and less than a handful of Guatemalan army regulars were doing lookout duty on the fringes. I talked to a couple of the men, and they explained to me what they were doing. I also overheard a conversation about 20 feet away in which the colonel was asking one of the men whether they needed anything and an ensuing discussion on how the work was progressing.

After 30 minutes or so we boarded the helicopters and flew back to the Nebaj airfield. Next to the airstrip was a huge encampment of several thousand refugees from the civil war. Harris and Alfred explained that these were Ixil people from the mountains and hills around Nebaj, Cotzal, and Chajul. Many of them had lost loved ones and had seen their homes destroyed in the crossfire between the Guatemalan army and the guerrillas. We were allowed to walk among the refugees and see first hand their dire living conditions.

As I walked down a path in the camp, I saw an Ixil man walking up the same path toward me. From a distance I could see that his intense, dark eyes were fixed on me, and they made it impossible for me to look away. We stopped and conversed. I asked him about his housing. He replied that he and the eight members of his family were a little crowded in their tiny makeshift shelter. But he added something that took me by complete surprise, "Don Raimundo tells us that in heaven we will live in mansions." I asked if by Don Raimundo he meant

---

[8] The helicopters we rode were actually civilian Bell helicopters armed with a machine gun mounted on the side opening. I saw no other weaponry on the aircraft.

Ray Elliott, to which he nodded and smiled, and was delighted to know I knew Don Raimundo as well.

I then asked him about clothes and blankets to keep warm in the chill of the highlands nights. He told me they could always use a few more items, but after a pause he again added, "Don Raimundo tells us that in heaven we will not lack for any clothing." In my do-good state of mind, I persisted. "Do you have enough to eat?" His reply came again, "Well, yes,[9] we could use some more food, especially the children. But Don Raimundo tells us that in heaven we will never be hungry again." I finally asked him, "What is your greatest need right now?" His reply stunned me then, and I still remember it today clearly:

> Do you know when Don Raimundo is coming back to Nebaj? We miss so much hearing him teach from the scriptures.

I realized then, and in the many times I've thought of that encounter over the years, that this man had long ago transcended the years of material deprivation and physical suffering and had his eyes set heaven-ward. He knew there was a loving God who would some day provide for his family's needs and who would wipe away all his tears. In stark contrast to my entirely temporal frame of mind, he was already wholly engaged with the eternal.

This diminutive-statured man I had met and conversed with was in reality a towering spiritual giant. I learned then that even if no one else cared about the well-being of the Ixil Indians, there was a God in heaven who loved and sustained them day by day, moment by moment. They felt God's presence among them as if he stood there in person.

Before we ended our conversation I asked him for his name. Later – back in the city – I related the encounter to Ray and Helen. Tears came to Ray's eyes as he recalled and told me about

---

[9] "*Si, pues*"

his long time friend who now missed him so much after he and Helen had to be evacuated from Nebaj because of the war.

That time in the Nebaj airfield refugee camp produced another unforgettable memory. I came across what looked like an awkward scene involving one of the men from Dallas. Knowing I spoke Spanish, he asked me to help. I found out that in his compassion, this middle-aged businessman had taken a $20 bill from his wallet and had offered it to a young mother with two children in tow. To his surprise, the woman had reacted very angrily. I asked the woman about this, and in what little Spanish she knew she told me that the American man must have thought she was a prostitute, and she wanted him to stop trying to give her money. The Dallas man was shocked, of course, to hear that his gesture of kindness had been completely misunderstood, and apologized profusely through me, until the woman gave him a faint smile and walked away with her children.

There was something so American about this little scene: American generosity at its spontaneous best, coupled with American cultural ignorance at its naïve worst. Throw in a little American charity – so well intentioned, but so often mindless to how giving money alone can produce unintended and unpleasant consequences.

Later that afternoon we all boarded the military transport plane and flew back to Huehuetenango, from there returning to Guatemala City by bus. We gathered in a lounge at La Aurora airport for a debriefing of the day and several from the group commented on what they saw. The entire group, minus one, saw what Harris Whitbeck had hoped we would see: Ríos Montt's change of course from a scorched earth strategy to the guns and beans approach appeared to be working. The Ixil people were benefitting both from the arms to protect themselves, and the food for work that improved road access to their communities. The BBC radio reporter, however, summarized what she saw in such a way that she appeared to have gone on a different trip. She spoke no Spanish, but insisted, based on what she had seen, that it was obvious that the men on the mountainside were nothing more than slave labor – working at gunpoint. It did not matter to her that the men themselves had weapons and could easily have overwhelmed the few soldiers on the scene. Nothing anyone else said would change her mind. I'm sure that night she filed a report that was broadcast to listeners around the world describing how the Ixil Indian people had been enslaved by the Guatemalan army.

That night I joined the Dallas contingent for dinner with President Ríos Montt at the presidential palace. We sat around a long table – my seat directly opposite the president. This was my first encounter with the man. Though a high-ranking general in the Guatemalan army, he was dressed in business suit and tie, and chatted freely with us. At one point he looked at me intently and said, "Mr. Li, they tell me you want to buy land for the poor. I know one farm you should start with – Finca La Perla." La Perla was a gigantic spread of land – 8,000 acres – north of Chajul in the Ixil region, and owned for generations by the Samayoa family. The current patriarch of the family was reputed to be a hard, pistol-packing *patrón*, widely hated and a particular target of the guerrillas. He had moved to the city because of the civil war, and some portions of his land had been overtaken by "*invasores*." These were not just squatters; they had been organized by a leftist political group who wanted to make an example out of La Perla and show others how to take land back from oppressive landowners.

I answered the president by telling him there were no roads to La Perla, and the only access for us would be by small plane. Without a moment's pause he replied, "Mr. Li, if you buy La Perla, I'll see to it that a road is built there right away."

In talking to Alfred later about this conversation, I found out that La Perla was a symbol of everything that was wrong about the Guatemalan land tenure and rural economic system, and it was a favorite object lesson used by the guerrillas to recruit Ixil men to join the revolutionary struggle. From Ríos Montt's viewpoint, the sooner La Perla could be bought and put into some kind of ownership by the poor farmers, the better.

The thought of buying La Perla gave a jolt to my entrepreneurial heart. What a wonderfully symbolic statement it could be if we bought this notorious farm from an infamous landowner and helped the poor workers and farmers in the region to become its new owners. What a shining light it might be in a region of political and historical darkness. As a first project, it could serve as a dramatic example of what could be done by private individuals answering the biblical call to care for the poor, and to strive to correct four centuries of injustice and oppression.

But legal training in analytical thinking and plain common sense prevailed. There were more than enough reasons to avoid La Perla as a first project.

We had no idea whether the Samayoa family would be disposed to sell La Perla. Even if they were willing to sell, the cost would be staggering, and we had no organization or infrastructure to carry out such a large project. The problem of the *invasores* was a sticky one. Although our objective – land ownership by the rural poor – and theirs might coincide, this could be a political minefield because of the leftist politics behind the squatters movement.

Furthermore, La Perla was a producing coffee farm; if we bought the farm from the Samayoas, where would we find the expertise to run the farm and all of the complex dealings involved with growing, roasting, and selling coffee beans? I was still trying to answer the question of whether private land distribution was feasible – there was no way I was ready to take on one of the largest coffee plantations in Guatemala with the political baggage that came with it.[10]

This trip had taught me that in the maelstrom of complexities here in Guatemala and all of Central America, our outsider's need to make sense of a tangled mess often leads us to see only what we want to see. That, at one level, explained the diametrically opposite conclusions drawn by the BBC reporter and by the rest of the group during our tour. What we saw on the surface made up one reality. Underneath it all was a complex web of 400 years of oppression, injustice, violence, corruption, and governmental and societal indifference to poverty and suffering. To top it all off, it was also a microcosm of the Cold War being waged between the Soviet Union and the U.S. The guerrillas and the Guatemalan army were surrogates fighting a global war in the Guatemalan countryside.

To most of the western press, Ríos Montt was presumed to be the stereotypical brutal military dictator. News reports commonly referred to him as the "Butcher of Central America." But what I came to know about him in person and through Alfred, Harris, and others painted a completely different picture: he was a man who cared deeply about the plight of the indigenous people and who grabbed the opportunity to address some of the root causes of misery in his country.

---

[10] Years later, one of the younger Samayoas approached Alfred and asked if Agros would be interested in buying La Perla. The old man had died, and the children no longer wanted to keep the farm. His asking price for the entire 8,000-acre spread was staggering by Agros' measure. At that time Agros had only seven villages, and our project size ranged from 150-800 acres. On my next trip to Guatemala Alfred and I flew by small plane to La Perla, taking with us Dave Olsen and Wanda Herndon, two Starbucks executives. I thought Starbucks might play a role in helping us if we bought the property with its huge coffee producing capacity. La Perla was a spectacular piece of property, but cooler heads prevailed again. It was in a different stratosphere in terms of project size and cost.

It was during this very early stage of exploring the feasibility of private land redistribution in Guatemala, that both Alfred and I began to think that we might be able to work, in some collaborative form, with the Guatemalan government. It seemed to us that the Ríos Montt presidency gave us a window of opportunity to work under favorable circumstances.

In the dinner conversation at the Presidential Palace, Ríos Montt had made it clear he would extend whatever help we needed if we would buy La Perla. Perhaps he might be open to alternative ideas other than La Perla. Alfred's position as his special representative on rural development issues could open all sorts of doors for us. Other friends were also in position to help. Might we even begin a project with land that the government owned? I wondered if the government might release some of its land for us to do a pilot project? This might compromise the "private" part of the program, to be in partnership with the government, but I was willing to rationalize this in order to get a head start and obviate the need to raise the capital to buy land from private owners. I thought we could switch to buying privately owned land after we had proven the feasibility of the idea. Besides, the goal was to get land into the hands of the rural poor, and if some of that land came from a government sympathetic to our objective, why not? In a sense, we could help the Guatemalan government do what it ought to be doing anyway.

Little did we know that the "window" would be slammed shut later that year, and all my rationale for a partnership with the Guatemalan government would be turned on its head.

6

ROADBLOCK

After three trips of encountering nothing but green lights, I decided on another trip in April 1983 to begin the groundwork for an actual project.

Soon after my arrival Alfred and I consulted a Guatemalan lawyer knowledgeable in real estate matters. In my work as a lawyer in the U.S., I knew exactly what it took to buy and sell property, whether residential, commercial, or agricultural. Title insurance removed the risk of a flawed title; U.S. law required recording the deed of transfer with only the county recorder. Priority of right could easily be determined by priority of recording date.

I found out from the lawyer that in Guatemala titles were recorded in the municipality in which the land is located. This legal requirement dated back to Spanish colonial times. In more recent history the government enacted another law whereby land titles could also be registered in the capital, Guatemala City. This duplicate registration system opened up countless opportunities for the unscrupulous and dishonest to cheat illiterate indigenous landowners out of their land. Such people could make a spurious registration with the national government to land registered only at the municipal level by an indigenous owner, then bring a lawsuit to challenge the real owner's registration. Most indigenous people had no idea how to navigate the Guatemalan legal and judicial system and would end up losing their land to the spurious claimant, thus giving rise to the Ixil definition of "justice" Ray Elliott had explained to me.

Title insurance did not exist in Guatemala. In order to verify a "clean" title, one engaged a lawyer to search property records both in the municipal and national registers and examine the claims against title to the subject property.

The lawyer also advised us that Guatemala law required any property purchase to be paid in quetzals. This would present some interesting issues for us to consider in light of exchange rate issues and manipulations.

The official exchange rate in Guatemala at that time had the dollar and quetzal at parity, which was a laughable fiction. The black market discounted the quetzal by about 30 percent. During that time, quetzals could be purchased at about a 20-25% discount at U.S. airport currency kiosks. No one but naïve tourists would go to a bank to exchange dollars for quetzals at the official 1:1 rate.

After discussing this issue with our ad hoc committee, we agreed to do our best to abide by Guatemalan law in all our dealings, which ruled out buying quetzals on the Guatemalan black market. However, we also agreed we should exchange dollars for quetzals from U.S. banks at the best discount we could get.

The Elliotts and Behrhorst urged us to be sensitive to the social and cultural considerations of the indigenous people in a first project. Knowing that past government land reform efforts had failed because the indigenous people were excluded from decisions affecting their own lives, we strongly agreed.

That night in my hotel room as I recalled the conversations of the day, I felt a growing sense of excitement that we were on our way to a pilot project. That seed of an idea from February 1982 was beginning to take on some substance.

I was inspired by the challenge to work in the Ixil region, notwithstanding it was the epicenter of the civil war. Other NGOs had pulled out of the Ixil Triangle because of the risk of harm. So be it. If this idea came from God, then it didn't matter that the guerrilla war was being fought around us. The Ixil people were both innocent bystanders and hapless victims of this war. The thousands of refugees at the Nebaj airstrip made that abundantly clear. These people had escaped with nothing but their lives and the clothes on their backs.

I also came to see that my friendship and the mutual trust developed with Alfred Kaltschmitt had grown exponentially with each successive trip. He, and others I met early on who doubted my intentions, gradually came to believe that I really meant what I said about helping the rural poor in Guatemala.

I learned more about Alfred as we worked together, shared meals, and drove from place to place. His father had worked for the United Fruit Company in Nicaragua,[1] where Alfred lived as a child. For an extended period of time during his twenties and thirties, he lived as a disenchanted young man and ran with a "hippie" crowd. He and his rebellious friends had their beliefs shaken to the core, literally, during the massive 1976 earthquake that devastated great swaths of Guatemala. The grandmother of one of his friends, who they ridiculed as being a religious nut, had prophesied that a huge earthquake would hit Guatemala, and she had moved herself out of her house into her back yard in preparation for the earthquake. When the earthquake came shortly after the grandmother's prophetic utterances, they converted to Christianity en masse, and began holding worship

---

[1] United Fruit Company was a dominant force in agriculture in Central America during the first part of the 20th century. The company had a reputation for interfering in local politics to its own advantage and is one of the sources for the derogatory term "Banana Republic," a reference to a poor country with a corrupt government unduly influenced by United Fruit Company. Alfred's family recollects that the company was run in benign fashion, contrary to its infamous public reputation; workers and their families were well taken care of and felt fortunate to be employed by UFC. Alfred's family's first-hand experience in this respect is another indication of the complexity of political and social issues in Central America, and that extremely negative popular stereotypes of multinational companies do not always tell the full story.

services in Alfred's home. That group of friends eventually grew into what later became the Verbo Church. Most of the pastoral team I met during that first session at my hotel room in October 1982 were "reformed" hippies.

On my return flight to the U.S. I began handwriting on a legal pad the outline and initial content of what I titled "Report on Proposed Land Redistribution Project in Guatemala." So much progress had been made to this point I thought it was time to put together a white paper for Art Beals at World Concern and for potential donors. We would soon need to come up with funding to buy one of the potential pilot project sites. I had penciled out a rough budget totaling $137,300 for the pilot project, which included a half-time project coordinator for three months.[2]

I also made plans for a June trip to Guatemala to keep up the momentum we had developed. Everything had gone so well I had no reason to think there was anything that could stop us from going ahead. Raising the money did not seem like an insurmountable challenge. $137,300 was a rather modest amount of money to help so many families get a new start on life. My optimistic side had taken over by now.

Dark Clouds Gathering

The first rain clouds on my succession of sunny days came with news of serious political turmoil in Guatemala. Shortly before my scheduled trip in June 1983, Ríos Montt declared a state of emergency in response to threats of a *coup d'état*. This was no

---

[2] As I look back now, I am embarrassed by the staggering naïveté under which I was operating back then, to think that the land purchase, community organization, resettling of 60 families, providing them seeds, building materials, tools, and animals, could all be accomplished in 90 days, and for only $137,300!

false rumor emanating from Costa Rica. My friends in Guatemala uniformly counseled me to postpone my trip. The news stunned me out of the unfailing optimism that had overtaken me and presented me the reality of Guatemalan politics and society.

It got worse soon after. In early August that same year, Ríos Montt was indeed overthrown in a coup led by army general Humberto Mejía Víctores. Ríos Montt was not sent into exile as was the usual custom in military coups, but returned to civilian life as an elder in the Verbo Church instead.

I was anxious to know whether my friends would suffer repercussions from their close association with Ríos Montt. I thought especially of Alfred and his Ministry of Development assignment. His official ID made it easy for us to travel in the Ixil region or indeed anywhere in the country. Would we still be able to travel freely? Were we back to square one?

When it appeared that things had settled somewhat, I decided it was time to go to Guatemala and find out for myself whether we could still work in that country. As my departure date in September 1983 approached, I wondered how I would find the country, and how my friends like Alfred, Harris, and others who had been close to Ríos Montt fared. Our adopted son Brian Huotari, a news cameraman and producer for KING-TV in Seattle, came with me on this trip to get a first hand look at what I was getting involved in.

Our red-eye flight to Guatemala City had a stopover in Mexico City. At the airport there I came across an American NGO worker I had met on an earlier trip to Guatemala. He and his wife had left Guatemala a few days after the coup because there was no way of knowing how the coup would affect the various projects he was involved in. He was now going back to Guatemala to find out what could be done. He mentioned something that was rather alarming to me, something that I had not previously known or even thought about. He said that all international calls were recorded, both incoming and outgoing. He told me a friend of his had called the phone company to complain that he had been charged incorrectly for an international call. The phone company located the tape of that call and played it back to him. He heard his own voice and realized that he had indeed made the call.

On another alarming note, this man also mentioned that the intelligence branch of the military had a very extensive network, and kept extensive files on anyone remotely involved in efforts that might be considered politically questionable. He said that he had seen a file on himself as a result of an inquiry he had made into the renewal of a permit for his airplane. He said it was a thick file that detailed much more than just the flights he had made in various parts of the country.

If all this was true, I wondered, what sort of a record or file was kept on our land project and how were our efforts interpreted? I confess to some paranoia after that conversation. I went through my briefcase at the Mexico City airport and purged my Guatemala file of any materials that might even remotely appear to be questionable or critical of the government.

The connecting flight to Guatemala City was once again occupied by just a few forlorn souls, not unlike my experience in October and December 1982. Travel had begun to pick up as foreigners had begun to feel safer about going to the country. But the coup had brought jitters again to anyone thinking of traveling to Guatemala.

The tension was immediately evident when Brian and I got off the plane the morning of September 21, 1983. The airport was even more deserted than usual. The soldiers with submachine guns were not new, but the air seemed thick enough to cut with a knife. The immigration and customs officials didn't smile – they seemed on edge.

We were greeted outside the customs inspection area by Alfred, who dropped us off at the Camino Real Hotel and indicated he would be back later that day. After finding our rooms and settling in, I sat on the bed and felt, for the first and only time in all the trips from October 1982 to this day, a fear I could not explain. The air itself seemed oppressive.

I contacted Walter Schieber and Adolfo Lau and made arrangements to meet with them. Alfred came later in the afternoon to have a long conversation in my room.

Alfred believed that the situation had regressed to where it was before the 1982 coup that had brought Ríos Montt to power. He told us some extremely distressing news, that Chepe Pajarito, executive director of Behrhorst's ULEU Foundation, had been kidnapped and murdered by the army just a week or two earlier. The men who came and took him were well known figures at the army base. Alfred felt that the army would move against anyone involved in development-type projects with the Indians. While they tolerated and invited relief help such as food and blankets, they apparently would not tolerate education, literacy or land redistribution.

According to Alfred, the military commanders of each military district were given far more power now than they had under Ríos Montt and acted like warlords in their districts. The military had a very definite idea of how the country should be run, and their primary objective was to prevent communism or any leftist cause to exist in the country. He believed the U.S. had been actively involved in the coup because Ríos Montt had refused to join the U.S. "team" and preferred to steer Guatemala through a more independent and neutral course. The U.S. was particularly disturbed that Ríos Montt had refused to participate in a united effort against the Sandinistas in Nicaragua.

Alfred's conclusion at that time: a land project might still be carried out, but we had to completely rethink how to do it.

After Alfred left, Brian and I had a chance to talk about what we had heard. I was feeling quite depressed about the situation, almost to the point of calling it quits and going home on the early morning flight the next day. For the first time in all my trips to Guatemala I also felt a clear sense of personal danger. I wondered if the room was bugged and if all of our conversations had been heard.

To this day, I have been blessed (or some might think cursed) with a contrarian indifference (or arrogance) to certain risks. In my first trips to Guatemala, what scared other people away from the country gave me an adrenaline boost that actually sharpened my mind and solidified my resolve. But that indifference dissolved on this particular night in Guatemala City.

I didn't want to be scared, but the feeling of fear was undeniable. With so few passengers arriving on each flight, I thought it would be easy for the new military government to track every arriving visitor. Would my association with people who had been close to Ríos Montt attract the attention of the security forces and the notorious paramilitary "death squads?" If Mark Pearlman had been gunned down in a Sheraton Hotel in San Salvador because of his passion for land reform, what would prevent armed thugs from bursting through my hotel door and doing away with another American lawyer who believed the poor should own their own farmland? Would I become the second 1970 University of Washington law school graduate to be murdered for taking on the land tenure system in Central America?

Per routine, I picked up the phone and asked the hotel operator to connect me with the international operator so I could place my "arrived safely" call to Cyd. These were pre-cell phone days, and the Guatemalan telephone system was built on a woefully outdated infrastructure. It might take 10-15 minutes just to get a dial tone, and then a call, when made, might not get through because the trunk lines were so clogged. Businesses, large and small, employed motorcycle-riding messengers to deliver messages across the city rather than suffer the unreliability of the phone system and the waste of time just trying to get a call through.

My anxiety level, fueled by an imagination wandering down dark paths, increased during the 20-30 minute wait for the international connection. When I finally had Cyd on the line, in typical male protector fashion, I did not let her know anything about my jitters and told her everything was just fine. I did ask her to pray for our situation and to get friends to pray, too.

My mental wanderings conjured up even darker alleys after the momentary sweetness of the phone call with Cyd. I began to question my own motivations for being there at all. Who did I think I was to take on 400 years of institutional injustice? Had my stupid arrogance as a 16-year old re-surfaced now in my 37-year old psyche? Who was I to brush aside the dangers that stopped others from traveling to Guatemala? Did I have some kind of messianic complex, or, just as bad, some perverted martyr's death wish? What would happen to my wife and two young children if I suffered Mark Pearlman's fate? Would my do-good intentions do any good for a forsaken family headed by a widowed young mother?

After thrashing myself thoroughly with a mental cat o' nine-tails, I unpacked my suitcase and, as a probably useless security measure, put a heavy desk chair under the room door handle. I took out my small black Bible Cyd had given me a few years earlier. It went with me wherever I traveled. I was ready to look for any comfort the scriptures could give me.

Thinking I would start with the Psalms where I might find some consoling verse by King David, I opened the Bible and saw I had opened to Jeremiah chapter 32 instead. A quick glance caught something about Jeremiah buying a field, which sounded intriguing. I was not very familiar with the Old Testament prophets at that point in my life, and what I read both surprised and stunned me. Over the years I have gone back to mine the riches which I stumbled upon during that moment of despair and doubt. I continue to be amazed at the depth of those riches.

Buy This Land

Chapters 32 and 33 in Jeremiah come as an unusual historical interlude amidst the prose and poetry of God's warning, chastisement, and promise to the remnants of His people. The time is 586 BC, a desperate moment in the life of the kingdom of Judah. Judah's northern sister kingdom of Israel had fallen to the Assyrians over 130 years earlier.

A few years earlier, another king of Judah, his court, and the whole upper crust of Jerusalem had been taken captive to Babylon. Judah was now a vassal state of Babylon with a puppet king sitting on the once glorious throne of David. Now even that last vestige of nationhood was about to be wiped out, the consequence of King Zedekiah's ill-conceived plan to rebel against and overthrow Babylon by invoking the help of Egypt. The alliance with Egypt had forestalled the inevitable, but not for long. After Egypt's armies went home, Nebuchadnezzar, king of Babylon, had renewed his attack on Judah. His armies had overrun all of Judah and now had laid siege against Jerusalem, the last unconquered city. Siege mounds reached up to the top of the city walls. The most fearsome and savage warriors of that time were poised to swarm over the mounds to overwhelm the starving and much-weakened defenders.

Jeremiah, at the time, was under arrest and imprisoned in the courtyard of the king's guard by order of King Zedekiah. His crime was his inability to tell anything but the truth to the king. The king had wanted to hear a prophetic word of God's deliverance and comfort. Jeremiah told him nothing of the kind:

> Behold, I am about to give this city into the hand of the
> king of Babylon, and he will take it; and Zedekiah king of
> Judah will not escape out of the hand of the Chaldeans,
> but he will surely be given into the hand of the king of
> Babylon.[3]

What was Jeremiah's state of mind at that point? Here he
had prophesied the end of his own nation; there was no hope for
deliverance. Yet was not the throne of David eternal? What
about God's covenant with King David that his house and
kingdom would endure forever and that David's throne would
be established forever? If Jerusalem were destroyed, and the
remnant of Judah either killed or taken to Babylon in captivity,
what hope was there that either the nation or the throne would
endure?

In this darkest of moments, a surprising thing happened.
Jeremiah's cousin, Hanamel, came to visit him in prison, and
offered to sell to Jeremiah a piece of property he owned in
Anatoth, just a mile north of Jerusalem in Jeremiah's home
town.

Could there have been anything more inappropriate under
Jeremiah's circumstances? He had no family, no children, and
was at the time in custody by order of the king. The Babylonian
army was about to overrun the city and bring an end to the
nation Judah. Anatoth, where Hanamel's land was situated, was
already occupied by Babylonian troops. The land was not then,
and never could have been, of the slightest use or value to
Jeremiah.

But Jeremiah bought the land with all appropriate ceremony.
He made full payment in silver that was properly weighed. The
purchase price, 17 shekels, was not "panic value" but full price.
The deed was sealed, and in the custom of the day, a copy was
made. The sealing of the deed was literal – the original could

---

[3] Jeremiah 32:3-4

only be read by breaking the seal to unfold the document. The deed was then delivered for safekeeping to Baruch, Jeremiah's personal secretary, with instructions to place it in a sealed earthen jar to protect it from dampness and preserve it for posterity.

Why on earth did Jeremiah buy the property? Prophets were not wealthy men. Whatever Jeremiah had in monetary wealth was probably carried on him or Baruch. In today's balance sheet terms, the purchase took a big chunk out of his liquid assets, and his net worth took a sudden, sharp turn into fixed non-income producing assets. It was not a smart move under the circumstances when the Babylonians were disrupting the real estate and all other financial markets.

Jeremiah was a great prophet, revered then and now. We would all root for him to have made a killing out of that purchase. But that didn't happen, and needless to say, the investment turned out to be a total loss. Jeremiah never made a profit out of it. He died a few years later in Egypt after his prophecy came true and his people had been marched off in captivity to Babylon.

What was this all about? Why did Jeremiah buy a worthless piece of land knowing it made no business sense whatsoever? Jeremiah asked the same question after it was all over. He asked God why He had told Jeremiah to buy that land from Hanamel.

> Behold, the siege ramps have reached the city to take it; and the city is given into the hand of the Chaldeans who fight against it, because of the sword, the famine and the pestilence; and what You have spoken has come to pass; and behold, You see it. You have said to me, O Lord God, "Buy for yourself the field with money and call in witnesses" – although the city is given into the hand of the Chaldeans.[4]

---

[4] Jeremiah 32:24-25

God's answer immediately set the tone for the great lesson to be learned by Jeremiah and all generations thereafter about the nature of God and how He chooses to act in the affairs of man:

Behold, I am the Lord, the God of all flesh; is anything too difficult for Me?[5]

Pity Jeremiah. God's first response to Jeremiah was in the form of a question that is unanswerable, the type of question that is better answered by silence than by words of any kind.

Just as I brought all this great disaster on this people, so I am going to bring on them all the good that I am promising them. Fields will be bought in this land of which you say, 'It is a desolation, without man or beast; it is given into the hand of the Chaldeans.' Men will buy fields for money, sign and seal deeds, and call in witnesses in the land of Benjamin, in the environs of Jerusalem, in the cities of Judah, in the cities of the hill country, in the cities of the lowland and in the cities of the Negev; for I will restore their fortunes, declares the Lord.[6]

So Jeremiah now knew. He was told to buy Hanamel's land as a sign that God would restore the fortunes of Judah some day. That's not all God had to say. Knowing that Jeremiah had wondered whether God would break His covenant with David, God continued with more unanswerable questions meant to eradicate any doubt on Jeremiah's part, and indeed, to shame him for doubting at all:

---

[5] Jeremiah 32:27
[6] Jeremiah 32:42-44

If you can break My covenant for the day and My covenant for the night, so that day and night will not be at their appointed time, then My covenant may also be broken with David My servant so that he will not have a son to reign on his throne, and with the Levitical priests, My ministers. As the host of heaven cannot be counted and the sand of the sea cannot be measured, so I will multiply the descendants of David My servant and the Levites who minister to Me.[7]

How is a man to answer God's challenge to make the day into night, and night into day? It is an impossibility. God was making it clear to Jeremiah: so it was impossible that He would break any covenant promise, much less His promise to David.

Through the following long discourse that resembled God's response to Job in the whirlwind, He made clear to Jeremiah:[8]

- He was indeed the God of heaven and earth;
- Jeremiah's nonsensical land purchase was a sign of the grace and mercy God would extend to the people of Judah;
- Houses and fields, vineyards and flocks would one day again be bought and sold in this land of desolation;
- He would never forsake His covenants with Abraham, Isaac, Jacob, or with David.
- He would one day forgive the people their sins and restore them to their fortunes.

Jeremiah was God's chosen servant to carry His message during the darkest moment in Judah's history. For all of this,

---

[7] Jeremiah 33:20-21
[8] Job 38:1

God used a mundane real estate transaction involving a few pieces of silver between two cousins.

God was challenging Jeremiah: Do you trust me, Jeremiah? You who are my prophet, do you believe that I am God? Do you believe that I will never forsake my people, never break my promise to them? Do you trust me enough to empty your pockets of silver to buy a worthless piece of land just because I told you to do so? Is my word good enough for you, Jeremiah?

If you can break the cycle of day and night so the sun does not rise and the moon does not shine, then so can my word be broken.

Reading that story in my hotel room in Guatemala, those words of a Hebrew prophet written some 2,500 years earlier came to life and brought me an indescribable peace of mind. My fear dissipated. I came to realize that God's answer to Jeremiah, and his message conveyed through that simple real estate purchase, was just as true today as it was then. All our dreams to help the poor buy their own farmland may indeed be preposterous, and we may never accomplish what we hope, and we may fail miserably, and we may lose all the money invested in the effort. It may make absolutely no sense to think of buying land in the Ixil Triangle of Guatemala. It may seem like utter foolishness. Jeremiah's purchase of Hanamel's land made even less sense. But good sense was of no relevance. This simple real estate transaction had everything to do with God's redemptive plan for the people of Judah.

And just as God had used Jeremiah's purchase as a sign of future restoration and blessing, so I came to see that night that God could use our imperfect efforts as a sign of His present and future justice and righteousness in a country bound tightly by 400 years of injustice and oppression. We might not change the course of history. But He could.

Behold, I am the Lord, the God of all flesh; is anything too difficult for me?

The gauntlet thrown down by God to Jeremiah in 586 BC became the answers to my doubts and fears two and a half millennia later. As I read those two chapters from Jeremiah over and over again that night to make sure I was not imagining things that were not there, I was overcome with a sweet sense of assurance. My mind came to a place of profound peace and contentment.

Of course we ought to continue our efforts. How could we stop now? So what if the land we bought was in the most dangerous area of the country? Wasn't it worse for Jeremiah who bought land that the Babylonians had already taken? So what if it made no sense? So what if a new military government had come into power?

Then and there, it seemed that the thickening dark fog that had enveloped me from the time I stepped off the plane lifted to show a bright dawn and blue sky. The anxiety and doubt went away, and to this day, they have not shown their faces again. There have been harrowing experiences in the intervening years, but I have not again felt the fear that beset me that night.

The notion that buying land in war-torn regions might serve as a sign of a loving God's mercy and grace to the poor has stuck with me as an inspiration for all that followed. In a very real sense it also took away another fear – fear of failure. I came to understand that night that any effort of ours to serve the poor in response to God's mandate throughout the scriptures was in itself a success, not by any tangible measure, but simply by the measure of obedience. Jeremiah's land purchase was not successful in investment terms. But as an act of obedience, his willingness to engage in what others in the king's guards courtyard that day might have ridiculed as foolishness stands out as an unmistakable and memorable milestone in the history of God's dealing with His people.

That night, the sense of calling that first came when I followed Juan Carlos Ortíz's verbal rabbit trail became crystal clear. I had an assignment of indefinite duration, undefined job description, and unknown outcome. Go do it. You're a lawyer trained to take on a case with its given facts and applicable law. Go do the best you can with what you have.

More Input

Meetings with Ed Greenberg over the next two days gave us a great deal more detail and insight into what was happening in the country. Ed now occupied the position Alfred had held as the government's chief coordinator for rural relief and development. Ed recalled very clearly what my interests were and our prior conversations on land redistribution during earlier trips. He said no formal government policy had been adopted yet on the Indians or on assistance to the Ixil highlands. He discouraged any efforts that would involve the government but strongly encouraged proceeding with the land project on a completely private basis.

He also shed some light on the Pajarito case (the executive director of Behrhorst's ULEU Foundation who had been kidnapped and murdered by the army) and on Carroll Behrhorst, including what he described as some highly confidential information. The government had evidence that ULEU had been infiltrated by guerrilla sympathizers and that Pajarito was suspected of aiding the guerrillas. Apparently Pajarito allowed medical treatment of guerrillas at the Behrhorst clinic and also maintained medical supplies for the guerrillas under the clinic name. Moreover, a second physician at the Behrhorst Clinic had also disappeared. He was also suspected of being involved with the guerrillas.

While Ed felt it was too early to tell which direction the government was headed, he did not believe this government would be opposed to the land project, particularly if done privately and quietly.

Toward the end of our meeting, he made an impassioned plea to me. "Mr. Li, do not abandon us. We need people to have solidarity with us. The indigenous people were amazed and happy after the 1976 earthquakes, because it seemed the whole world took notice and sent help. For the first time they felt they were not alone in the world."

He told me that in the late 1960s the Guatemalan government had tried, with $15-20 million of funds provided by the U.S. government, to institute a land reform program in Nueva Concepción, Escuintla. It was a total failure and loss. The program was imposed from top down. Nobody had thought to ask the indigenous people what they wanted. The land plots were too small, and the attempt to implement a cooperative completely backfired.[9] Greenberg told me about the saying

---

[9] I recently discovered, through a Google search, de-classified reports, formerly secret, written by the American Embassy in Guatemala in 1969, in which the Nueva Concepción land reform project was mentioned. Reading between the lines, one can tell that those land reform projects were further burdened by the weight of mind-boggling Guatemalan government bureaucracy and what the Embassy characterized as "inter-agency rivalries." The "Joint GOG/USAID Rural Development working group" was meeting twice weekly and included no fewer than eight government agencies having their hands in the till, including the Ministries of Agriculture, Finance, Public Works, the National Planning Council, the Bank of Guatemala, the Institute of Agrarian Transformation, the Organization for Community Development, the Social Welfare Organization. These were additionally "supplemented" by representatives of the National Agrarian Bank, the National Institute for Production Development, the Interamerican Cooperative Supervised Credit Agency. The Embassy report added that "we have prepared the way for possible participation in the future of an FAO representative and of spokesmen for the private sector." One wonders how anything could possibly have been accomplished with such a hydra-like "working group." -U.S.

among the poor farmers who were supposed to benefit from the Nueva Concepción program: *"si acepta un favor, se pierde su libertad."*

"If you accept a favor, you lose your freedom."

This was my first one-on-one conversation with Ed Greenberg. He was very cordial towards me, very supportive of the land project concept and seemed very eager to help in whatever way he could.

Brian and I also spent time at the Chinese Embassy with Ambassador I. C. Loh, a meeting set up by Enrique Lee. I had met the Ambassador at the Double Ten reception on my first trip back to Guatemala in October 1982, and because of his respect for my father, he took an interest in my activities in Guatemala. He had even considered recommending that the Chinese government in Taipei fund the project I was advocating. Ambassador Loh told me that the Chinese government had a large agricultural mission in Guatemala, which included two demonstration farms. The ROC provided considerable financial and technical support to Guatemala as part of their dollar diplomacy strategy. The Ambassador felt that the concept was a sound one, but that it had not been developed sufficiently in order for it to be successfully implemented.

He made the point that production would never be the problem. In other words, getting the land into the hands of the indigenous poor and helping them to properly cultivate the land would be the easy part of any such project. He questioned, however, whether sufficient or any consideration had been given to a realistic marketing plan. He said it was one thing for the indigenous people to be taught to grow vegetables which they would not eat themselves, but quite another thing for them to be able to get those vegetables to the proper marketplace in order to

---

Embassy Memorandum transmitted to State Department August 13, 1969, titled "Implementation of IRG/COIN Working Group Action Plan for Guatemala."

get the highest price. He pointed out the example of one Chinese resident in Guatemala who grew Chinese snow peas that sold for $5.00 a pound in New York City. This man regularly shipped 5,000 pounds of these peas to New York and made an enormous amount of money off the trade. Ambassador Loh felt that we completely lacked any such thinking or planning.

Thus he had thrown out the idea of recommending the project to the Chinese government. He bluntly told me he had no confidence in the chances of such a project succeeding in Guatemala. He simply did not believe there was any competent management personnel in the country to run a program of that kind and to be able to deal with all of the complicating factors.[10]

Our time was basically a monologue on his part. I was of a younger generation and, under Chinese custom, I could not dialogue with him as a peer or question any of his assumptions or conclusions.

From the Chinese Embassy we proceeded to the Ministry of Development, where Ed Greenberg set up a meeting for Brian and me with General Fuentes, the cabinet minister in charge of rural development. Fuentes had a low-key manner and came across very sincere and knowledgeable. He had survived several changes of government and was highly respected. After the usual courtesies and after Ed had briefly told him about our land project (with which he was already familiar) I asked him if he thought we should still proceed with the project. His answer was very positive, but he also counseled that it be done without any government involvement. Governments come and go, he said, and he chided the people who had been close to Ríos Montt for thinking that his government would be around long enough for them to accomplish all of their good works.

---

[10] What an ironic twist that the Ambassador's example of growing and exporting premium crops such as snow peas, which he thought was beyond the capability of indigenous farmers, is exactly what Agros farmers in Guatemala and Nicaragua are doing today with the help of our national staff.

He then philosophized on relief and development, particularly in the context of foreign organizations coming to Guatemala and the attitude that they adopt. He said foreigners should first understand that Guatemala exports such things as coffee, bananas, cotton and other agricultural products. He drew a graph on a piece of paper showing how these products might amount to $400 million in sales per year in exports, primarily to countries that he designated as "ET" countries – countries with energy and technology. (As he wrote ET on his chart he looked at me with a twinkle in his eyes. Since the movie *ET* was then a worldwide hit, he wanted to make sure I got his little joke.) He said the ET countries, in turn, would export to Guatemala energy and technology amounting to $2 billion per year. Of that $2 billion most of it would go to the energy and equipment required to produce the $400 million per year in exports. He said that this imbalance was a problem that was almost insurmountable to a country like Guatemala. He asked whether any country from the ET group would offer to pay Guatemala higher prices for its exports and reduce the costs of their imports into Guatemala simply because Guatemala was an underdeveloped country.

"Do you see our difficulty, Mr. Li?" he asked. Then he looked at me straight in the eyes and said, "That is why, Mr. Li, if the Soviet Union tells me today they will buy our oil for twice the price paid by the United States," and here he paused again for effect as I awaited what would be his punch line, "then tomorrow I will tell the world I am a Communist!"

He next drew a picture of a tree with its roots under the ground. He used the picture to illustrate the relationship of the northern and southern hemispheres of the American continent. The upper part of the tree (northern hemisphere) bears all the fruit, flowers, leaves and beauty, he said. The lower or underground part of the tree (southern hemisphere) has worms and diseases attacking the root system. He asked, "Is it right for someone from the top of the tree to come to the bottom of the tree and accuse the bottom with being afflicted with social injustice and oppression? Can the upper half of the tree do without the lower half of the tree?"

We had a moment of humor when he asked if I could look around his office and identify anything that was 100% made in Guatemala. I pointed to the coffee table that sat between us – the type where a slab of a tree trunk had been taken to make the top of the table. It looked like the work of local artisans. He laughed, and responded "But the resins used to produce the surface of the table were imported materials." As I looked around the room he pointed to a small flag of Guatemala sitting on a corner of his desk and said "That flag is not even Guatemalan; it was probably made in Japan or Hong Kong." Realizing his question was a set-up, I resorted to a different tact. "That plant," I said, pointing to a large potted plant growing in one corner of his office, "that was surely made in Guatemala." Just as I was relishing my little triumph, Ed Greenberg interjected, "But the fertilizers used to help the plant grow were imported from Mexico!" We all had a good laugh about that.

The general ended our meeting by offering all the help that he and his office could provide including letters of safe conduct, travel permits, military authorizations and the like.

That evening as I replayed this conversation in my mind, I realized General Fuentes had given me a quick master class on the fundamental economics of a poor, developing country, and how it tied into the global geopolitical struggle between the two superpowers. Here was yet another layer of complexity in what was already a highly complex situation.

That afternoon I had a long talk with Alfred. Alfred had previously suggested that I talk to everyone else before he would give me his impressions and opinions. Having fulfilled his request, I asked him to share what he had in his mind. He indicated he had no strong feelings of either going ahead with the project or not going ahead with it. He said his heart was very much in the project and perhaps too much in it. But he was also troubled about the coup and recent events such as the Pajarito kidnapping. He suggested that I wait for a few months and then come down again and evaluate the situation.

Our conversation also covered the subject of a paper Alfred had written entitled, *The Comín – An Agricultural Democracy*. He had sent it to me in June after I canceled my trip that month. During his tenure as the president's special representative on rural development, he took a trip to Israel to look into the kibbutz system of agricultural cooperatives. Ríos Montt had been very interested in how the Israelis had so successfully built up their agricultural sector in spite of being such a small country in such an arid land. He wanted to see if the Israeli experience could be applied in the rural regions of Guatemala. The result of that trip, and Alfred's thinking about it, was a white paper on *Comunidades Integradas* (integrated communities), shortened to the catchy name "Comín."

The paper advocated government action to implement agricultural communities, proposing first that the country's land reform laws be completely rewritten. The paper advocated the creation of a Land Bank that would finance the purchase of large tracts of land at low interest rates to enable poor peasants to buy land and subdivide into small family parcels.[11]

I expressed to Alfred that the Comín concept might have worked, and worked well, in Israel where ethnic homogeneity and an ethic of integrity in society and government prevailed, but in Guatemala it had little chance of succeeding. On the

---

[11] Ray Elliott wrote a highly critical analysis of Alfred's paper. Ray believed the stated social and economic goals of the Comín system, crafted with the heavy involvement of government legislation and Land Bank rules, would once again, as in so many instances in the past, preempt and trump any plans or wishes of the poor rural farmer. Past efforts had never solicited the views, wishes or aspirations of the indigenous farmer, and Ray saw in the structure of the Comín system the same disregard for the opinions of that population.

lighter side, I pointed out to Alfred that the name "Comín" was perilously close to "Comintern," the shortened name used to refer to Communism International. The realization startled him, and we shared a few laughs about it. Whatever we ended up doing in the Ixil Triangle to help the poor buy land, we agreed we would not be calling it by the Comín name. It took him a while to stop using the term, however, so I kiddingly threatened to fine him any time he mentioned the name "Comín" again.

In the period of three short days I had managed to hold conversations with and listen to the counsel of all the key people who had expressed support or willingness to help over the past year. Add to that the views of General Fuentes and Ambassador Loh, and my mind was filled to overflowing. I took copious notes, and each night before going to sleep wrote down recollected tidbits of conversation and impressions. Brian and I also debriefed one another at the end of each day. By the end of the third day I was physically and mentally exhausted and ready to go home.

Brian and I both recall the palpable relief we felt when our flight lifted off the tarmac at La Aurora airport. Up to that moment and throughout the three days in Guatemala it had constantly been in the backs of our minds that at any moment we might be detained by military or paramilitary types for questioning or worse. As usual, the return flight provided several hours of uninterrupted time for writing and thinking about the just-ended trip. This flight home was a sobering time. Our early plans to work in collaboration with, or maybe even with the help of, the Ríos Montt government had been shot to pieces. We were very much back to the drawing board. I decided this was not the time to make a decision on whether the project should go ahead or not. Perhaps in another three or four months I might travel again to assess the situation. If we were to go ahead at some time in the future, the conclusions drawn from this trip had made it crystal clear that we should work privately, without government support, and as quietly as possible. Over the course of the past year, we had drifted more and more into accepting the idea of a partnership with the government.

Two factors had heavily influenced our thinking. The first was that Ríos Montt had been very enthused about the concept and wanted the government to push it. He had needed an idea and a program like this to give his government credibility. Second, we had been all too willing to accept the benefits of a close relationship with the government in power. It seemed so ideal to be able to get a road when you needed one, transportation by air force flights or army helicopters when we needed transportation; protection from the military when we traveled through guerrilla territory. We could cut through or avoid so much bureaucratic red tape because we had the blessing and full support of the government in power which ruled as a military dictatorship.

Now that the Ríos Montt government was ejected from office, I did not consider the time and effort wasted, however, because much groundwork had been laid, especially in relationships with key people who would undergird a private effort – Alfred, Walter, the Elliotts. I realized we needed to distance ourselves from Behrhorst because his organization had come under suspicion of aiding the guerrillas. We had done basic research on feasibility, and had even identified potential land to buy. As Walter had expressed, the only thing we had lost was time. But we had gained valuable experience and learned some hard lessons in the process.

I thought of traveling again in early 1984 to reassess the situation. By then the course of the new government should be defined and there would be a better indication of the general political situation with elections approaching.

For the first time after returning to Seattle I did not make plans for the next trip. So far after one year, five trips, several thousand dollars of travel expenses, and even more in law firm income not generated during the times I was gone, I had zero to show in terms of helping the poor to buy land. My mind at this point was not so much filled with disappointment as with questioning what all this meant – was this really worthwhile, or was it all just an enormous waste of time, money, and energy? Would it amount to anything at all?

For the next few months I turned my attention back to minding business at the law firm and at home. A long business trip to Taiwan and Hong Kong in January 1984 and other business and personal issues pushed Guatemala to the recesses of my mind.

7

BUEN SAMARITANO

In the midst of a beautiful Seattle summer in 1984 word came to me from Alfred and others that a certain normalcy had returned to Guatemala, and perhaps it was time to talk about resuming our efforts. My mind, I confess, had wandered away from Guatemala for a while, and I had no idea whether we were permanently stymied there insofar as private land reform was concerned. It took refocusing on what we had done, and where we had left off, for me to schedule a trip in late July 1984. Ten months had passed since my last visit.

I returned to Guatemala for a short stay of three days, during which I consulted all my contacts. The Mejía government had been in place for almost a year and my friends in Guatemala had uniformly laid low during that time. Now the tensions surrounding the coup in August 1983 had eased, and there was a general feeling that the political atmosphere was right for picking up the pieces and starting anew.

A new friend emerged out of that trip – Bill Taylor. Bill was then teaching at SETECA, the Central America Theological Seminary, in Guatemala City. He had lived most of his life in Guatemala and spoke Spanish like a native. He was enthused about the idea of private land redistribution and promised to help in whatever way he could. He also said he had some friends I should meet on my next trip, since my stay was so short this time. These friends might be able to help. Little did I know how significant a role Bill's friends would play and what great "help" they became.

Back in Seattle and thoroughly encouraged by the open doors I had encountered, I not only made plans for a longer trip in late September 1984, but also decided it was time to set up a nonprofit legal entity to bring some formality to the work that had been lacking up to then. I think in many people's eyes it was, up to that time, a one-man crusade on my part. Some may have admired my one-track-mindedness; others probably thought I was crazy. It seemed that a new legal entity would better reflect that there were others involved as well.

After drafting articles of incorporation for a 501(c)(3) corporation, I searched my mind for a name descriptive of this vision to help the poor buy their own farmland; a word or a set of words that captured the idea in simple and easily remembered form.

A few years earlier I had taken a class on biblical Greek taught at Mercer Island Covenant Church by a good friend, Connie Jacobsen. In order to increase my reading proficiency in Greek I often read from the Nestle/Marshall Interlinear Greek-English New Testament. During that time I came to understand how much of the English language owed its roots to Greek and Latin. The same could be said for the Spanish language. I began to search for a word or phrase in Greek or Latin whose meaning might easily be discernible in either English or Spanish.

It did not take long to come to the realization that the word "agriculture" in English was not only almost the same word in Spanish (*agricultura*), but the word had roots in both Latin (*ager*=field; *cultura*=cultivation) and Greek (*agros*=field).

Agros.

So simple. Yet so expressive of what we hoped to do. Land. Farms. Poor farmers owning their own land. As a final touch on the articles of incorporation I inserted a passage from Psalm 24 in the text:

The earth is the Lord's, the fullness thereof, the world, and all who dwell therein.

I had been reading and thinking about this psalm for some time. If the earth is the Lord's, I wondered, then should not the poor share in it and reap its bounty just as the rich do? Perhaps social and economic injustice distorts the truth of the Psalmist's declaration, but it must be our calling to correct the distortion.

Washington law required a nonprofit organization to have a minimum of three initial directors. Richard Barrueto, my law firm partner Rob Tulloch, and a good friend, Joel Van Ornum, all consented to serve as co-directors with me. And so with a four-person board the legal existence of Agros began.

My next trip to Guatemala in late September 1984 became the real starting point for our work. And for Agros.

I met right away with Bill Taylor who told me a story of some highly creative entrepreneurship in helping the poor.

In the late 1970s Bill Veith and Steve Sywulka, two enterprising and unconventional North American missionaries who cared deeply for the poor in Guatemala, thought land ownership was crucial to the well-being of poor rural farmers and decided to do something about it. They applied for and received a grant from World Vision to buy 800 acres of land in the remote Ixcán region of Guatemala, not far from the Mexico border, and settle the land with poor farmers – of Kanjobal and Caxiquel descent – who did not own land. The land was purchased, the families moved on to the land, simple wood houses were built, and coffee and cardamom were planted. But before their new lives had a chance to take root, the long arm of the civil war swept over the region, and the families of *Buen Samaritano* – the name they had give to their village, meaning the Good Samaritan – fled for their lives across the border into southern Mexico.

Bill arranged a meeting for me with Bill Veith the next day. Steve Sywulka was traveling outside the country at that time. At the meeting, after I had finished explaining why I was traveling regularly to Guatemala, imagine my surprise when Veith took off his glasses and began sobbing. Tears streamed down his face. After an awkward minute or so, he composed himself, looked at me, and told me he believed I was an answer to his long years of praying.

It's a humbling thing to be called an answer to someone's prayer.

He told the updated story of Buen Samaritano. After living as refugees in Mexico for several years, many of the families had taken up the Ríos Montt government's offer to escort them back to their village. When they arrived they found most of their homes and crops destroyed. Some of the homes left standing had guerrilla booby traps set in them, including Vietnam-style concealed pits with sharp bamboo stakes that would impale anyone who fell in. I could tell Veith cared deeply about the people of Buen Samaritano. He had come to know the people, the families, and the children. They were his friends. His heart ached over their hardships and struggles, knowing that they lacked the means to do anything but eke out a meager subsistence on some corn and bean plantings.

Would I consider a quick trip to Buen Samaritano to see it for myself, and consider whether we would help the people there, Veith asked, eyes still red from earlier tears. The answer came easily. How could I not? I was deeply moved by Veith's love for the people, and impressed that he and Steve Sywulka had thought through and implemented a model for land ownership by the poor long before I stumbled onto the idea listening to Juan Carlos Ortíz.

The next day we were on a Cessna 180 operated by Missionary Aviation Fellowship (MAF), flying to Buen Samaritano. From the capital, it was a flight of about one hour

20 minutes. At an altitude of 9-10,000 feet, I felt like I could reach out and touch the beauty of the Guatemalan countryside. My spirit soared much higher than the airplane – it seemed that with this first opportunity to work with a village, the real adventure had begun.

The Ixcán region of Guatemala is even more remote than the Ixil Triangle. The Ixcán River originates high in the Cuchumatánes and meanders north across the Mexican border. The Buen Samaritano village was in the middle of nowhere, with no road access. The closest thing to a road that could be used by four-wheel vehicles was some 20 kilometers away in the town of Barillas. In this region, people walked everywhere. If they had coffee or cardamom harvests to sell, they carried the sacks on their backs using foot trails through dense jungle to Barillas. The more fortunate few might own a pack animal.

The alternative to flying by MAF plane to Buen Samaritano was an eight-hour drive from Guatemala City to Barillas, then hiking by jungle trail for another 8-10 hours. The local residents could make that long hike in shorter than eight hours with a heavy pack of harvested coffee or cardamom on their backs, or supplies and seed for the return trip. For Americans not accustomed to long foot jaunts in tropical jungle landscapes, 10 hours might not be enough. MAF charged a variable rate for their flight, one price for foreign (think U.S.) NGO personnel, and another for Guatemalan nationals working for a Guatemalan nonprofit or humanitarian agency. I did not begrudge the discriminatory rate; I understood MAF had to "tax the rich" to support their work which was primarily on behalf of the poor. If I had been riding with them just for sightseeing or tourist purposes, I imagine the fare would have been even higher.

As we approached Buen Samaritano, MAF pilot Jeff Nelson pointed out the village to me in the distance. He then circled the village at low altitude to alert the villagers of our arrival, and to remind the men of the village to clear the landing strip of rocks or fill in holes created by rain or small animals. What a thrill it was to see the village from the air – the small houses laid out neatly, forming the four sides of a large rectangle in the middle of which a rough soccer pitch was clearly visible, goal posts on each end. At each corner of the rectangle was an elevated guard tower, unoccupied.

In the back of my mind I was conscious of the possible presence of guerrillas in this remote jungle area, and that small planes flying at low altitudes made an easy target. This thought came back over the many subsequent flights to Buen Samaritano and to the Ixil region. But other than some gunshots we thought we heard at the airstrip on one trip in 1985, to my knowledge we were never shot at. I am certain it had something to do with the wonderful reputation of MAF, an organization that was thoroughly apolitical, and the fact that MAF pilots were regularly called on to conduct missions of mercy, dropping in on remote and tiny landing strips to bring out people in need of emergency medical care.

After landing we were greeted by a small band of men with old rifles slung over their shoulders, acting as both greeting committee and civil patrol squad. A few children tagged along as we hiked from the airstrip for about 20 minutes through the jungle to the village. We passed through coffee and cardamom plantings under the jungle canopy. I marveled at the beautiful flora of every kind growing everywhere I looked, including the largest ficus trees I had ever seen. I thought of the sickly ficus and other plants in my office in Seattle that I struggled to keep alive. Yet here they grew robustly, wild and untended.

I was drenched with sweat by the time we reached the village. The heat and humidity of the lower elevations of the Ixcán were quite a contrast to the temperate cool of the Ixil highlands. Bill Veith introduced me to the village leadership; his rapport with them was obvious. They loved this man who had helped them buy the land, and now was trying to bring them more help to rebuild all that had been destroyed in the civil war. Many of the approximately 40 homes were of makeshift construction – just enough sticks and larger pieces of scrap wood to make up walls that would support corrugated tin roofing overhead. A few of the homes were deserted – I found out these were the ones booby-trapped by the guerrillas. The people did not want to live in them because of their belief that bad karma lingered in those houses.

By the looks of the gaunt children with glazed eyes, some with bloated bellies and blond streaks in their dark hair, it was obvious that malnutrition pervaded the village. The sole source of income for the people came through meager crops of coffee and cardamom from plants left over from before their flight to Mexico. They did not even have the means to buy seeds to plant subsistence crops of corn and beans.

At Buen Samaritano I experienced my first taste of indigenous hospitality in the midst of poverty. We were invited into the home of the village leader and sat around a roughly hewn table to talk about the situation in the village. I noticed the leader's wife across the small one-room house cooking at a makeshift stove, and another woman making tortillas over the lid of a steel drum propped above a small wood fire. After we had talked for about half an hour the women served us a lunch of chicken and potato soup, tortillas, and a very sweet and hot corn-based drink. It was meager fare by our North American standards, but in this setting it might as well have been a lavish banquet. They had spent out of their minimal resources to buy the chicken and potatoes for our lunch. Their own fare – every day, every meal – was tortillas and beans. Sometimes even the beans would be missing. I dealt that day with powerfully conflicting emotions – touched and humbled by the generosity of my impoverished new friends, and burdened by feelings of guilt. I knew that in my wallet that day I probably carried more cash than any of these villagers could earn in a year's hard labor – if they could find the work.

After the return flight to the city we discussed with Bill Veith what the people of Buen Samaritano needed: seeds to plant corn and beans for their subsistence, and new coffee and cardamom plantings to renew their main cash crops; building materials to shore up their dilapidated homes into healthier living spaces; basic medical and dental assistance to reset broken bones, pull rotting teeth; a school and teacher for the children; a community building for gatherings and church services. Just as important, it seemed they needed to know someone cared enough to come alongside and give them encouragement as they struggled to rebuild their lives.

It did not take long for me to decide this would be our first project in Guatemala. Here were people in desperate need and on the edge of starvation. They had returned from Mexico at the government's invitation, but the same government had no capacity to extend any help for their survival. The land was already bought, so there would be no capital expenditure required of us for land purchase. A key consideration in my mind was Bill Veith: a trustworthy intermediary for whatever financial and practical resources we could provide to the people of Buen Samaritano.

We came to learn that the title to the Buen Samaritano property was held by a Guatemalan non-profit entity named *Asociación Cristiana de Beneficencia*, formed at the time the property was purchased. ACB had been inactive during the time the people had fled to Mexico.

After our return from Buen Samaritano I met with Veith, Taylor, and Walter Schieber to discuss how we could get help to Buen Samaritano. We were joined by Hugo Morales, a lawyer and also member of the ACB board. The needs were compelling.

Hugo informed us that because ACB had been inactive for several years, there were unpaid taxes and overdue legal filings and reports that must all be brought up to date. Walter expressed a strong sentiment that we should be good corporate citizens and do everything required by law. He said too many NGOs had acquired a bad reputation in Guatemala by circumventing the law and brought accusations of illegal actions upon the organizations.

I explained that I had, just before the trip, completed the paperwork for creating the nonprofit entity in the U.S. to raise funds for this and future projects, and told them I had named it Agros Foundation. We agreed that rather than set up another nonprofit organization in Guatemala at that time, whatever funds I could raise in the U.S. by way of Agros Foundation should be channeled through ACB for Buen Samaritano.

On this trip Bill Taylor also introduced to me Salvador González, a young man who had recently graduated from university with an engineering degree. Bill thought he might be a good coordinator for the Buen Samaritano work. Salvador spoke good English, and on Bill's strong recommendation I agreed to hire him on a half-time basis for a term of three months to act as our project staff.

Before my return to Seattle Alfred took me to visit Efraín Ríos Montt. The recently ousted president of Guatemala now lived a rather quiet and unassuming life. After leaving the Presidential Palace he moved back to the house he had lived in for many years before his brief leadership tenure. His home was a modest structure in a quiet residential neighborhood. He had by this time resumed his work as a full-time elder at the Verbo Church and showed none of the trappings of great wealth attendant to those who had sat as a president/dictator of a Central American country.[1]

---

[1] During the mid to late twentieth century when military dictatorships ruled so many Latin American countries, a deposed dictator was typically viewed as a continued threat and *persona non grata* by a new regime and would usually be sent into forced exile. Many chose Spain as the favored haven to live out

On arrival, I saw one, maybe two bodyguard types who blended into the background.[2] Ríos Montt greeted Alfred and me warmly. He was dressed casually in a short sleeve Hawaiian-type shirt and slacks. We were offered coffee and sat down to chat in his living room. He remembered me and even recalled when we had first met over dinner at the Presidential Palace. I recall there was some banter about La Perla and how he wished we had bought that farm, and his promise to build a road there if we did buy it.

In answer to my questions on how he saw his country in its present circumstances, he began to sound like the Sunday evening television preacher I recalled from his time in office. He answered that until the Guatemalan people refused to tolerate the corruption endemic throughout government and society, the country would always remain gripped by poverty and chaos. At one point he asked me, "Skip, do you know the key difference between my country and yours?" Sensing he wanted to share something out of the ordinary, I asked him to tell me the answer, and he went on to say:

North America was settled by people looking for God. Latin America was settled by people looking for gold. That is the fundamental difference between your country and mine, and from that history emanates all the good the United States has experienced, and all the evil we have experienced in Guatemala.

---

their retirement years. Others chose Miami or one of the Caribbean islands. The mental anguish of involuntary exile was in most cases soothed over by the luxurious living made possible by riches grafted during their time in office.

[2] The Spanish word for bodyguard is "*guardaespaldas*," etymologically drawing a picture of one who guards your back (*espalda*). Presumably, a frontal threat should be handled by oneself – a threat from behind, more likely to be a sneak attack, would be the bodyguard's responsibility.

He was speaking in Spanish – his English was almost non-existent – but after saying this he added, with a smile on his face, that in English, this important concept comes off even better.

God.

Gold.

He enunciated each word in English carefully, then reverted to Spanish:

Do you see how one small letter has made all the difference in the world? The people who first settled North America looked for God and built a society on that premise. Look at the great nation you have now. The people who first came to Latin America looked for gold, and instead of building, they killed, they raped, they destroyed, they stole, they took treasures away with them back to Spain. Look at what miserable consequences we suffer today in Latin America because of them.

Point taken. The very brief lesson he just taught me had my mind working in overdrive. I doubt I said anything coherent in return. After about a 45-minute visit, Alfred and I said our farewells and left this remarkable man, both of us rolling over in our minds what had been said.

The conversation with Ríos Montt made for much pondering that night in the quiet of my hotel room. It was one of those memorable and thought-provoking experiences sprinkled along the path of my Agros adventure. There was enough content packed in his brief exposition on the beginnings of North America and Latin America to form the subject of Ph.D. dissertations in history, religion, economics, and sociology. His little lesson could be written off as simplistic and reductionist. But great truths are sometimes simply stated. Ríos Montt offered this insight not as a comprehensive explanation of the histories of North and Latin America, but to boil a very complex question down to one of its essential components.

The Puritans, maligned today in so many quarters and painted with a broad brush dipped in hues of cruelty, hypocrisy, fanaticism, and just about any other unsavory color, did in fact build great foundations for a new nation. So much about the American identity, both individual and national, traces back to Puritan religious and intellectual thought. The richness and complexity of that thinking is nowhere better expressed than in the founding of Harvard University, and the place that great institution has taken in the life and history of this country.

In contrast, the Spanish *conquistadores* bequeathed to Latin America an identity and legacy founded in violence, greed, corruption, and betrayal. Generations of Latin Americans have struggled to overcome that identity. Idealistic politicians and great leaders alike, with stars in their eyes, have aspired to bring about reformations of the Latin psyche and culture. But over a decade into the 21st century, they found their fondest nationalistic and cultural dreams constantly displaced by nightmarish reverberations from the horrors of the 16th and 17th centuries. This great struggle manifests itself as a consistent theme in so much of the magnificent prose and poetry of Latin America's greatest writers.

Early Funding

With a real project to work on now, a nonprofit entity incorporated and in process of getting its 501(c)(3) status approved by the IRS, a board of directors, a few supportive friends, and World Concern as a highly motivated partner, Agros began to take up more of my time. In January 1985 we completed Agros' Form 1023 tax-exempt status application and sent it to the IRS. The narrative description of the organization's activities and purposes required by the application was answered in this way, indicating my early thinking on Agros:

> Agros Foundation ("Agros") was formed as an international Christian relief and development organization designed to help the rural poor in Third-World countries help themselves by providing for individual farm ownership, education, vocational training, and basic services.... Agros would provide funding for land redistribution efforts...coupled with consulting services through local staff. While no assistance has yet been provided, it is planned to begin in 1985. Agros anticipates assisting other Third-World land redistribution programs in the future guided by the experience gained in this initial project.

Other than the early gift from World Concern for the feasibility study, most of the initial funding came out of my own pocket. My law firm had only five lawyers and Rob Tulloch was my only partner. We were located on the top floor of the Exchange Building in Seattle.

From the time I started my law practice as a sole practitioner in 1977, Cyd and I had made the decision to set aside a charitable giving fund of 10% of the gross income of the firm. It was easy and highly satisfying to set aside the money. As each day's receipts were deposited into the firm bank account, I wrote a check out of that account to be deposited into a separate "tithe" fund. The amount of the fund grew steadily, and from that Cyd and I were able to give freely to charities or individuals in need. My Guatemala travel expenses were also covered. When Rob became a partner, his ownership of the firm was 20%, and we continued the practice of setting aside 10% of the gross income of the firm – only now he controlled his separate 20% fund, while I controlled 80% of the total amount.

During those early days Richard Barrueto became a comrade in arms, and our friendship flourished. Richard owned and ran an industrial resins and epoxy supply business with a small office just south of downtown Seattle. He and his wife Meredith (Mimi) not only gave generously to Agros, but Richard also had a wide circle of friends whom he pulled into becoming Agros donors. Moreover, he began to travel regularly with me whenever I went to Guatemala. His companionship on our trips was priceless. We spent many happy hours together, especially with Walter and Heidi Schieber at their home in the city or their Lake Amatitlán beach house. Richard and Walter had been such close friends growing up in Guatemala – I sensed their friendship deepened even more as Richard traveled with greater frequency back to his native land. I loved hearing him banter in Spanish with Walter. As I said before, Richard had picked up a high-class Spanish sometime, somewhere, that rolled off his tongue beautifully. Richard was a fine amateur musician and played a lovely cello, so I attributed his refined Spanish accent to having an acute ear for exact tones and timbre.

The brand new Agros organization did no fundraising in those days, being sustained by a handful of board members and close friends. We had sufficient funds to cover the estimated amounts needed to render aid to the people of Buen Samaritano, and to pay Salvador González for his coordination work.

1983 had ended with political uncertainty and doubt over whether I had been wasting time, effort and money. Year-end 1984 seemed filled with hope and the actuality of beginning work to help the poorest of the rural poor in a village called Buen Samaritano.

I returned to Guatemala for another short visit in mid-January, 1985. We had collected some money by now, so I was able to hand Walter Schieber a check for close to $10,000 for the Buen Samaritano work.

As a routine I took a side trip to Buen Samaritano each time I traveled to Guatemala. January was a good month for travel in country. The Guatemala rainy season corresponded to Seattle summers, while our winters meant it was dry season in Guatemala. This made a difference because flying to Buen Samaritano by MAF plane was not to be taken for granted. The MAF pilots listened closely to weather reports from their hangar in the private aviation section of La Aurora airport – not only the official government weather reports, but also radio reports from their contacts on the ground in the places where they would be landing and taking off. If the forecast called for rain or even low cloud cover in either the capital city or the flight destination, there would be no flight. Many times over the years I was warned that I may land in Buen Samaritano, but there was no assurance that the plane could come back to pick me up. Jeff Nelson was, in particular, good about giving me the option; however, my schedules were tight enough that I would decide against the flight to Buen Samaritano unless I had reasonable assurance I could get out the same day. I knew of others who had been stranded there for days on end when a weather system would unexpectedly move over the Ixcán region and stay fixed there.

In early March 1985 Rob Tulloch surprised me one day with news that he had been contacted by a donor who wished to remain anonymous. The donor gave him a $10,000 cashier's check as a gift to Agros Foundation for the work in Guatemala. I was overwhelmed. This unsolicited anonymous gift more than covered our projected 1985 costs for the promised aid to the people of Buen Samaritano. What tremendous encouragement this would be to the friends in Guatemala – Alfred, Walter, the Elliotts, Bill Veith and Bill Taylor. I recalled Bill Veith's tears streaming down his face when we first met. Here was further answer to his prayers.[3]

1985 saw three more trips to Guatemala – April, August, and November – and flights to Buen Samaritano to check on the progress of work there. I discovered the pleasure of friendships developing with people each time I showed up at the village. I'm not sure they understood where I came from, and why exactly I was there. But the "chinito" did come frequently enough that they came to know me, and welcomed me warmly.

During these trips I discovered the downside of supervising an employee from 3,000 miles away. Communications between Seattle and Guatemala were necessarily sparse because of the high cost of long distance telephone calls. Letters posted from Guatemala took 10-14 days to reach me in Seattle. Letters I sent to Guatemala took even longer and had a 50/50 chance of never reaching their destination at all. My law firm had a telex address, but there were few telex outlets in Guatemala. Besides, telex communications were treated like telegrams; you were charged by the number of words and lines used, so only very brief messages were sent by that medium. In any event, it seemed to me that very little work was accomplished while I was in Seattle. A flurry of activity would take place the week before I arrived and while I was there. When my return flight took off for the U.S., I could count on no discernible progress until I arrived on the scene again.

This pattern began developing early and frustrated me no end. I tried a number of times to call Salvador by phone, but could not reach him. Richard said he had planned a trip to Guatemala in February and offered to have a straight and hard talk with Salvador about our expectations for him as a paid

---

[3] About 15 years later Frank and Patti Holman authorized Rob Tulloch to disclose to me that they were the anonymous donors. Frank is a fellow lawyer in Seattle and son of preeminent Seattle lawyer, legislator, and judge Francis Holman. Patti is a Seattle family therapist.

employee. Key concerns at the time included the need for an agronomist to help with crop plans, regular visits by doctors, nurses and dentists, a schoolteacher for the children, and a pastor to address the people's spiritual needs. We had also directed Salvador to hire an engineer/surveyor to mark out the property lines so that we could properly prepare deeds for the families; and to determine the amount of back taxes owed on the property.

Salvador had maximum freedom, minimum supervision, and little motivation to work hard. It eventually became clear that Agros' mission of helping the rural poor was not something Salvador could put his heart into.

Meanwhile, I met with and spent many evenings with Alfred and his family during these trips. Alfred was not involved at first in the work at Buen Samaritano. Bill Taylor had counseled distancing our work from the Verbo Church and its nonprofit affiliate Fundapi. There was no deliberate shunning of Alfred. In fact, our personal relationship continued to deepen.

Alfred had lost his credentials with the Ministry of Development, and with it, his unrestricted access to the Ixil Triangle and other rural regions. His time now was mostly taken by his pastoral position in the Verbo Church. Others who had been in position to help us in the Ixil had gotten the boot as well. Harris Whitbeck was back running his various businesses. Fundapi had, according to Ed Greenberg, made the critical mistake of not getting a formal "*convenio*" (agreement) with the Ministry of Development while Ríos Montt was in power. At the time, they had all the access and authority they needed without going through the formalities other organizations had to go through. But when the boom was lowered on Ríos Montt, Fundapi was out in the cold. The new government would not approve any entity so closely associated with Ríos Montt to work in the rural areas of the country.

My attention turned from Central America to Asia in late March and the first half of April in 1985. After a week in Taiwan and Hong Kong on client matters, I traveled to Shanghai for a two-week lecture stint on international technology transfer at Jiao Tung University. My first trip back to Guatemala in 1982 had uncovered some emotions within me I hadn't known existed. As my flight made its descent into Shanghai in March 1985, a whole new set of emotions flooded my mind. I was returning to my family's roots. I had left Shanghai as a two-year old; I was now returning as a grown man of 39.

This was still in the very early days after the Chinese mainland had opened itself to foreign travel. In a very real sense, the physical Shanghai – its buildings and infrastructure – had not changed in 38 years. When I first walked into the Peace Hotel downtown close to the Bund, I felt like I had walked into 1947 Shanghai. It was as if the hotel had been preserved in its same state for all those years. The lighting, furniture and fixtures in my room were still 1930s to 1940s vintage. The university sent a car to pick me up at the hotel the next day, and while driving through the streets of Shanghai and its suburbs and seeing the rice fields and small farms on the edge of the city, I realized China in 1985 was still very much a Third-World country; not as poor as Guatemala, but significantly behind in its development compared to its Asian neighbors Japan, Korea, and Taiwan. Travelers to Shanghai today, with its towering skyscrapers, would not recognize the Shanghai I returned to in 1985.

I arrived back in Seattle on Easter Sunday. The next two weeks I worked frantically to catch up after being gone three weeks from the office and from home, and by the end of the month was on a plane again headed to Guatemala. Contrary to my usual pattern, I made very few notes or journal entries about the trip; I have hardly any recollections of it, other than a continued feeling of frustration over the very slow pace of progress to the work at Buen Samaritano. By this time the exchange rate had risen to 3:1 and was still rising. This was helpful to us whenever we paid quetzals for goods and services for Buen Samaritano. However, we also faced increasing requirements by vendors such as MAF for payment in U.S. dollars.

Good news awaited me on my return to Seattle: the IRS had granted provisional approval to the tax-exempt status application for Agros Foundation.

In August I went to Guatemala again, this time taking with me Dr. Leeon Aller of Snohomish, WA, and son Peter, who was 12 at the time. Leeon was a family physician introduced to me by Kent Hotaling. He was excited to see how he might help us from a medical standpoint.[4] Leeon and Peter went with me to Buen Samaritano, which was a real eye-opener for Peter who had lived in upscale Mercer Island during all his young years and had never encountered poverty at this level before. One particular experience at Buen Samaritano stands out in my mind.

Prior to our arrival there I warned my young son that the people might serve us a meal during our time at the village. I also told him how improper it would be either to decline what they served or to leave anything uneaten. I could tell that Peter, as a North American pre-teen with typically narrow tastes, was uneasy at the prospect. Sure enough, some time later we were each served a bowl of chicken and vegetable soup, together with the milky warm corn drink. Under my watchful eye Peter ate and drank all that was proffered to him, and did so without showing any distress.

---

[4] This was the beginning of many trips to Guatemala for Leeon, who often took his wife Virginia. Eventually Leeon established a clinic in Barillas. I remember many occasions traveling to Guatemala when I took an extra suitcase filled with medical supplies, including syringes, vaccine sera, and various other implements to stock up Leeon's clinic.

As we talked about the experience later that evening back in our hotel room in the capital, he asked if I saw how he had eaten every bit of the lunch served to him. I told him yes, I had noticed, and how proud I was that he had been such a trooper. He then asked, "Dad, why was that chicken so tough?" I had a good laugh, and then explained to him the drumstick that took him so long to chew was the hardened muscle of a chicken that had spent its life wandering freely, escaping from dogs and little children, jumping onto low hanging branches, and generally running around having a good time. What a great contrast to chickens that are cooped up in narrow spaces for all their lives before finding their way to grocery counters in the U.S.

More importantly, we both marveled at the generosity and graciousness of the people of Buen Samaritano. They had prepared a meal out of their abject poverty and served it to us even though we could easily have done without it. Over the years, this scene was repeated often in other Agros villages. It has helped me to understand the depth of faith of some of these gracious people. Their faith was manifested by an amazing generosity, sharing freely what little they had with us.

On a trip in November 1985 news came that Buen Samaritano had been attacked twice by guerrillas and the civil patrol had fought them off both times. In the first action, one of the villagers was shot in the leg. Agros paid for MAF to fly him and three family members to Guatemala City for emergency treatment.

The news brought the reality of the civil war close to home. It also made me all the more aware that the guerrillas had an active presence in the Ixcán region, and our flights in and out of Buen Samaritano would certainly be known to them. During one of my trips we encountered an army patrol taking a rest break in the village. I was a little startled to see the soldiers with submachine guns slung over their shoulders and grenades hanging from their belts, but decided the best policy for me would be to act normal and pretend that their presence didn't alarm me at all. I carried a small Olympus camera in my pocket, but decided against taking any pictures of the soldiers. By the time our business was done in the village the patrol had left, and I think everyone breathed a little easier.

Completion of Work

From 1985-86 the civil war intensified and guerrilla activity sharply increased. Army patrols were ambushed, it seemed, on a regular basis. The U.S. Embassy advised in as strong terms as possible that Peace Corps volunteers or other U.S. NGO staffers should stay out of the rural areas. AMOCO, the giant oil company, pulled its workers out of oil exploration activities in the Petén region. The army increased its forces at the Barillas garrison. So the news went, and it continued to get worse.

By this point I was inured to the risks of traveling to Guatemala or to Buen Samaritano. The anxieties I experienced during the first moments of the September 1983 trip, right after the coup that threw out Ríos Montt, had dissipated, and I simply did not devote much time to think about the possible dangers. We had a task to carry out and people in great need to help. Our work was just getting off the ground; as an organization and as individuals we maintained the lowest of profiles. We hoped that our quiet ways would not attract unwanted attention from the wrong people on either side of the civil war.

The people of Buen Samaritano were a hardy group who had survived enormous hardships and suffering. They seemed determined to tough out any new threats. This was a second chance they had been given to establish their lives on the land and they were not going to let anything get in their way. Within a couple of years of our beginning to help them, they had progressed enough to where a few families began payments on their land. ACB had set a very modest amount as the repayment goal, and the families, one by one, were able to achieve that goal. By now the survey work had been done and the legal descriptions for the parcels had been finished. We were able to begin preparing title deeds, awaiting the day when we could hand them out to families who had paid for their land.[5]

One interesting development during that time was when the French government donated solar cell batteries to Guatemala for use in rural areas. We became aware of these through MAF, whose pilots had heard talk of the batteries. Buen Samaritano received a number of these solar cell batteries and MAF helped us to fly them to the village. Technicians came to help the people install the batteries on the roofs of their small houses and connect the batteries to a single light fixture inside the house. On one of my visits to Buen Samaritano I went into several homes that had, for the first time, electrical lighting. The amount of light put out was small, but certainly enough to provide basic illumination.

Unfortunately the lights did not stay on for long because the people had no technical knowledge, tools, or training to repair the photovoltaic cells when they malfunctioned or wore out. They certainly did not have the funds to hire technicians to fly to the village to make repairs. Within a year's time I noticed none

---

[5] The Buen Samaritano families paid off their land loans one by one. The last family to do so did it in 1994. In 1995 we held the first Agros land title ceremony and handed deeds to 56 families. It was a great day for the villagers, and a great day for Agros. At the end of 1995 our Guatemala country director was visited by a delegation from Buen Samaritano. What, they asked, should they do with their money now that they no longer had to pay on their loans? Our staff quizzed them on what they thought would be most needed and prepared to recommend that they spend their money for those purposes. The villagers' response stunned us all when we heard the story later. They answered that they would rather buy more land so more families could join their village. They did buy more land and invited 18 additional families to join the community.

of the houses had lights anymore. This little experiment at Buen Samaritano brought to mind the meaning of the term "appropriate technology" as it is used in international relief and development work. The French government, in its largesse, had not thought through the sustainability of the technology they provided to the rural poor of Guatemala.

By March 1987, I met with the ACB board and we celebrated the end of our work in Buen Samaritano. There was strong sentiment to continue a relationship with the people there, and perhaps to provide other assistance in the future as appropriate. But my mind was ready to look for another land project, this time involving the actual purchase of new land. Some of the ACB members had very different ideas. Hugo Morales, in particular, laid out a detailed list of projects and initiatives, indicating he had given this quite a bit of forethought. These included housing for widows, aid to village pastors, legal aid to the poor, medical and dental care for the poor, and finally (almost as an afterthought, it seemed) dealing with land ownership and agricultural issues. The suggestion was also strongly made that future projects be conducted close to Guatemala City so that more ACB board members could be directly involved with the projects without the same travel and risk associated with Buen Samaritano.

Clearly, Buen Samaritano had brought the people of ACB and Agros together at the outset as strangers to deal with a particular project pushed by Agros, even though ACB had been the sponsoring entity of the village in the 1970s. Now that we were closing that first chapter, the original ACB members and I had very different ideas on future projects. The list they had presented as proposed areas of work, while commendable, seemed to me a general grab bag of ways to help the poor without any particular theme. I went home wondering if this meant the end of our partnership with ACB.

La Providencia

In late April 1987 Steve Sywulka stepped into the picture, a godsend, from my standpoint. Although he had been co-initiator of the Buen Samaritano work in the late 1970s with Bill Veith, Steve had not been actively involved in the ACB/Agros joint effort to help the people get back on their feet. Now Steve came to us with a written proposal to buy a property near the town of La Democracia, located on the Pan American Highway close to the Mexico border. The particular farm was called La Providencia and was known for good coffee production. The purchase would help in the resettlement of M'am Indian refugees returning from Mexico. Steve was a member of the Central America Mission emergency coordinating committee helping to provide relief and assistance to that particular indigenous group.

The Guatemalan government continued to make efforts to coax the refugees in Mexico to return to their homes. Vague promises of financial and housing assistance were made and some refugees even came to understand that the government promised them land. Predictably, government action did not match up with government promises. Steve told us that people were returning, but were living in destitute conditions because their homes had been burned and the land they had previously worked as sharecroppers was not available to them anymore.

The proposal interested me greatly because it involved a specific land project instead of general poverty relief, and especially because Steve Sywulka was advocating for it. In the few times I had met Steve up to that point, I found him a highly intelligent man, and yet another American who spoke Spanish like a native, and was totally comfortable in Guatemalan culture. His experience partnering with Bill Veith in the Buen Samaritano land purchase in the 1970s would be invaluable.

Steve's involvement at this point was also timely because a few months earlier, Bill Veith had been stopped by guerrillas as he was driving his car, told to get out of the car at gunpoint, and was manhandled and beaten. His glasses were smashed and they threatened to kill him. He was released a few hours later. Badly shaken by the experience, he and his wife Margie decided to move their family back to the U.S. Just as we were contemplating losing Bill's experience and passion for the people, Steve stepped in.

On a trip to Guatemala in late September 1987 Steve and I flew with MAF to Huehuetenango, and from there drove a four-wheel drive vehicle to La Providencia, at 5,000 feet elevation. The road was very rough and steep with an elevation gain of 2,000 feet. I thought to myself that this place should be called Providence Heights, the name of a suburban area on the Sammamish plateau to the east of Seattle. There we found some excellent coffee-growing land. La Providencia was a very large farm, but only a portion of about 100 acres was being offered for sale. The farm produced about 1,500 lbs. of coffee per acre per year. ANACAFE, the coffee growers association in Guatemala, had a program that provided production loans to coffee farmers in addition to technical assistance.

The asking price was Q60,000, equivalent then to US$30,000, which was a fair price. The land could support about 25 families. Our enthusiasm for this land was only dampened by uncertainty over the land title. The owner claimed he could not find the registrations for the property. Back in the city we discussed this, and Hugo Morales expressed that this was not an unusual situation and felt that the risk did not seem unreasonable.

Back in Seattle, the Agros board met and approved support for the purchase of La Providencia. We communicated that action to ACB and waited for news of the purchase of the land. Richard Barrueto took a trip to Guatemala in November and came back with the disturbing news that there had been no follow-up on the land purchase. At this point we realized it was essential that we hire someone in Guatemala who could be trusted to get work done — a self-starter who did not need to have a supervisor looking over his shoulder.

Help wanted

Richard and I returned to Guatemala in December intent on finding the right person. On our red-eye flight down, we drafted a job description and talked about the attributes in the person we were looking for. It did not take long for us to realize the person who fit the bill perfectly was Alfred Kaltschmitt. Before the plane landed in Guatemala we had agreed that our number one objective of this trip was to offer the job to Alfred and persuade him to accept it.

On arrival we first met with Walter Schieber over breakfast. When we explained to him what we felt we needed in someone to work for Agros in Guatemala, he immediately proposed we ask Alfred Kaltschmitt. Coincidentally during our breakfast meeting, Alfred called, and we arranged to meet with him for lunch. We didn't beat around the bush with Alfred. As we explained the purpose of our trip — to find someone who could work for Agros in Guatemala — Alfred immediately suggested Walter Schieber. We told him Walter had just as quickly suggested his name, and that we agreed with Walter. We explained that we had not asked him before because we did not believe he would be available or open to taking the job.

Alfred answered by saying he had been feeling restless during recent months. His responsibilities as a full-time elder/pastor at Verbo church had been switched around frequently, and the 12 years of building the church, which had started in his home, had worn him down. He also was longing for more freedom in his work. That morning he had prayed to God for direction. Had we asked him about the job two weeks earlier, he would not even have considered it. If we had arrived two weeks later, he would be gone on a three-week vacation. Thus the timing seemed to be perfect for him to reconsider his situation. He added that he had recently started to think about getting the Verbo church involved in land redistribution.

As we talked further, Alfred got increasingly animated over the idea and told us he really wanted to say "yes" right away, but he needed at least to talk to his wife Patricia first. The following evening while Richard went to Schiebers for dinner, I joined the Kaltschmitt family for a meal, during which the subject was given a thorough going-over. Patricia expressed excitement for Alfred to take the Agros job; she had been feeling his restlessness for some time and agreed the constant switching of responsibilities at Verbo was frustrating for him.

We also talked at length about compensation, which was the only reservation Richard and I had with Alfred. Hugo, Walter, and Steve Sywulka all had opined that the job we described should carry a salary of Q800 to Q1,500 per month. During our first meeting with him, Alfred had asked for Q2,500 to Q3,000. Alfred strongly disagreed with the numbers cited by the others. He said the lower salary amounts would correspond to a Guatemalan working for a nonprofit organization who was not required to lead an organization or be bilingual. English-Spanish bilingual Guatemalans working for foreign companies were paid much more than Q2,500-3,000. He saw himself as far more than a field representative, but someone who could be involved in developing the vision, leading the work, and getting others excited about Agros.

The following morning Richard and I looked in the job listings in the classified ads of *Prensa Libre* newspaper. We saw several ads offering from Q45,000-65,000 per year for bilingual positions in companies engaged in international trade or doing business with the U.S. As we discussed this further with Walter Schieber that morning, we agreed that what we wanted from

Alfred, his leadership experience and capabilities, plus his heart for the rural poor, indeed justified the Q2,500-3,000 monthly salary range he asked for. Thus we reached agreement with Alfred, and his hiring launched Agros into a period of sustained growth in Guatemala.

Not long after Alfred took on the executive director position he persuaded his good friend Kurt Meyer to get involved with us. Kurt ran a successful business growing and exporting bromeliads – plants that grow and thrive without roots in soil, such as orchids. His plants and flowers were of high enough quality to be in great demand in Europe. Not surprisingly, Kurt had an encyclopedic knowledge of flora of all kinds. On many later trips to visit our Agros villages, Kurt would sometimes abruptly ask the driver to stop in the middle of nowhere. He would leap out of the car, go over to the side of the road, and excitedly show us some rare or not so rare variety of bromeliad or other plant, give us its Latin genus name, and tell us all about its scientific classification and related orders. Kurt brought some tremendously valuable agricultural know-how and learning to the organization.[6]

At year-end 1987, I was tremendously encouraged by the evidence that Agros was growing out of its fledgling status as an organization and was prepared to fly in earnest. In June 1987 we had received formal approval of our tax-exempt status as a 501(c)(3) organization. This was by no means a given, since our board had in the early days provided most of the funding out of our own pockets and the IRS required proof that the organization was supported by the public, not just a few individuals. There was a period of time in 1986 when Richard Barrueto and I enlisted just about every friend we knew to send at least a token donation to Agros so we could expand our list of

---

[6] Kurt Meyer served on the Fundación Agros board (the Guatemalan arm of Agros) for many years, and acted as chairman of the board during a period of time. I lost a great friend and colleague when he died in January 2012.

"public" donors. Richard was far more effective than I was in getting contributions; I suspect he had far more friends than I did. The final determination letter approving our status meant we were in the clear, much to our collective relief.

Our board of directors by now had gone through some expansion. Since 1983 we had picked up several new members who contributed needed skills to the board: Wes Anderson and Leeon Aller (1986), Richal Smith, Perry Lovelace, and Dick Nelson (1987). (It was at Dick's house where I had first met with Juan Carlos Ortíz.) Wes provided a pastoral element to the board. Leeon (physician), Richal (civil engineer), and Perry (energy/environmental consultant) were all interested in program elements in Guatemala and contributed according to their professional backgrounds. Dick was an entrepreneur with recent expertise in public relations and fund raising. We also elected Richard Barrueto as board chairman, taking over the role from me. I felt it important that someone else now serve as chairman as the organization began to expand its scope.

The public relations firm of Burgess and Associates, headed by a good friend Tim Burgess (now a Seattle City Councilman), produced our first corporate brochure in December 1987, a bi-fold piece laying out the basic facts of Agros' work in Guatemala. On the project front we had finished our assistance program to the villagers in Buen Samaritano. We had also provided financial help in the successful resettlement and reconstruction of a smaller village, *El Manantial* (The Spring) – also in the Ixcán region. And now we were actively negotiating the purchase of the land in La Democracia.

Unfortunately, within a month of starting his job, Alfred found out the owner of La Providencia had sold the property to another party after having promised to sell it to Agros/ACB. I am sure someone else offered more money. He also reported to us that he was besieged with requests for help of various kinds. Already, Perry Lovelace had gotten involved with a cardamom-drying project in Buen Samaritano and Leeon Aller had begun work in setting up a clinic in Barillas. ACB was pressing to get involved in providing housing for widows and legal aid to the poor. Now we had a request from Buen Samaritano for a hydraulic pump, and other refugees from Mexico were requesting help to buy tools for carpenters and loans so they could get into the cattle business. We also had requests for funds to buy corn mill grinders, scholarships for young people to go to school or attend university, and funding for reforestation projects.

The Agros board and Alfred agreed that as an organization we needed to concentrate on buying land for the poor, together with providing some initial agricultural assistance in the way of seeds, fertilizer, tools, and tin roofing for houses. Board members were free to pursue additional projects on their own, not in Agros' name – Leon Aller's clinic in Barillas being a prime example. For other requests that did not fit into the narrow mission of land ownership and basic agricultural assistance, we agreed we should refer the applicants to other organizations that had the capability of meeting those needs.

By mid-1988 Alfred and I began discussing the possibility of doing a new project in the Ixil Triangle. He had always felt that was the area of greatest need in the country and I concurred. He began traveling again to the Ixil Triangle to search for a possible project site. By the fall of 1988 he said he had found a strong possibility near Chajul that was worth exploring.

Little did I know then what a significant step this "strong possibility" would become for Agros and its work.

8

IXIL TRIANGLE

Among all the places I have lived in or visited, the Ixil Triangle has an allure all its own.[1] You can find spectacular scenery in its mountains and valleys, including lovely waterfalls and winding rivers. But more than anything else, the people draw you in. Descendants of the Mayans, the Ixil Indians are a physically handsome people. I have sometimes wished I could sit in a town plaza, unseen, and take candid photos all day long of the faces of men, women and children who pass by. The women's traditional dress and hair coverings dazzle with color. The children's smiles can melt a cold heart. But more than their physical appearance they are a people of easy and unpretentious grace and charm.

All the more tragic then that the beauty of the land and its gracious people were so devastated by the 36-year civil war. This is where the war raged hottest and the people suffered the most.

The Ixil region encompasses an area that includes three towns in the *altiplano* (mountain plateau) area of the Quiché Department some 250 kilometers northwest of Guatemala City: Nebaj, San Juan Cotzal, and Chajul. Nebaj, the largest of the three, sits at the southwestern corner of a scalene triangle. Cotzal, the next largest, lies 13 crow-flight kilometers northeast of Nebaj, and Chajul in turn sits five kilometers northwest of Cotzal and 15 kilometers from Nebaj. The region is mountainous and even the short distance between Cotzal and Chajul is divided by a mountain range. Roads to the area and

---

[1] Ixil is pronounced *ee-sheel.*

between the villages are very poor. In 1988 the paved road from Guatemala City went 150 kilometers to Huehuetenango. From there the 60 kilometers to Nebaj started as a gravel road but deteriorated rapidly into roads pockmarked with large and small potholes created by torrential rains characteristic of the area during the winter season. After crossing the Rio Negro at Sacapulas the road narrowed considerably and began a very steep ascent over the Cuchumatánes range.

At points on those roads your heart might drop almost as precipitously as the ledge of the precipice you behold outside the car window. Your tires seem just inches away from driving off the road and into oblivion as you negotiate yet another hairpin turn or drive around a stalled bus or truck on the shoulder. The trip from Huehuetenango to Nebaj can easily take three hours or more of mostly torturous driving. In these mountain roads of Guatemala it is not unusual to see the rusting carcasses of buses lying at the bottom of a ravine, grim reminders of the macabre descriptor "Orange Crush" given to colorful buses plying dangerous rural roads in the developing world, overloaded with passengers, freight, and animals.

The Ixil people, their language, culture and religion can all be traced back to the Mayans. Generally, they are characterized as being individualistic and independent people with strong ties to the land they live and work on. Their religion is animistic, in which every object has a reason for being and a spirit residing within it. The spirit world is a real world to the Ixil and governs all aspects of life, including birth, death, sickness, marriage, ownership of land, and harvests. Not surprisingly, shamans and witch doctors wield very powerful influence and control over the life of an Ixil man or woman. They are looked on for leadership not only in spiritual matters, but in all areas of life. Sickness and healing are directly related to sorcery, good and evil.

The Mayan calendar is still observed ritualistically and is interpreted by those trained and designated for that function.

Every day has a name indicating those events and occurrences that may or may not take place on that day. For example, there are days when it is forbidden to marry, to borrow money, or to plant seeds. There are severe social sanctions exercised by the community against individuals who deviate from the norm; such individuals are believed to invite retribution by the spirits upon the entire community.

Early Ixil converts to Christianity were shunned by families and friends and subjected to harsh consequences. But once brought to an understanding of the gospel's message of unconditional love, combined with their already existing belief in an all-pervasive spirit world, the Ixil man or woman became a firm and unwavering believer in a God of the universe who is Lord over all things and all aspects of life. That faith helped many Ixil Indians to endure the most adverse of circumstances, particularly during the long years of warfare in their region. Ask an Ixil believer how he was able to survive the physical and mental anguish and suffering of those war years, and his face will likely light up; he will tell you about how God comforted him at even the most difficult moments.

Until Ray Elliott devised a common written form for the Ixil language, the Ixil spoke three separate dialects, one for each of the three towns. Ray's written Ixil, which he taught the Ixil to read and write, unified the Ixil tongue since dialectal differences disappear in the written form. He then translated the New Testament directly from the Greek to the Ixil. Today, most Ixil men speak enough Spanish to get along in the world of farms, work, and shops. A very small proportion of Ixil women speak Spanish.

My last visit to the Ixil Triangle had been in 1983, before the coup that unseated President Ríos Montt. Now in 1988, the civil war in the Ixil region continued to rage without abating. Allegations of massacres of the Indian peoples continued – even though Ríos Montt, the supposed "butcher" of Central America, was long gone from the presidency.

Through his contacts Alfred became aware of a large group of people in need of land who had located a 280-acre parcel near Chajul for sale. After negotiations with the owner in September 1988, Agros bought the property and began the first Agros project from scratch. We paid Q38,000 (US$14,000). The seller had owned the property for 20 years and was hesitant to let it go, but was swayed by the fact that the sale would result in benefitting poor families from the region.

The property could potentially accommodate up to 40 families. Alfred worked with three pastors in Chajul to help decide which families would be asked to join the project. We specified that each family should be headed by a man or woman of good reputation, not a drunkard, known to be hard working, and not the owner of any other land. We quickly found that the three pastors, instead of working in harmonious collaboration to help us identify families, each wanted to exert greater influence in the process to benefit the families of his own church. Alfred soon found himself immersed in conflict resolution.

The Agros board in Seattle made the decision to travel to Guatemala together to hold joint meetings with the ACB board and take the opportunity to inspect the property in Chajul. Plans were made and a party consisting of Richard Barrueto, Richal Smith, Joel and Diane Van Ornum, plus guests Del and Judy Wisdom embarked together on October 27 for Guatemala. Del was an old schoolmate from Seattle Pacific University, and ran a very successful farming operation in Basin City in eastern Washington. We had reconnected a few months earlier, and he expressed great interest in what we were doing in Guatemala.

Those few days in Guatemala in late 1988 were particularly memorable for me because Agros had just bought its first parcel of land and was about to test, for the first time, the ideas we had developed to help the landless rural poor. It was the first step in a process that would help them build a new life and break away from the generations of poverty they had known. In Buen Samaritano we had helped the villagers complete something that had been started years earlier by others. Now we were blazing a new trail, from buying the land to selecting the families, to actually carrying out the ideas we had been discussing since that first trip in October 1982.

After a day-long drive from Guatemala City to Chajul, we slept that night in a house rented by Wycliffe[2] and the next morning hiked to the property about two miles outside of town. The anticipation built in me as we neared the property and I wondered in my mind what the land would look like. When we finally reached the property boundaries, climbed over a fence to be greeted by the eight leaders chosen for the village, I could hardly contain my excitement.

As we began to walk the length of the land, the men pointed occasionally to boundary markers and talked about its features. I recall walking through lovely green clearings with gentle hills bounded by some forests of tall pine trees. There were no planted crops and it seemed the land had been used for grazing purposes.

At one point Del suddenly walked off to one side, got down on his hands and knees and peered intently at the grass. He then dug with his hands under the sod, grabbed a handful of dirt, brought it up to his nose, and took a deep breath. The reaction among the local men was instant and electric. They converged on Del like metal shavings drawn to a powerful magnet. I had no idea what Del was doing, but they did. They knew instinctively he was a farmer – that he was one of them.

Del told me he was looking for bugs in the grass and that the presence or absence of insects can reveal important information about the land. That deep breath he took was to smell the soil for alkalinity, another important indicator of the quality of the

---

[2] The house later became affectionately known as the "Chajul Hilton."

soil. For the rest of that walking tour the men stayed close to Del, asking him questions and in turn answering his questions about their local agricultural practices. I became the interpreter and thoroughly enjoyed the interaction between a veteran and successful North American farmer and a group of Ixil Indian men who had worked on farms owned by others all their lives, and who were now looking forward to farming their own land. I marveled then and now how, in an instant, all the seemingly insuperable barriers of culture, language, and economic disparity between Del and these men had vanished. Here was brotherhood built instantly on a common love and understanding of the earth, the soil, and what the land meant to one's whole life and existence.

Back in the city we discussed a development plan and a working budget for the new Chajul project. Initial estimates were $55-65,000 for the year, representing a significant amount of money since Agros had been raising about $25,000 annually to cover activities to that point. There was no hesitation in our minds, however, that we could and would meet the fundraising goal. I think the other board members shared the excitement I felt at starting our first project, and we were of one mind that we would do whatever had to be done to raise the needed funds – and more, if necessary.

And I sensed excitement among the people who were part of that first community now that an unprecedented opportunity had come upon them to some day own their own land. In fact, they had already chosen a name for their yet-to-be constructed village and community: *El Paraíso* – Paradise. Perhaps each man and woman harbored different meanings of the name in their hearts. For me the name had a profound significance that I still cannot adequately describe all these years later. I thought of the 35 families we started with, their desperate struggle for survival – physical and mental – and their seeming hopelessness in the midst of great suffering. I then thought of their aspirations now that land ownership was something proffered to them – not a handout, not easy, not simple, but even then, an opportunity more than any of them could have dreamed of. I thought of their children and how different their lives might be from their parents' lives because of this opportunity.

Paradise. It was as if the very thought of this great chance gave them a glimpse of heaven and allowed them to imagine, for the first time in their lives, that an impossible dream might actually become a reality.[3]

In those early days of the new Chajul project we recommitted as a board that Agros would maintain a focus on land. Land was our distinctive. Along with land we knew we needed to help the people with housing, seeds, animals, and tools. After all, the people we were helping had no means of their own. Moving on to the land and joining the Agros project meant they would no longer be earning even the meager wages they had been paid as laborers on farms owned by others. Until they could harvest crops to be sold in the market, they had no other means of income. We discussed how Agros could act as a conduit for other needs of the people, including medical help, water projects, reforestation, and soil conservation.

The work plan for El Paraíso included surveying and defining the agricultural lots to be owned by each family, and

---

[3] Years later, the people changed the name of their village to Xetzé – an Ixil word meaning "place of the big tree." Remembering my emotional attachment to the El Paraíso name, I was saddened at first to hear of the change. But then I pondered how, in the natural progression of their lives, the villagers perhaps wanted a name that did not express as much a future aspiration as it did a present contentment. Perhaps this was now a place of peace, where a great tree need not be cut down for firewood, as in days of yore, but could be admired for its beauty and majesty. I pictured in my mind how men and women could find shade under the rich canopy of a big tree and take a moment's rest from their labors. I thought of how children might enjoy climbing the tree and look out in the distance and see sights they might never see from the ground. I even imagined the home this tree would be to birds and the happy songs they might sing to cheer a saddened heart.

planning and designing the residential lots and community land. The community land would include an all-purpose community building for meetings and other uses, a school, a church, and an open space for a soccer field.

Heeding the advice from the Elliotts to listen to what the people wanted (and not just act on what we thought they needed or wanted), we solicited the villagers' views on the location and design of their homes, which they shared with great enthusiasm. We quickly found that they were dissatisfied with our original house design to accommodate an average family of about six people. The houses were very small by U.S. standards, and measured a total of approximately 8x12 meters, or about 860 square feet each. But to our surprise, the people didn't object to the small size – they were accustomed to living in even smaller spaces. They objected to the absence of a porch! Where would the women do their weaving? Thus we changed the design so that each house had a porch about six feet deep, running the length of the house, and accounting for almost 25% of the floor area of the total structure. Each porch had a roof overhang that would shelter the lady of the house from rain as she did her weaving. The resulting plan and structure might not have impressed any architectural student of small or minimalist dwellings, but it made the people very happy.

The house design issue was a happy problem and a chance to hear what was important to the people. The most nettlesome problem continued to be the friction between the three pastors we had chosen to help lead the project. We had purposely chosen to approach the three pastors in Chajul because we knew we had to work through leaders in the local community; the alternative of just showing up in town one day to announce we were going to select families and give them the chance to farm their own land seemed absurd. In very poor rural communities like Chajul there were no business or educational leaders we could approach, and we did not want to go through the municipal government. The local priests and pastors were the *de facto* leaders of the community.

In approaching the three pastors we sought to avoid the appearance of favoring just one church or making our work appear to be a denominational matter excluding others. We also thought this would present an opportunity for pastors in the same town to work together in harmony as an example of inter-church collaboration for the benefit of the poor in their congregations.

We discovered this was far easier said than done. From the very outset the three pastors quarreled. Alfred Kaltschmitt's principal contact of the three had taken it on himself to act as the leader of the group since he was the first one contacted. He began to make executive decisions on process and outcome that rubbed the other two pastors the wrong way. Hard feelings followed harsh disagreements and, before we knew it, Alfred was spending too much of his time in Chajul mediating the disputes between the three pastors. Our board minutes and my personal notes from late 1988 through 1989 make repeated mention of Alfred's mediation efforts. Whenever we thought the group had finally resolved their differences, some other issue would flare up and Alfred would be at it again, trying to make peace among the three.

Things reached a low point at a meeting between Alfred and all the El Paraíso village participants in Chajul in early 1989. Rumors had been flying around town that Alfred was dishonest and corrupt and would cheat the people. Alfred heard the rumors and felt personally threatened by what was being said. He asked for and received police protection from the mayor of Chajul to attend the meeting. At that meeting one of the pastors threatened to pull out of the project altogether and take the people from his congregation with him. A number of people from all three churches complained to Alfred that the land should have been a gift and they should not have to repay anything.

At a crucial point during the proceedings Alfred took a courageous stance that was nothing less than a stroke of divinely-inspired genius. He told the assembled people that since so many were unhappy Agros would suspend the El Paraíso project altogether for six months to a year. He invited anyone who was unhappy with the project to leave permanently and not return. He laid out conditions for how the project would resume and said that he would look for people who were willing to abide by the conditions and who were thankful for the opportunity. He said the conditions included agreement among all participants and told everyone he was fed up working with ingrates and backbiters.

To his great surprise a number of people immediately spoke up and said they would gladly accept all the conditions and would be eager to participate if and when Agros chose to resume the project; they said they knew many others who likewise would want to participate on all the conditions stated. As things turned out the "suspension of activities" was minimal and the project resumed under far better circumstances.

This little sideshow proved a disproportionate distraction and taught us valuable lessons on a number of fronts. We learned that the religious strife bubbling beneath the surface in the Ixil Triangle (and in many other parts of the country as well) – pagan/Christian, Catholic/Evangelical, Evangelical/Evangelical – had to be factored into dealing with the layers of complexity in working with the poor in the region. I would love to say that the unhealthy rivalry stayed at the leadership level and that the people got along fine. But that would be misrepresenting the situation. I would love to write that sharing in common abject poverty removed pettiness and intolerance among the people, but that would be ignoring basic weaknesses in human nature among the rich or poor. It had been naïve of us to think that the opportunity to overcome generational poverty in their lives would, in itself, motivate people to work together for the common good without being distracted by petty envy and grabbing for an advantage over others. But our experience with conflict resolution in Chajul taught us to put some aspects of community development and leadership training high on the list at the very early stages of future projects, even before the families were selected for a new village.

As the work at El Paraíso proceeded we encountered other serious problems as well. During the time of strife between the pastors we discovered that timber was being stolen regularly from the forested portion of El Paraíso. We could not determine who the thieves were but suspected some of the men who had complained the loudest, and who had spread the lies about Alfred. Alfred's solution was to hire six men to guard the forest at Q60 per month plus permission to sell a little firewood on the side. On one of his trips to Chajul he visited the military garrison with the hired watchmen and introduced them to a lieutenant and explained what the men were hired to do. He also asked the lieutenant to send an army patrol through the forest from time to time to help keep the peace there. The thefts of timber stopped.

Guerrilla activity increased during this time in the Ixil Triangle and across Guatemala. The head of the Industrial Bank in Guatemala was killed in a guerrilla attack and his son was seriously wounded. Helen Elliott reported that she barely missed a guerrilla ambush on the road outside Nebaj. The targets of this and other ambushes in the Ixil region were usually army patrols or members of the National Police. But civilian casualties from attacks on both sides were not a rarity.

El Paraíso was not spared. The vice-president of the village committee was killed in an ambush while on civil patrol duty. The other leaders on the committee decided that they would all pitch in to help the man's widow and young children stay as part of the community and take ownership of the land the family was to be allotted.

I narrowly missed a guerrilla ambush myself. On one of my increasingly frequent trips to the Ixil Triangle, as we drove on the road between Nebaj and Chajul, we came upon the wreckage of a National Police pickup truck that had been attacked by the guerrillas probably 10 minutes before we reached that point in the road. A couple of cars had stopped to lend aid to the wounded. Since the army would probably show up very soon as well, the better part of discretion told us we should move on and not remain at that location.

After many of the simple wood-framed houses (with porches) had been built, a large tractor belonging to the government was brought in to clear a space for the community building and level the site for a soccer field. An armed guerrilla contingent came to the site and, per their usual practice assembled the people for a quick political indoctrination lecture on the evils of the government and reasons why the people should join the guerrilla cause. As the story was related to me a couple of days after the encounter, the men had responded by saying that they were working on land they would own for the first time in their lives and had no desire to go into the mountains to live like animals – the way they had when they escaped the fighting in the early 1980s.

The guerrillas threatened to confiscate the tractor battery because it was Guatemalan government property that should belong to all the people. The men protested, saying that the tractor had been used to clear land for their houses and that they were going to use it for the community center and their soccer field. How were they to do all that without a battery for the tractor? And where would they find the money to replace the battery if the government accused them of stealing it? In the end, the guerrillas removed and took the battery, but left money with the villagers as a "payment" so no one would accuse them of stealing.

I considered the significance of this encounter. First, I was thankful the guerrillas had tried to "win" the hearts and minds of the people rather than launch an attack on the village. But more than that, I was thankful for how the people had responded to the guerrillas' demands. Even at this early stage in the project our people acted and responded like they knew they were now working for something they had never had before. They were able to articulate to the guerrillas that this opportunity did not require them to take up arms. They pointed to their houses. They showed the guerrillas the agricultural land where they had planted seeds for crops – crops that would be theirs alone and not belong to a *patrón*. They had a future for themselves and their children, so why should they take up arms and "live like animals" in the mountains?

For almost three decades the Ixil Indians had been caught smack in the middle of a deadly struggle. The protagonists on both sides claimed political righteousness. The army told the Indians the guerrillas were Communists who would destroy the country; the guerrillas told the Indians the army was an oppressor who kept the land in the hands of the rich at the expense of the poor. Not to support one side meant you favored the other side and you became a target to be shot at.

For the first time the men and women of El Paraíso could truly say they were neutrals – after all, they were working for themselves and depended on neither side for their living. As the tractor battery incident showed, the guerrillas seemed to understand that this group of people had found a third way, one that involved no weapons, no violence, and no taking of sides. And on the other side, it seemed that the Army understood enough to leave the people alone, too (other than making sure the men did their turns on civil patrol). The commander of the local army garrison even helped persuade an obstinate adjoining landowner to agree to have a road built from Chajul to El Paraíso that would partially cross over his land.[4]

As work progressed in El Paraíso I noticed with each visit further progress in the fields and in the community infrastructure – a school building, a community building with an attached health clinic, a church, a lush green two-acre agricultural demonstration plot – and in the lives of the people. The children greeted us with great joy on our arrival and walked hand in hand with us. It was not unusual to have a couple of children grasping each of my hands as we walked around the community. The village was built on a hilltop and one could see the surrounding landscape from several points. I came to favor one particular vista point that overlooked the agricultural fields and at some point during each visit, I would sneak away from the group to take in the sights, sounds, and smells from that spot. We had done so little at that point and were still in the earliest stages as an organization. But as I stood at that vista I felt that even if Agros did nothing else – if it were to shut down operations after El Paraíso – I would die content to have helped the men, women and children of at least one village overcome crushing poverty.

Within 10 months of commencing the work at El Paraíso Alfred came to us to say there was another property for sale closer to Nebaj and urged us to consider starting a second village there. The board agreed and negotiations soon began. By this time Alfred had enlisted the part-time services of an agronomist, Mario Morales, to help the people of El Paraíso in their crop plans and ongoing work. Mario would later play a huge role for Agros as country director for Guatemala. By now we had also set

---

[4] The first time I drove to El Paraíso after the road was built, the view took my breath away as I approached the village. After the last turn in the road the whole scene unfolds before your eyes. In the foreground, you behold a beautiful field planted with neat rows of crops (this was the demonstration site) and in the background, on top of a hill, you can see the village itself with all its houses.

up the Guatemalan legal entity to buy the land and execute the Agros model: *Fundación Agros*.

Guatemalan law made it difficult for a foreign NGO to operate in the country without a domestic, autonomous legal entity. With ACB board members looking in different directions to help the poor, work on setting up the new entity began soon after we purchased the Chajul property. The process of creating a new NGO in Guatemala was not nearly as simple as it was in the U.S. It literally required an act of the Guatemalan Congress to approve the new entity. It was a happy day when I was given the newspaper clip announcing the approval of Fundación Agros by the Congress.

It ended up taking another two years before we managed to buy the land to start the next village. It was not near Nebaj, but in the outskirts of Cotzal, the third town in the Ixil Triangle. In late 1991 we went to see the land and well do I remember that view. Coming up the road from Nebaj toward Cotzal and at a particular bend in the road, I beheld a lovely green valley that was to become the new village of Los Ángeles. What an exhilarating sight it was. The property measured 110 acres of gentle slopes situated right alongside the road going into the town of Cotzal. It even had a stream running through it. As we later walked the length of the land with a few of the men who were leaders in the newly forming group that would participate in the project, my mind leaped ahead to visualize the families who would call this land their home and look on this beautiful ground as their means of living.

The third village in the Ixil Triangle came two years after Los Ángeles. This was the property Alfred found in 1989 near Nebaj. It was not until 1995 that we were able to persuade the owner to sell it to us. This land was also situated right next to the road beyond Nebaj toward Cotzal and Chajul. It had a more uneven topography than either El Paraíso or Los Ángeles, but to see the looks in the faces of the people and to hear them talk about their dreams, you would think this land was the Garden of Eden itself. In fact, this group of people also named their village *El Paraíso*. Conveniently, the people of Chajul El Paraíso had by then renamed their village to Xetzé.

I vividly remember speaking to one elderly Ixil man who talked about having walked for two days from a distant hamlet to come and participate in the meeting that led to the formation of the community. His face was lined with the signs of hardship and suffering endured for a lifetime. He spoke of the many beloved family members he had lost to the war. But his countenance glowed as he thought of a new beginning, even at his age, in this new "paradise."

With the establishment of the Nebaj El Paraíso, Agros had begun to earn a name and reputation in the region. We were no longer unknown. Signs at the entry point of each village identified it as an *Agroaldea* sponsored by Fundación Agros. The term *agroaldea* was coined by us, combining agro+aldea (village) to identify the village with Agros. It is not, strictly speaking, a Spanish word, but it is easily understood by any Spanish speaker to indicate an "agricultural village" branded, in a sense, with Agros.

The new project in Nebaj also indicated Agros was acquiring some momentum, and we grew not just by reputation, but also in our experience and learning. The model that we once only talked about on paper now had some "legs" to it. We now had a proof of concept for what had at one time seemed such a wild-eyed idea. It helped too that the people of Los Ángeles and El Paraíso were industrious, enterprising, and wide open to new ideas and new ways of doing things. This was in very sharp contrast to the people of Chajul, who seemed so much more resistant to change. This was not just a contrast of villages, but of three towns with distinct cultures, even though all the people were of Ixil descent.

The Right People

The rapid pace of growth in activity in the Ixil Triangle and the opportunities opening up to Agros elsewhere in the mid-1990s meant that we needed to strengthen the organization not just in Guatemala, but in the U.S. as well. Fundraising became a fact of life that none of us had really wanted to deal with up to that time. We were having too much fun starting and working on new villages.

In 1991 we had added Bernie Stender to the Agros board. Bernie was a retired U.S. Marine Corps pilot and had flown F-4's in the Vietnam War. He was as honest as the day was long and tireless as a fundraiser for us. Bernie visited the Chajul Xetzé village in its early days and his heart broke at the sight of the children. Bernie served as treasurer, and during board meetings when we actually passed a hat around to cover a deficit, Bernie's hat was the one we used; his own check was always the first one in.

Hat-passing at board meetings was no longer enough to fuel the engines of a rapidly growing organization. We began engaging consultants by the mid-1990s to help us raise funds.

We were tremendously encouraged during this time by an extraordinary and completely unexpected gift of $200,000 from a donor couple received in late December 1995. This gift was designated for purchasing land for new projects and was a milestone in our development.

Don Valencia was a key addition to the board in 1996, a man who had recently moved from Sacramento to Seattle, having been recruited by Starbucks CEO Howard Schultz. Don was a scientist by training who had run his own medical research company that specialized in immunology. He loved hiking and backpacking in the Sierras and over the years acquired a taste for coffee. He grew more and more dissatisfied with the instant coffee he took on his backpacking trips and decided to do something about it.

Don began tinkering in his own kitchen with processes to convert ground coffee beans into an extract that could be preserved and made into a fresh cup of coffee later by adding hot water. Over the course of about four years he succeeded in developing his own process, producing in his kitchen instant coffee that replicated the aroma and taste of freshly brewed coffee.[5] His instant coffee was so good that while on a trip to Seattle with his wife, Heather, Starbucks baristas at the Pike's Market store admitted it was revolutionary. Word of his work filtered up to Howard Schultz, who could not believe Don's extract could taste like freshly brewed Starbucks Sumatra coffee. The rest is Starbucks history and lore told by Howard Schultz in both his books on the Starbucks story.[6] Schultz ended up persuading Don to move to Seattle to take on the position of Senior Vice President in charge of research and development at Starbucks.

I met Don shortly after he moved to Seattle in 1993 and we became fast friends, regularly meeting for lunch at Don's favorite Vietnamese restaurant in Seattle's international district. Although he joined the board in 1996, he was so consumed by his Starbucks schedule over the next two years that he seldom attended board meetings. If you had told me back then that one day Don would be a key Agros board member who added huge value by his participation, I would have wondered what you were smoking. Little did I know how wrong I would be, and furthermore, what a huge part Don would play in my life.

Corky Morse and David Carlson were other key additions to the Agros team in 1995. Corky had been in the business world

---

[5] Heather Valencia tells of her kitchen at their Sacramento home being filled with vats of coffee and other liquids involved in Don's experimentation projects.

[6] *Pour Your Heart into It* (1997), and *Onward* (2011).

for a number of years, was well connected on the eastside of Seattle, and personally brought in key donors to the organization. David was a fluent Spanish speaker who first served Agros as a board member. When it became clear we needed to beef up staff capability in the U.S., he resigned from the board and took on a full-time job as our first executive director. David, or "Dahveed" as he later became known by Agros villagers, had an amazing network of friends in the Puget Sound region. He also had a great gift for establishing close relationships with people.

We had learned one great lesson by that time – how important it was to have honest people, not just trained and experienced people. This was especially true in the upper management positions where people had supervision of funds. Most NGOs in Central America and the developing world have experienced the heartache of hiring people who viewed the work as an opportunity to fatten their own wallets.

In the mid-1990s, Global Partnerships, a Seattle microfinance organization, began working in Guatemala as well. GP was founded by good friends, Bill and Paula Clapp. About two years after they began their work in Guatemala, Bill called me one day to ask if I would spend some time with him and his GP staff, particularly to address the issue of finding the right people "on the ground" in the country. They had unfortunately had a succession of national staff people whose vision was blurred by seeing dollar signs when North Americans came to their country with money to help the poor. At the time Agros seemed to have an outstanding team of nationals, including a Guatemala country director who was especially beloved by Agros volunteers who spent time in the villages.

I remember speaking to the GP staff about the importance of finding people who had a heart for the poor and who looked on serving the poor as a calling. I still believe today what I then told Bill Clapp's staff, but in the intervening years have learned the hard way how difficult it is to see what motivations really rest in a person's heart.

We came close to de-railing as an organization in Guatemala in year 2000 when we discovered our "beloved" country director was using Agros funds to run a separate and secret for-profit construction business. By this time he had been in his position as country director for several years. Everyone, it seemed, sang his praises. What made his moonlighting operations especially grievous was that we discovered, after the fact, that funds intended for community programs or small business or productive loans were never applied to the intended purposes. People in our villages who should have gotten loans or had other community-building programs in their villages told us they had never known this kind of help might have been available to them. Instead, the money had been used as a slush fund for a construction business and other personal uses. The malefactor had the nerve to deny any wrongdoing even though his computer hard drive, when searched, disclosed file upon file of secret construction business transactions using Agros funds. He had even started a second business – trucking freight to and from the Ixil Triangle – at the time his dishonesty was exposed.

An audit disclosed the funds he embezzled were primarily derived from a Spanish government grant. U.S. donor funds were not used. But his treachery cost far more than any sum of money. The cumulative effect of about five years of his double-dealing meant untold opportunities lost for the people we served. In conversations and meetings with Fundación Agros board members during those days, even mention of the person's name was repulsive to us, and to avoid saying and hearing his name we began referring to him as "*el ingrato*" – the ungrateful one.

The Guatemala organization was in turmoil for almost all of 2001, dealing with the man through the legal system and auditing the books and records to uncover the extent of the corruption. We promoted Mario Morales to be the new country director in the second half of 2001. Gradually, integrity was brought back into the organization.

9

EXPANSION

By 1990, eight years from the inception of the idea to attempt private land reform, the Agros name began to spread from the remote rural regions of the Ixcán River and the Ixil highlands. We were still operating under a very low profile and generated little publicity either in the U.S. or in Guatemala. But it seems the wind itself must have carried the word because we began getting inquiries from unexpected places.

Nicaragua 1991

In 1991, out of nowhere, a pastor in Nicaragua wrote to Agros asking us to consider his country.

Nicaragua had been embroiled in civil war for almost 27 years. From 1961 – 1979, the Sandinista National Liberation Front (*Frente Sandinista de Liberación Nacional* - FSLN) fought and finally ousted the long-entrenched Somoza family dictatorship. Not long after that, disenchanted elements of the Sandinistas (known later as the Contras) waged war against the government headed by Daniel Ortega and the FSLN. The war between the Contras and the Sandinistas lasted until 1988, ending with the signing of a peace accord.

After taking the reins of power from the Somozas, the Sandinista government implemented their land reform policy by expropriating enormous quantities of land from the Somoza family and other large landowners. They turned many of the properties into cooperative farms to be run by poor peasants. At the same time they placed huge land holdings into nonprofit organizations that they controlled.

The peasant cooperatives had no capital to maintain the production of export-quality crops and cattle that had once come from these large farms. Eventually the cattle were sold and trees cut down and sold as well. Some land lay fallow while other land was used for planting corn, beans and subsistence crops where there had once been a thriving coffee farm or sugar cane plantation. Through their shortsighted policies, mismanagement, and corruption, the Sandinistas destroyed the agricultural economy of the country. Driving along the Pan American Highway one could see long stretches of arid, brown landscape where in years past there had been forest groves or bustling crops.

Having aligned itself politically with Fidel Castro's Cuba in Latin American politics, Nicaragua soon became dependent on subsidies from the Soviet Union. The country, once a serfdom ruled by the Somozas, had now acquired a new overlord in the USSR. When the Soviet Union imploded in 1989 the spigot of cash and goods from the Communist bloc ran dry. Desperate for cash, Nicaragua invited huge Russian trawlers to scoop up everything that moved off its coasts, depleting its fishing resources. It allowed trees everywhere to be cut and the timber sold.

On the Agros board Dick Nelson became the enthused advocate for expansion to Nicaragua. A businessman who had started and run his own companies, Dick's eyes would light up at new entrepreneurial opportunities. The 1991 letter from the Nicaraguan pastor prompted Dick, Del Wisdom, and Alfred Kaltschmitt to visit Nicaragua to explore possibilities for Agros. Once back in the U.S., he fondly recalled the visit and became visibly animated when talking about the possibilities of Agros starting a project there some day.

But with the growth of new villages and activities in Guatemala consuming our resources, that "some day" turned out to be six years later. In the summer of 1997 word came from another pastor, Filemón Morán, that there was a 200-acre property for sale in the Rivas region of southern Nicaragua. Filemón knew of many poor families in church congregations within a short radius of the property who could become the core constituents of a first Agros village. He urged Agros to send someone very soon to meet the owners and tie up the property because other parties were known to be interested in buying the land.

Filemón's communication might as well have been the firing of a sprint race starting gun for Dick Nelson. Within a short time Dick, wife Meri, and Corky Morse flew to Managua. None of the group spoke Spanish. A translator who was supposed to have met them in Managua had left the city a few days earlier, and Filemón, who was scheduled to meet them at their hotel the next morning and escort them during their time in the country, spoke no English.

Later Dick told us how he had stayed up most of that first night piecing together the few Spanish words he knew to describe Agros and our mission. Next morning, the presentation that had taken him hours to prepare the night before lasted only five minutes, after which Dick and Corky used the most rudimentary "Spanglish" they could conjure (supplemented by hand signals) to communicate further with Filemón. Against all odds they succeeded. During that trip they visited the land identified by Filemón and talked about what it would take to start a first project there. They promised to report on their trip and recommend that Agros move forward and buy the land.

Dick and Corky excitedly recounted to the board their anecdotes of extraordinary experiences on the trip and their impressions of the land and people. Some board members expressed serious concern that moving ahead in Nicaragua might dilute our very limited resources already badly needed for the villages in Guatemala. These concerns were echoed by our board counterparts in Guatemala. The U.S. team had enough trouble raising funds and sending the required monthly program budget for Guatemala during those days; how could we think of diverting scarce resources to begin a new village in a new country?

But at that particular time the U.S. Agros board happened to be loaded with entrepreneurial types – people who had successfully started and run their own businesses and who tended to look past short term financial or logistical challenges to envisage bright possibilities in the future. The memorable line from the 1989 movie *Field of Dreams* – "if you build it, they will come" – might well have been a tag line for many of us who were entrepreneurially-minded. "If you go there, funds will come" is probably how some of us on the board regarded the proposed expansion to Nicaragua.

Is it faith or foolishness that propels some of us into the unknown? Is making sure each step is carefully measured before taken a mark of prudence or lack of trust in God? Is it subsequent success or failure that validates the one approach over the other? Those are questions that hover over our personal, business, and other life choices for which I am convinced there are no right or wrong answers.

After much discussion the board voted to go ahead. I think we all were aware as we voted that Agros had reached a crossroad – two very distinct paths that would, over the course of years, lead us in diametrically different directions. Dick, his daughter Missi, and Corky then made another trip to Nicaragua to tie down the property. I remember receiving at least two long-distance phone calls from them at crucial points during their trip when, because of their language limitations, they needed my help to understand their negotiations with the property owner – including confirmation of the terms of sale demanded by the owners. They settled on an all-cash purchase price of $30,000 to be paid in U.S. dollars, and left a cash deposit with the owners to seal the deal. The owners agreed to a four-week closing date to allow the Agros board time to raise the necessary funds for the purchase.

On a Friday afternoon 10 days before the scheduled closing date, we received an urgent telephone call from Filemón saying that the sellers wanted to advance the closing to that weekend, or no later than Monday. They had received another cash offer higher than ours from a buyer who was prepared to fork over hard cash immediately. In a token gesture toward Agros they had agreed not to do the deal with the other buyer until the following Monday.

If this had been a transaction in the U.S. there would have been a legally enforceable purchase agreement signed by the parties that would have precluded the unexpected shortening of the closing date. But this was a real estate deal in Nicaragua and while we had legal rights, litigation to enforce contract terms would likely cost a lot of money and get us nowhere. At an emergency board meeting that early afternoon we agreed to try to get the deal done.

We actually had sufficient funds in the Agros coffers to close the deal. But could we physically get those funds in cash into the seller's hands over the weekend? The sellers would not accept a check from us. They could not have cared less if it had been a check issued by the Federal Reserve Bank and signed by then Fed chairman Alan Greenspan. Wire transfers were out of the question. Wiring funds was an accepted and reliable way of sending and receiving funds within a 24-hour period in the U.S. and countries with long established banking rules, customs, and law-abiding business and banking practices. But wiring funds to a bank in a developing country like Nicaragua was different.

Experience had taught me that we faced nothing but serious grief and deal-breaking delay if we tried to wire funds to the sellers, even if the sellers had been willing to accept wired funds. Few people even maintained bank accounts. Most people dealt in cash and a smart seller of land would accept nothing short of hard U.S. currency.

We had learned some hard lessons during earlier years of transferring funds to Guatemala. As a result, those of us traveling to Guatemala would carry checks for program budgets with us, drawn on the U.S. Agros account for our Guatemalan counterparts to deposit in their local bank. There might be a delay of a few days in accessing the funds but not nearly the kinds of delays from wire transfers.

After the board voted approval I called Wanda Wong, our banker at U.S. Bank, and told her we needed $30,000 in cash, preferably in new $20 bills – older bills would be subject to suspicion of their authenticity by the Nicaraguan sellers. What banker in her right mind would say yes to that kind of request on a Friday afternoon? An unusually customer-service minded banker, that's who. Wanda was a godsend for that occasion. She told me over the phone she would scrounge up the cash and call other branches to garner enough if she had to. We then called David Carlson, perfunctorily asked him what plans he had for the weekend, then informed him to forget about those plans because he would be taking a red-eye flight to Nicaragua via Los Angeles Saturday night. David, ever the willing warrior, immediately agreed. Our next call was to Dan Smith, the travel agent who had arranged so many flights for Agros folks for almost 10 years. Dan found a seat for David on both L.A. and Managua legs.

Wanda Wong successfully collected the money from her own and other branches within a couple of hours, and David met her at her branch to take the bags of cash, which had to be counted out to satisfy good banking practice. That night, David stuffed the cash in money belts he had bought that afternoon and fastened them around his waist and up and down both legs. Being tall and lean (bordering on skinny), with bulging money belts strapped to various parts of his anatomy, he was transformed into a stocky man. He had to wear loose-fitting clothes to cover it all.

During one of several phone conversations with David before his departure, I told him he would have to declare the cash to a U.S. customs agent in Los Angeles before he boarded his flight to Managua that night. That was an absolute must. Anyone boarding a flight to Central America carrying that much cash would immediately come under suspicion of being involved in the drug trade or some other illegal activity. If the U.S. customs agents found out he was carrying that cash and was trying to board the plane without declaring it, David would surely have been detained and not allowed on the flight. Moreover, the cash would likely have been confiscated.

I also explained to David that when the flight arrived in Managua, Nicaraguan law also required that he declare how much U.S. currency or other cash he had with him. But at that point, I told him it would be entirely up to his own conscience whether he declared the cash – if I were in his position, I added, I would not declare it.

Anyone familiar with travel to third world countries where corruption is rife would have understood my reasoning. Filling out and signing a customs declaration that said you were carrying $30,000 in cash on your person would invite one of two very unhappy possibilities. If you were lucky you might be detained by local customs agents for questioning. You might endure some browbeating and verbal threats aimed at extracting a bribe so you would not have to sit in a jail cell for a few nights. After prolonged negotiations during which you were left to sit in a small room stewing by yourself, you might successfully negotiate your way into a relatively modest "fine" or "fee" of, say, $500 to $1,000.

But if you weren't lucky, there was a strong possibility that after you were released to leave the airport you would be held up and robbed of all the cash before you got anywhere. A person in that situation had to consider that one of the customs officials might have "friends" outside the airport who would be tipped off to the "gringo" with significant cash on his person.

David, being an experienced third-world traveler, knew exactly what I was talking about. He arrived in Los Angeles past midnight and as he told the story later, proceeded duly to the U.S. Customs office to declare the cash. The office was closed because of the late hour so he wandered around a nearly deserted LAX asking and searching for a Customs agent. He finally found an elderly man dressed in Customs office uniform in a quiet area of the terminal and managed to get a form filled out and handed over to the officer. He described the officer as having not the least bit of interest in his cash or his declaration and looking slightly annoyed at having been interrupted.

Sunday morning I got a phone call from David informing me he had arrived safely in Managua and had gotten through Nicaragua customs without any problem. Filemón was at the airport to pick him up. An appointment had been set up that afternoon to meet the seller, hand over the cash, and sign all the legal documentation. Word was relayed to other board members – we were all praying for David's safety and the success of his unusual mission.

Sunday evening another call from David gave us the news we were hoping for. The deal had been closed. David later described the scene vividly. He, Filemón and our lawyer showed up at the store owned by the seller and his wife and were ushered into a dark back room with no windows and illuminated by a single low-wattage light bulb. They sat on stools or benches under the light and David proceeded to count, bill by bill, the cash as he handed it over to the sellers. They then signed the legal documentation that had been prepared by our Nicaraguan lawyer.

Agros had no legal standing as an organization in Nicaragua as yet. Thus the transaction was closed with David Carlson shown as the buyer. David, over that weekend, had become a landowner in Nicaragua.

After closing the land purchase David agreed to the board's request to live in Nicaragua for three months during the summer of 1998, in order to build relationships with nationals who might eventually serve on a country board of directors to oversee our work in their country. Thus the entire Carlson family lived in Managua that summer.

I took my first trip to Nicaragua in March 1998 to take stock of the newly bought property. Seeing the country from close up, the sense of lethargy and hopelessness in the rural areas was palpable. We drove by large swaths of what appeared to be top grade agricultural land lying fallow. In some places rough fences gave indications of how large farms had been cut up into smaller parcels. Occasionally we saw mechanized plows or tractors and trucks abandoned in the fields, rusting symbols of yet another failure of land reform carried out in name only. The Sandinista government might have listed land reform as one of their crowning achievements, but the absence of capital and technical assistance needed by the people to sustain the agricultural production from the land destined the effort to failure. Once again bright hopes ended in despair and destitution.

The southern region of Nicaragua is a fertile farming area blessed by level topography, plenty of sunshine, and a source of unlimited irrigation water from the vast Lake Nicaragua. Named *el mar dulce* (the sweet sea) by the *conquistadores*, it is said that Spanish soldiers coming upon the lake for the first time believed they had reached the Pacific Ocean. Looking upon the lake one can understand why – the water extends far beyond the horizon and the wave action close to shore is the same as what you would see on an ocean beach. They were shocked when their horses walked up to the lake and began lapping up the water, and amazed when they tested the water themselves to find no trace of saltiness.

On our arrival at the property, accompanied by Filemón, we were greeted by a few of the families that had begun moving on to the land. The men had horses readied for us to tour the property. We were grateful for the horses because our riding tour showed what appeared to be a vast property that took considerable time to reach its outermost boundaries. I thought for sure the property was much larger than had been reported to us.[1]

The people of the first village named it *Futuro del Mañana* ("Tomorrow's Future"). We later discovered that one of the men had said that becoming an owner was a lifelong prayer answered. He had been born on the property and grew up laboring there alongside his family. As a young man, he had stood one day in the middle of the field he was working on and cried in despair over the difficult toil that brought so little income to support him and his family. He had prayed that God would one day let him own a property like this one, a parcel from which he could reap harvests for his own loved ones and not for someone else as a hired laborer. His prayer to own his own land had not only been answered, but the land he now owned was the one where he had stood that day and cried out to God.

---

[1] Some weeks after my trip another board member who had just returned from visiting the new project brought back an engineer's surveyed drawing of the property. Looking at that drawing, I had to laugh out loud. It revealed a very long and very narrow strip of land, resembling the shape of a slightly crooked noodle. No wonder it took us so long on horseback to reach the farthest boundaries! That drawing led to the property being affectionately known among Agros board and staff as "Nelson's Noodle," in tribute to Dick and his pioneering efforts.

To this day Futuro holds a special place in my heart, because it opened the door for our work in Nicaragua, and prepared our thinking for expansion into other countries as well. The Nicaragua staff, well prepared and motivated, has also been a source of creative thinking that has worked its way into the Agros model.

El Salvador 1998

In 1996 the Agros board, believing that we had developed the right model and learned enough in our efforts up to that time, decided to expand the work significantly either in Guatemala or another country. The board voted to embark on an aggressive growth path and adopted a three-year plan to push our annual operating budget from $65,000 in 1996, to $150,000 in 1997, tripled in 1998 to $450,000, and again tripled to $1.2 million in 1999.

During that time I began to commit increasing time to Agros in order to manage the growth. Our small staff operated out of the second story of an old building in the University District of Seattle just two blocks away from my home. The vacant ground floor had been occupied by a wonderful little Italian restaurant that had shut its doors a couple of years earlier. Internet communications had improved enough that I could maintain contact with the law firm and clients by e-mail and phone while working out of the Agros office.

In September 1998 we received a communication from Jeff Abbott of Habitat for Humanity asking if Agros might be interested in doing a joint project in El Salvador. Jeff worked out of Habitat headquarters in Americus, Georgia, and oversaw their work in Central America. This inquiry, coming at a time when the Agros board had decided on a path of expansion, seemed providential. Habitat was a major NGO with great credibility, and we were delighted that they would even know about our existence, much less ask to work with us in El Salvador. I had long admired Millard Fuller (the lawyer/founder of Habitat) from a distance and was excited at the possibilities.

Three of the Agros board members at that time – Don Valencia, Mike Geertsen, and I – were scheduled to travel to Guatemala November 4-12 as part of the University Presbyterian Church service team destined for La Bendición in the Ixil Triangle.[2] Plans were set to meet the Habitat team in Ahuachapán, a Salvadoran city a short distance across the border from Guatemala. Don, Mike and I would fly there by MAF on Monday, November 9, have our meetings with the Habitat team, then take a bus from Ahuachapán to Guatemala City November 11 for our flight back to the U.S.

Hurricane Mitch, the killer storm of the 1998 hurricane season in the Caribbean region, blew away our best-laid plans. Guatemala and El Salvador were not hit nearly as hard as Honduras and Nicaragua, where thousands died in the floods and landslides caused by torrential rains. But the storm caused havoc to roads everywhere in Central America and flights all through the region were suspended for several days. The weather system lingered over Central America even after the winds died down. Our UPC team kept a watchful eye on both weather reports and flight cancellations, uncertain whether we might have to cancel the trip altogether. There was a strong possibility MAF might not be able to fly us from the Ixil to our rendezvous with Habitat in Ahuachapán because of the thick cloud cover that would not go away. So we developed a Plan B for Don, Mike and me to drive to Guatemala City and meet the Habitat folks on November 9 at a hotel near the airport. The Habitat

---

[2] La Bendición (The Blessing) was the next Agros village in the Ixil Triangle after El Paraíso Nebaj. The land was purchased and the people began work there in 1997.

team would maintain radio contact with Agros staff in Guatemala City until then.

The Delta flights from Atlanta to Guatemala City on November 2 and 3 went all the way to Guatemala, circled, and turned back to Atlanta because the weather made it impossible to land. As the UPC team boarded our flight in Seattle early morning November 4 we had no idea whether our connecting flight in Atlanta would be able to take us to Guatemala City that evening. Nor did we know as we took off from Atlanta whether we would also be turned away after making the three-hour flight to Guatemala City. About 30 minutes from the capital the pilot informed us that we had been given clearance to land even though a thick cloud cover blanketed the city. Soon after the plane began its descent the ride became very bumpy, and I think all of us were on edge wondering if we really could make it. When we finally touched ground, we all let out a cheer – as much about venting pent-up nerves as the satisfaction of making it. We found out the next day that the November 5 Delta flight from Atlanta had been turned away and diverted to Panama City. So in the course of four consecutive days, ours was the only Delta flight that made it into Guatemala City.

Someone on the Agros staff who greeted us told us we were the first flight on any airline from the U.S. to make it through to Guatemala City after Mitch had shut down all flights in the region. Our team's spirits were buoyant because we had made it into the country. Moreover the long drive to the Ixil Triangle through torrential rains came off without hitch (though we did have to deal with detours around road closures caused by mudslides). The most challenging detour was at Sacapulas where floods had damaged the bridge over the Rio Negro and we had to ford the river with our 4-wheel drive vans.

After our arrival in the Ixil Triangle we maintained radio contact with Agros staff in Guatemala City, who in turn kept in telephone and radio contact with Habitat. We developed Plan C at that time – to meet in Antigua, where our UPC team was scheduled to spend a day at the tail end of the trip. The El Salvador team would drive to Antigua that day from San Salvador because their scheduled flight had been canceled.

After a daylong drive from the "Waldorf" in Cotzal,[3] the UPC team arrived in Antigua in the dark of early evening. As we hauled our luggage from the vans parked on the street and started to walk to the Hotel San Jorge entrance, we noticed a group of four suitcase-laden men converging on the hotel entrance from the opposite direction. On arriving at the hotel door at the exact same moment I asked one of the men if they were from Habitat for Humanity. Indeed, he replied.

What an astonishing first introduction of the two organizations, Habitat and Agros – considering the enormous logistical difficulties of travel and the continually torrential rains during our stay – that we should arrive at the same hotel in Antigua at exactly the same moment! I think every one of us knew how special the moment was and sensed the beginning of another great Agros adventure.

Later that evening Don Valencia, Mike Geertsen and I met with our Habitat counterparts seated round the table. The conversation proceeded first in English to accommodate Don and Mike. But at one point Mario Alfaro of Habitat looked intently at us and apologized that he would have to speak in Spanish in order to express what was on his heart. He then told us about what he considered a major cause of social disruption in El Salvador – the migration of poor landless rural people into the cities to look for work and a means of survival. Habitat worked mostly in the cities and was encountering waves of new arrivals

---

[3] "Waldorf" was the name we gave to a house in Cotzal rented by Agros to serve as our Ixil regional office. The house had two large rooms where bunk beds were placed for groups of U.S. volunteers. Needless to say, this house and the one dubbed "Chajul Hilton" were both named with obvious tongue-in-cheek.

from the countryside. Entire families would come into the cities, principally San Salvador, and settle in the rapidly growing slums around the city's fringes where there were no power, running water, or sewer systems. Each day they would search for work — even the young children.

At this point Mario took off his glasses and tears began streaming down his face. He described how young girls would be taken into households as servants, separated from their families, and become helplessly vulnerable to physical and sexual abuse from predatory employers. Many of these girls ended up in prostitution because that was the only way they could earn money. The young boys wandered the streets begging and looking for handouts. Many would end up in gangs and resort to crime because they, likewise, had no other way to earn money for themselves or their families. This was all too common a story among the urban poor in his country. He talked about the helplessness he and the other Habitat staff felt because they understood that at the root of this urban migration was a lack of economic opportunity in the rural regions. Their work in providing decent, low-cost housing in the cities did not even begin to touch the underlying causes of poverty. What was worse, they knew of countryside rumors that said if you go to the city there were people who would build you a new house. The rumors were false, of course, but it made the Habitat staff feel like they were unintentionally contributing to the migration of some of the rural poor to the cities.

Habitat, he explained, was not allowed by its charter to buy land for the poor. When they heard about Agros they realized what a difference they could make if they could collaborate with Agros to provide housing while Agros helped the rural poor to buy farmland. His impassioned plea for Agros to work with Habitat in El Salvador made quite an impression on us. He went on to explain that Habitat staff had identified a parcel of property in the Suchitoto region to the north of San Salvador.

This area was ground zero for many of the battles and skirmishes of the Salvadoran civil war. He offered whatever help Habitat could provide if Agros would consider buying that land to begin a project there. At this point I think those of us on the Agros side of the table, having heard Mario's deeply moving appeal, were ready to sign and seal a deal on the spot.

But a huge red flag went up when we asked how much the land cost. Mario mentioned a figure of over 11,000 *colones* per *manzana*, which kicked in the oft-recurring conversation over differing *manzana* measures in different countries and even in different regions of the same country. When we finally came to agreement on the proper land measure and multiplied the unit cost by the total number of *manzanas*, our Agros team came to the sinking realization that the land price alone for this 264-acre parcel would cost US$200,000, a staggering figure to us. We had been paying one-fifth that amount for land of comparable size in Guatemala. Our entire Agros budget for 1998 was only $400,000. The cost of this one parcel in El Salvador came to half that amount, and we hadn't even figured in additional costs for building a team in El Salvador and the non-land components of an Agros village.

I think the Habitat team saw the shock on our faces, and their hearts must have sunk too. We told them about prices for comparable land in Guatemala and wondered if we could start with cheaper land elsewhere in El Salvador. They explained that land prices in their country were much higher than in other Central American countries because El Salvador was such a small country. Land was scarce and thus came at a premium. For that reason few agricultural parcels came on the market for sale, and if they found land for sale elsewhere the price would not be any better.

With spirits much dampened, we agreed to adjourn for the night and meet again the next morning. Don, Mike and I had a triple room at the San Jorge. We talked late into the night but were unable to overcome, in our minds, what seemed like an impossibly high entry barrier to working with Habitat in El Salvador.

A night's sleep brought us unity and resolve the next morning. We were in complete agreement that God's hand was in this encounter with the Habitat team, from the simultaneous arrival at the hotel in Antigua under difficult travel circumstances to Mario's eloquent and passionate appeal for help. We were convinced God was challenging us to say yes to our new Habitat friends. When we gathered with them again that morning we told them of our resolve to find a way to be their partners in El Salvador and agreed with them on the next two steps for both sides: (1) approval by each organization's board, and (2) a follow-up meeting in El Salvador early in the new year to work out details of a joint venture.

On the flight back to Atlanta Don and I were seated together in the back of the plane. He confessed he had intended that this would be his first and last trip for Agros and had planned to resign from the board after we got back to Seattle, pleading lack of time to devote to Agros. However, what he saw and experienced on the trip had turned his thinking upside down. He not only wanted to stay on the Agros board but felt the need to devote much more time to Agros. He said he planned to call Heather after we landed in Atlanta and was concerned how she might react to this change of heart. His Starbucks responsibilities already cut significantly into his family time; what would she think of him wanting to spend more time with Agros as well?

But Don walked back from the pay phone bank in the Atlanta airport with a broad smile on his face. "Skip, you'll never believe what Heather said. She was not upset at all that I want to devote more time to Agros. In fact, she told me she had been praying that this trip would make me rethink priorities in my life and the way I use my time."

The flight home to Seattle was a happy one for both of us. It marked the conclusion of a great trip and the beginning of an exciting new stage for Agros. A few days after our return from Guatemala, Don informed me that he and Heather had decided to fund the entire purchase price of the new land in El Salvador. They asked to be designated as anonymous donors.[4]

Early February 1999 Don and I fulfilled step two of our Antigua agreement with the Habitat team by traveling to San Salvador to work out terms between the two organizations. We toured the property in Suchitoto and also looked at other land that might become available. The smaller geographic dimensions of El Salvador were evident in the shorter driving distances. Where it might take five to six hours to drive from Guatemala City to the Ixil Triangle, Suchitoto was only a one-hour drive from San Salvador.

We met at the Habitat offices in San Salvador with eight members of their national board. Through introductions and conversations I became aware that two of the men seated side by side across the table from us had fought against one another in the Salvadoran civil war – one a former army soldier and the other a guerrilla. Their faces showed the strains of years bearing arms but their hands were now joined in bringing decent housing to the poor of their country.

The Salvadoran civil war had raged from 1980 – 1992. A little more than six years after the conclusion of the war the national reconciliation that had taken root and blossomed was remarkable. The strong economic pulse of the country was clear indication that the people had buried the hatchets of the past and were moving on. The country still had significant problems, but I sensed a vibrant and renewed spirit of hope in the people we encountered.

---

[4] Heather Valencia has since given permission to disclose Don and her as the donors.

Over the next months the land in Suchitoto was purchased, 24 families were jointly selected by Habitat and Agros staff, and the first Agros village in El Salvador took shape. Many of the families were displaced refugees from the civil war; a few others had been made homeless by Hurricane Mitch. The families included men who had fought on both sides of the civil war. Now they were uniting to build new lives for themselves and their families. The people chose the name for their new village: *El Milagro* – The Miracle.

As our activity grew in El Salvador, we eventually hired Mario Alfaro as country director. During the two years that Mario worked for Agros, he fulfilled a personal wish to help the rural families of El Milagro develop self-sufficiency and break the cycle of poverty that drove so many of the rural poor to migrate to urban areas.

A second village followed very closely on the tails of El Milagro. In 2000 we bought a 140-acre parcel, also in the Suchitoto region. When the 18 families who formed the new community, *San Diego de Tenango*, first approached us for help in buying land, we found out they had an unusual story to tell. They had all come from a town called Cabañas, but were forced to flee across the border to Honduras when the Salvadoran civil war made their lives impossible in their home town. When they returned they found they could no longer live in Cabañas, so they found a piece of land to rent in the area of Tenango. One of the community, a young man, had purchased a one-half acre parcel of property there and invited the other families to live on his land while they farmed the rented land. When they heard about Agros' work with the people in El Milagro they asked for help in buying the rest of the land.

Having just successfully completed the joint venture with HFH at El Milagro, we told the people that we could collaborate on a second joint venture with HFH to build their homes as well. We were quite surprised when they responded by saying they would rather not have HFH build their houses. They had looked at the cinder block construction of the El Milagro houses and told us they would rather build their own houses out of adobe. Their reasons? They told us (1) the HFH houses were too hot, and they felt adobe construction would make the homes cooler; (2) the cinder blocks would shatter if hit by bullets, whereas adobe walls could withstand and absorb the impact of bullets far better. We were astounded at their answers, but agreed not to build HFH houses in their village. Seven years after the conclusion of the civil war, the memories that lingered from that era had stayed fresh in their minds.

The importance of the November 1998 trip to Guatemala with the UPC team and the encounter with the Habitat friends grows with the passage of time and hindsight. We had committed to work in another new country on the heels of starting our work in Nicaragua. The financial and logistical demands of expanding from one country to three in the space of 12 months piled exponential burdens on our small staff, our board, and on me personally.

With this new push into El Salvador and the joint venture with Habitat, the board voted in late 1998 to begin a search for a full-time president to manage the growth of the organization. In the meantime, and until we had found someone to take that role, I would have to spend even more time on Agros.

Two weeks after returning from the November 1998 trip to Guatemala I told my partners at the law firm that I had decided to devote close to full time to Agros during the first three months of 1999. For that time, I would work at the Agros office and only come to the law firm if a client matter required my presence there. I would still maintain e-mail and phone contact with the firm and clients but my primary focus would be on Agros. Several board members wondered whether I should quit my law practice altogether and take the presidency role myself. Dick Nelson particularly urged me to do so.

Cyd and I pondered whether this was the point in my life to make a dramatic professional switch. Son Peter was finished with college and earning his own living. Joseph was then studying piano performance at a conservatory in New York City, so the high cost of his education and musical training, even with scholarships and loans, had to be considered. Kara was just about to enter a private high school so her educational costs also factored into the equation. More importantly, I loved my profession as a lawyer and did not feel any strong calling to leave it. My business card as a partner in a downtown Seattle law firm gave me an entrée into spheres of influence that might not be open to me as a nonprofit executive. I often found people more interested in talking about Agros and my involvement with the organization when they realized Agros was not my living but my passion. Had my business card indicated I was president of Agros, some of those doors may have been closed to me.

The 1998 trip brought about an even more radical change in Don Valencia's life. Within a few months, instead of resigning from Agros as he had originally intended, Don resigned his position as senior vice president for research and development at Starbucks. In the summer of 1999 Don and Heather and their two boys took up residence in Antigua for three months to immerse themselves in the culture and learn Spanish.

Don's resignation from Starbucks stunned a good many people who had difficulty understanding why he would give up such a high level executive position at one of the fastest growing companies in the country. Howard Schultz regarded Don as a key player in the effort to take Starbucks to new heights through his work in new product development.

Don and I were elected co-chairmen of the Agros board in 1999, and we served shoulder-to-shoulder until 2006 when he began his battle with colon cancer. The board initially asked Don to serve alone as chairman, but he only agreed on the condition that I serve with him. He felt comfortable running the "inside" aspects of the organization – finance and administration; I was much better at the "outside" role of vision casting and fundraising. We quickly settled into a smooth working relationship with almost instant mutual respect and trust.[5]

The November 1998 trip also resulted in the deeper involvement of other UPC team members. Theresa Schulz, a former Microsoft manager, and Mike Yukevich, a real estate developer, joined the Agros board a few months later.

In 1999 the board hired Greg Rake as our first president. Greg was a seasoned professional in rural development and had spent many years in Latin America. His Spanish was flawless and he brought with him an ethic of service and humility to the organization. He also embraced our organizational philosophy of listening to the people we served rather than imposing programs on them. He was exactly the man we needed during a time of aggressive organizational growth and expansion into new countries.

Mexico 2001

Mexico was the last place I would have chosen for Agros involvement. When the board voted in 2000 to target Mexico as a new country in 2001, I was a reluctant supporter for the idea.

I had long ago developed prejudices against Mexico. It started with my three years as a young boy living in Guatemala where I picked up the same kind of national resentment that so many Mexicans harbor against the U.S. – resentments against a

---

[5] The trip also marked the beginning of a deepening friendship between Don, Heather, Cyd and me. Two years after this trip, the Valencias moved two blocks down the street from our house in Seattle's University District and became involved in our work with university students as well. Don became my closest friend until his death in December 2007 after a valiant fight with cancer.

larger, more powerful and wealthier neighboring country. In my adult years my juvenile prejudices were reinforced when I read about a country with rich resources crippled by corruption and criminal violence, stifled by a self-serving bureaucracy, and impoverished by the greed of the powerful and wealthy.

Elected office often meant a license to steal and get rich. PRI (*Partido Revolucionario Institucional*), the political party that ruled the country for most of the 20th century, at times resembled a legalized crime syndicate in the way it bled the country of its tax revenues and eliminated opposition. To make things worse, those charged with enforcing the law and protecting the citizens were some of the worst predators. The police could not be counted on to protect citizens. Instead, highway and traffic stops by cops looking for bribes and worse were to be expected for anyone driving through Mexico.

The Mexican bureaucracy had a notorious reputation for its arrogance and disdain of common citizens. They acted less like public servants and more like overlords. I hated flying through Mexico City or on Mexicana Airlines – there were always delays and they never bothered to explain or apologize.

Mexico's national wealth dwarfed that of countries like Guatemala, El Salvador, and Nicaragua. It should have been a country with a strong and thriving middle class in which few were left wanting. It should have been a major economic power. But it was not. The rich were fabulously wealthy, the poor were dirt poor.

These were the broad and cruel generalizations stored in my mind. Of course, my mental picture of Mexico was grossly unfair and those who perpetrated the injustices were a small minority who preyed on the vast majority of Mexicans.

Early in 2001 while in Washington D.C., I met Jonathan Salgado, advisor to Pablo Salazar, the newly elected governor of Chiapas, Mexico. Jonathan served as pastor of a church in Tuxtla Gutiérrez, the capital of Chiapas, and Salazar, who was elected governor in late 2000, was a member of his congregation. Salazar had asked Jonathan to identify NGOs, including faith-based organizations, that might be willing to participate in helping the indigenous and poor of Chiapas.

Today the State of Chiapas embodies all the best and the worst of Mexico. With four million inhabitants Chiapas encompasses an area as large as the whole country of Guatemala. It is rich in natural resources and generates 80% of the hydroelectric power for the whole country with its three major dams. Chiapanecos should be well off, but for 70 years they suffered under central governments that took from Chiapas all it could and gave little or nothing back. And thus Chiapas, instead of being one of the richest, was instead the poorest state in Mexico.

PRI, with its iron grip over Mexican politics nationally and in Chiapas, routinely rotated the governorship of Chiapas to its party members. Chiapanecos observed wryly during the PRI era that every governor they ever had was an interim governor, as the PRI shuffled people in and out of the governor's office, rewarding party loyalty by giving each a turn at dipping a sticky hand or three in the public till. The last governor to serve an actual six-year term was elected in 1970. During the six-year term that expired in 2000, four PRI party members had rotated through the office.

The Mexican elections of 2000 produced massive shifts in the political landscape. Vicente Fox smashed PRI's 70-year monopoly on the Mexican presidency, and Pablo Salazar stunned everyone by breaking the PRI's 70-year stranglehold on Chiapas.

Salazar was a lawyer by training, and during his legal career had often represented indigenous people in their struggles and causes. In 1994 he was elected as a PRI member to the Mexican senate representing Chiapas. Six years later he renounced his PRI membership and a coalition of eight opposition parties from both left and right proclaimed him their candidate for the Chiapas governorship.

He ran without any money while the PRI spent a fortune trying to preserve its power. As the election drew near, gifts of cash, cars, TV's were given to people so they would vote for the PRI candidate. On a humorous note, it was said that Salazar supporters made a pact among themselves to accept the money and gifts – it was their own money that had been paid in taxes, after all – and then vote for Salazar anyway. The 53.7% majority he received indicates a lot of Chiapanecos did exactly that.

Jonathan Salgado invited me to bring an Agros team to visit Chiapas and meet with Pablo Salazar and his staff to discuss the possibility of Agros doing work in Chiapas. Greg Rake, the Agros President we hired in 1999, and Agros supporters Don Kunze and Gordon Bell and I took him up on the invitation. We arrived in Tuxtla on March 26, 2001, at a time when the international spotlight was squarely focused on Chiapas. One day earlier the Zapatista rebels who controlled much of rural Chiapas spoke before the National Congress to outline their grievances and demands.

Research we had done in advance of the trip told us that working in Mexico would not be easy due to the complex and highly divisive political, social, and religious issues. Mexican history textbooks proclaimed that land reform was instituted by the Mexican constitution and successive distributions of land to the poor over several decades meant that all Mexican peasants were already owners of their own land. Much of that land was consolidated into *ejidos*, legal entities best described as land cooperatives whose members owned the land communally. Knowing this historical background, we wanted to find out whether there was even any need for Agros to help the rural poor buy their own farmland.

We met with Governor Salazar our first night in Chiapas, and during the time we spent with him I realized I was listening

to an extraordinary man during an extraordinary season in the
political history of Mexico.

He confessed to facing enormously difficult odds against
succeeding in his six-year term. All the vested interests wanted
him to fail. The state legislature, still controlled by the PRI, had
indicated it would not approve his budget, so he had no money
to fund any programs. The press was highly critical of him, not
the least because one of his first executive orders was to cut off
long-standing state subsidies of the newspapers. Salazar said he
wanted the press to be free to criticize him so as not to oblige
him to fork over government handouts.

We explained Agros' mission to help the poor buy land and
build communities. Knowing we were a faith-based organization
his first question was whether we worked only with Christians.
He was pleased to hear we did not limit our work in that way
and that our selection process did not include a religious
prerequisite. "The poor come with no religious or political
labels," he said. We were glad to agree.

I had trouble sleeping that night, energized as I was by the
conversation with Pablo Salazar. Here was a bright, talented and
brave man with a vision to help the poor. He had set out on a
course nothing short of changing history. But the deck was
stacked solidly against him. Was this the right time and place for
Agros to begin work in Mexico?

The next morning we met with Rubén Velázquez, Salazar's
cabinet minister in charge of rural development. He briefed us
on the plight of the poor peasantry in Chiapas and why such
extensive poverty pervaded the rural regions even though the
people owned their own farmland. He sent one of his assistants
to accompany us on a helicopter tour of these areas and to visit
some ejidos to see first hand the conditions and circumstances of
the poor.

The helicopter took us over some of the most beautiful
farmland I had ever seen – rich, fertile valleys between two

mountain ranges, with sparkling rivers running through the valleys. But my heart broke as I looked at this otherwise idyllic scene. Next to the large, lush green irrigated fields in the foothills of the mountains, and stretching up to the sides of the mountains were tiny plots of dry, brown, rock-filled land. Who owned the large green fields? The rich. Who owned the small dry plots? The poor.

We saw miles upon miles of green fields. And we saw miles upon miles of tiny arid plots right next to them. Most of the small plots were so badly eroded that the rock structures underneath the earth showed clearly from the air. These were not scattered rocks, but lines of rock showing through the earth – much like the ribs of a starving man, an apt simile for the grinding poverty of the peasants in Chiapas.

What we saw from the air provided a bright flashing neon asterisk to the claims in Mexican history books that every Mexican peasant owned the land he tilled. Constitutional doctrine may embody an ideal. But reality may be something totally different. In Mexico, the visual images from our helicopter flight told the real story: (1) much of the land given to the peasants was dry, rocky, mountainous land, and (2) over the years the wealthy landowners had managed to bring the best of the land owned by the poor back under their control.

The old prejudices stirred within me on that helicopter ride. Why was capital so totally tied up in the hands of the wealthy? How was it possible that those so blessed by the riches of the earth could totally ignore their poor neighbors? How could these wealthy ones be so blind not to see that the seeds of violent revolution are sown by the rich living selfishly without regard to the poor?

We were flown to a grouping of ejidos over an area of 240,000 hectares (approximately 500,000 acres). We found that in 1994 the Chiapas government had bought this large tract of land from a private landowner as part of another land reform effort. But most of that land lay fallow right now. Later, as we walked over some of the land, we could tell the ground was parched for lack of water. It was the dry season. In June the rains would start and if any farmer were to reap a harvest this season they must plant soon. But where would they get the money for seeds and fertilizer? The dilemma faced by the people in these ejidos was the same faced by so many others across Mexico. The poor may have owned the land, but had no means to make it productive.

One poor farmer in the ejido told me there were three groups of rural poor: one group had given up altogether and migrated to the U.S. Another group didn't believe they could make it on the land and did what they had always done (work for the large landowners at subsistence wages). The third group, including himself, was determined to gut it out and make it on the land.

That day the people told us stories of a government that had acted as an all-powerful adversary – a government that had persecuted, kidnapped, and assassinated those who demanded a more just society. We heard how the government gave the poorest half of the population absolutely nothing but misery and grief unless those citizens organized themselves into mutual help groups large enough to be noticed. Even then, anything a group obtained from the government came only after hard negotiation. The government acted not in the role of helping the poorest of the poor live a more decent life, but as a heartless adversary.

We heard accounts of a government that exploited the religious differences of its population by pitting one religious group against another. Acts of violence carried out by paramilitary groups associated with the government were routinely blamed on religious strife.

Little wonder then that the Zapatista rebels operated and controlled most of Chiapas. The poor rural farmers had little reason to support or care about the fortunes of the national government. It was someone else's government, not theirs.

We also heard guarded optimism that change was in the air.

We watched and listened as a team of government rural development workers interacted with the people we were visiting. I paid close attention to the reactions of the people as they listened to the government agents. The agents were asking them what they needed and suggesting various ways to tap into available resources. I sensed conflicting feelings among the people – on the one hand, a sense of disbelief that the government that had acted for so long as a harsh adversary now was offering to help them; on the other hand, a spirit of cautious hope and optimism.

The people of this ejido knew that Pablo Salazar had turned his back on the PRI and they seemed willing to believe that this might make a difference in how the new government would treat them. But generations of neglect, broken promises, and betrayal at the hands of past governments also made it difficult for them to trust that things would be different.

The task facing Salazar was to convince the poor that their fate was tied inextricably to his. Their success would be his success. Their failure would be his failure. Neither could afford for the other to fail. If Salazar failed and the PRI returned to power, their lives would return to the despair of the past. Even worse, for once they had dared to hope – that hope, if crushed, would leave them more devastated than if they had not hoped at all.

These were my impressions after two short days in Chiapas. This was the setting in which Agros had been invited to work with the rural poor. Rubén Velázquez came to our hotel at ten o'clock the night before we left to request, in his own right and on behalf of the Governor, that Agros consider starting a first project. Just one. He confessed they desperately needed help, but did not want do-gooders coming to Chiapas promising to eradicate poverty and promising to do 100 projects. They knew those kinds of promises would only be broken. They would be content with an organization serious enough to do just one project; one successful project would encourage others to come – other NGOs who, at that moment, considered Chiapas too dangerous, too risky, too politically volatile for them to come and help the poor.

The trip home allowed me some time to process what had been an overload of people, experiences, images, and impressions picked up over 48 hours. I'm sure Greg, Don and Gordon did the same. By coming to Chiapas, we had some questions answered. But many more were raised.

If Agros accepted the invitation of Governor Salazar, we would have to change our way of thinking and be willing to work in ways we had not done before. They did not need Agros to buy land, which was our distinctive as an NGO. But they needed us, and they pleaded with us, to help the people in the ejidos by providing the capital needed to make the land productive. They did not expect handouts and suggested that whatever we invested could be in the form of loans which the people could and would repay.

The team came back and unanimously recommended to the Agros board that we begin work in Mexico. I was surprised at the complete turnaround in my own attitude toward working in Mexico. We decided to move ahead, believing the other components of the Agros model could be of significant help to the rural poor in that country.

Our research told us that Mexican law required us to operate as a national entity rather than as an international organization working in the country. Once again, Dick Nelson stepped into the role of entrepreneur and took the lead over the next three years to travel to Mexico and find and develop relationships with like-minded men and women who would serve as Agros Mexico board members.

Our due diligence also uncovered an urgent need we could address in our initial foray into Chiapas. As a result of religious strife a number of *evangélico* families in the Mitontic area had been expelled in 1994 from the ejido they had been part of. They went through a long process of applying to the government for recognition as a separate ejido, and finally, in 2000, had received some land for their new ejido. With land and a few resources provided by the government, they set themselves to the task of building new lives and named their community *San Miguel Mitontic*. We decided to help this group and Agros thus began its work in Mexico by providing training, technical assistance, and help in planning for their agricultural and community development.

Not long after beginning work with the San Miguel Mitontic community, we were told of another group that had split off from an ejido, in this case because of disputed titles to the ejido's land. These villagers formed a new ejido named *Espinal Buena Vista* and in 2005 asked for Agros' help. We were able to get involved with them on a number of fronts, including technical training in raising cattle and non-traditional crops such as flowers.

More recently Agros has actually bought land in the Comitán region of Chiapas in order to help two separate groups of indigenous Guatemalans who fled into Mexico during the Guatemalan civil war. As non-Mexicans, the people of Nueva Ilusión and Santa Fe Ajké did not qualify for land ownership through an ejido. Thus even in Mexico, the full Agros model, including land purchase, has been mobilized to help the rural poor.

Honduras 2004

In 1999 we began receiving indications of interest from donors who asked if we had any plans to expand our work to Honduras. One donor even made a substantial gift from a recently received inheritance to encourage us to explore beginning work in that country.

The first exploratory trip took place in 2000 when Greg Rake and David Carlson flew to Honduras, and with Norma Martínez, looked at land in different regions where we might begin. Norma was a Honduran national who conducted occasional training sessions for our national staffs in Guatemala, Nicaragua and El Salvador. She had a deep sense of empathy for the poor in her own country and was animated by the prospect of Agros taking its model to Honduras.

In 2002 there were two more exploratory trips. Theresa Schulz and then intern Laurie Werner attended regional staff training sessions in Tegucigalpa. At the end of 2002, Greg Rake and board member Craig Shuck went to Honduras and began a serious search for land that might be available for sale and people in the country we might rely on to help establish an Agros foothold in the near future. After they returned, the staff did further feasibility inquiries over the next 18 months.

Our research told us that in Latin America, only Nicaragua and Haiti had lower GDP's than Honduras. Not surprisingly, rural poverty was exacerbated by disproportionate land ownership between rich and poor. A 1993 agricultural sector census disclosed that 70% of rural farmers owned only 10% of the agricultural land. Moreover, the land owned by poor farmers had very low production from overuse and poor agricultural practices.

The history of land reform in Honduras was spotty, to say the least. In the 1950s the Honduran government enacted a land reform law that was never implemented, and indeed never had a chance. The *reforma agraria* legislation became one of the justifications for a military coup that sought to reverse what the army saw as a leftist drift in the country. By the 1970s the military government itself faced enormous pressure from the rural poor who resented the inequality in land ownership. Attempts were made to address the situation but little was accomplished. The movement of *invasores* steadily grew, creating chaos in the rural regions. In 1992 the Honduran government enacted legislation intended to "modernize" the agricultural sector of the country. Now, a little over a decade after the new law had been passed, experts opined that the modernization law did nothing of the sort; if anything, the concentration of land ownership had increased during that time.

Norma's hope was fulfilled in the summer of 2004 when more donors were found to begin work in her home country, including a substantial gift from an anonymous donor with special instructions to use the funds for a new project in Honduras. With funding thus secured, we bought a 140-acre parcel in the Otoro Valley region for $62,000 and began the first project. Agros Uno, the name given to that first village, did not get a good start. In retrospect we fault ourselves for not having done the family selection process correctly. The first group of families came from four different communities and lacked any sense of unity and willingness to work together for the common good. Individual families began to leave and eventually the national staff had to bring in an almost entirely new community of people.[6] We were much more careful the second time around, and the new community eventually adopted a new name as well, *Nuevo Amanecer* (New Dawn).

---

[6] When a family leaves, what becomes of any equity they have built up to the time of their departure? This is worked out on a case-by-case basis. "Sweat equity" is often offset by the benefits derived from living and working the land during their time in the project – including harvests and housing. The amount of any land debt assumed by a replacement family is also handled on a case-by-case basis.

A second project, Brisas del Volcán (Breezes of the Volcano), originated in 2005 in collaboration with a Honduran nonprofit organization working with families in the Santa Barbara area. The 22 families on this 117-acre parcel have some terrific territorial vistas because of the elevation of the property. One unusual promontory rises almost straight up with a vertical cliff face and is unique enough to have generated a good many legendary stories of spirits and gods inhabiting the place.

10

AGROS TODAY

People ask me if back in 1982, when I got so excited about the idea of helping the poor buy their own land (and it was just a seed of an idea then), I foresaw what Agros would become all these years later.

The truth is, there was no way back then for me even to dream about what might come out of pursuing the idea. Juan Carlos' message that afternoon at Mercer Island Covenant Church lit a fire within me I could not ignore. I had no notion of the outcome; I simply felt compelled to see if the idea could work. In retrospect, my early notes and papers on private land redistribution as a means of helping the poorest of the rural poor amounted to a very mediocre and skeletal sketch when placed beside the robust picture of what Agros has become.

In the Introduction I laid out some of the statistics that describe what Agros has become and a few indications of what the people in our villages have accomplished. All of us at Agros are thankful for and proud of what has been achieved. But my experience of the past 30 years tells me Agros will always be a work in process. I do not believe we will ever come to a place where we can claim to have seen all the problems and arrived at all the solutions. That would be sheer arrogance. Working with the rural poor in the world's poorest countries will always require a new set of eyes and fresh thinking.

If you examine the Agros model and visit Agros villages today, what you see is the product of at least three significant strategic shifts over the years. The first came to us very early when we realized we had to do more than help people buy land. We had to consider other impediments to a war-traumatized people trying to rise out of abject poverty. Thus non-land elements were brought into the Agros model: individual and community development, agricultural technical assistance, production loans, healthcare, education, and spiritual development.

In 2005, our Nicaragua country director proposed a second shift: that Agros change its strategy of buying uncultivated or open land and consider buying existing farms instead. While open or fallow land cost far less than a producing farm, it also meant that the path to income production was lengthier and more challenging. By paying a premium for a producing farm with existing crops, the people could harvest crops almost immediately and food security would not be as difficult to attain. The land loans would be much higher per family, but the repayment capability of each family would correspondingly also be much greater. The proposal made sense to the board.

With some trepidation over the much greater funding commitments required, we authorized the purchase of El Edén, an existing coffee farm in Nicaragua on 292 beautifully situated acres with a river running through it and even a 66-foot waterfall. The owner's house has been converted to a community building and there are even corrals for raising livestock. As soon as the people moved on to the land they were able to harvest the coffee crop that had just come to maturity. The significantly higher per-family land loans did not daunt the families. They understood clearly the advantages of buying an existing farm, and the first coffee harvest drove the point home right away.

A third strategic shift came in 2010. The issue of leverage had been considered and debated for several years. How could the model be scaled to benefit greater numbers of people, and correspondingly reduce the cost per beneficiary? With help from the country directors and the U.S. staff, the board eventually adopted a large-village plan designed to benefit not just more Agros villagers, but people in nearby and surrounding communities as well. The first project under this new strategy was begun in Nicaragua in the fall of 2010. It is the first of what we hope will be a new generation of Agros villages. And it best represents what Agros has become.

I saw this project first hand in March 2011. *Tierra Nueva* ("New Earth") is a beautiful tract of land in the Matagalpa region of Nicaragua. The 1,300+ acres parcel was bought in September 2010 with funding from the Dobberpuhl Family Foundation of Nashville, Tennessee. It consists of what had been five separate farms owned by the Picada family. I joined the Dobberpuhls – parents Joel and Holly, son Samuel and daughter Lily, and a number of others on March 14, 2011, to dedicate the land and the community.

As of that date 144 of the target number of 150 families had been selected. Eleven of those families had moved into the existing buildings on the land and another 33 families were living in makeshift, temporary quarters on the land. Many of these 33 families shared a sad story that has become more common in the beginnings of new Agros villages. They had all lived and worked on other farms. When their *patrónes* heard they would be joining an Agros village they were immediately fired from their jobs and evicted from their homes. In some cases their homes – even as rudimentary as they are on large *fincas* – were physically destroyed at the *patrón's* orders. With nowhere to lay their heads at night they asked and obtained permission from Agros staff to move to Tierra Nueva before the scheduled date.

Those who were already living on the land and others who made the special trip from elsewhere welcomed us when we arrived. We met with the families, including children of all ages, in an open structure with tin roofing over it, and the community greeted us with the usual formal "agenda," always beginning with a scripture reading and prayer. The scripture read by one of the elders in the community was the passage in Genesis where Abraham was called by God to enter into a new land from whence he would become the blessed progenitor of untold numbers of descendants.

At one point, a man named Noel Rodríguez was called on to tell the story of how he had come to be part of Tierra Nueva. His first words were:

I was bought by Agros.[1]

Of the countless stories I had listened to over these many years, that was the most unusual beginning I had heard. I never tired of hearing the accounts of so many who overcame enormous suffering and poverty to experience the pride and joy of working their own land and building a brighter future for their families. They inspired me and filled me with awe. But never before had I heard a statement like that.

I thought Noel Rodríguez meant it in jest, but his story had a fascinating twist to it. Here is what I recollect he said (my translation):

I was bought by Agros. I was born on this land and have worked on this land my whole life. One day last year the *patrón* told me to prepare three horses for the Agros people who would be visiting and riding to inspect the land. I readied four horses, one for myself so I could ride with them. Later the *patrón* informed all of us workers he had sold the land to Agros and we would all have to leave. I was very, very sad. Where would I go? My whole life had been on this land. I determined to ask the Agros staff if I could become part of the project. I pleaded with them. They told me to wait and they would see what

---

[1] *Yo fui comprado por Agros.*

could be done. I kept asking them. They told me to be patient. One day they finally told me I could stay and be part of the new Agros village. I was so happy! So you see, that's why I say I was bought by Agros.

Later I talked to the Agros staff and we all agreed that Noel's intimate knowledge of every corner of the land and its attributes would be invaluable in the development of the community.

The generations at Tierra Nueva span from newborn babes cradled by mothers to 86-year old Don Lino. Don Lino will live with his "young" 55-year old son and his family. I chatted with him while some of the women in the community served up a lunch they had prepared of tortillas and piping hot beans with a slice of goat cheese, to all present at the gathering. Don Lino wore a clean and pressed shirt with the Office Depot logo on the breast pocket. What route did that shirt travel to become Don Lino's prized dress shirt? His head was shaded by a handsome straw hat. I wondered about the stories he could tell of what his eyes had seen over 86 years. I wondered also what stories would be told by those newborn babes 86 years from now as the 21st century draws to a close – if any should live as long as Don Lino.

How will the work at Tierra Nueva benefit others in the surrounding region? From our tour of the village, we came to see several possibilities, including:

Water: Agros staff is looking into bringing a water line from the Nueva Esperanza Agros village to Tierra Nueva, over a distance of several kilometers. It will require help and coordination from the municipality. The new water line will allow approximately 650 families living between Nueva Esperanza and Tierra Nueva to tap in and have access to potable water.

Agricultural training: Agros staff will conduct "best practices" agronomy training with our Tierra Nueva villagers, and invite people from surrounding villages to join in the sessions.

Crop marketing: Agros staff will offer neighboring villagers the opportunity to participate in joint marketing of crops such as sweet peppers, chili peppers, snow peas and coffee in order to maximize market reach and prices.

During that welcoming ceremony, one of the young girls in the village, about 11 years old, was called on to recite a poem. She did so with a radiant smile on her face. The poem – *La Calumnia* (The Slander) – was penned by Rubén Darío (1867-1916), Nicaragua's national poet:

Puede una gota de lodo
sobre un diamante caer;
puede también de este modo
su fulgor oscurecer;
pero aunque el diamante todo
se encuentre de fango lleno,
el valor que lo hace bueno
no perderá ni un instante,
y ha de ser siempre diamante
por más que lo manche el cieno

My rough translation:

A drop of mud may
On a diamond fall
It might in so doing
Darken its glow
Yet though the whole diamond

In mud be immersed
Its innate worth
Is not lost for an instant
It must always be a diamond
Though mired in sludge

Her recitation was deeply moving to me on several levels. To me, she embodied the future of Tierra Nueva and even Nicaragua – a literate young girl, full of hope and aspiration. If Agros does its job well she will never suffer the constraints of poverty and illiteracy that plagued her parents' generation and earlier generations. The poem itself is a metaphor for Nicaragua's rural poor: generations of men and women whose innate worth and dignity have been obscured or entirely hidden by poverty – diamonds mired in sludge. It was as if the young girl expressed the heart and hope of her entire village, earnestly anticipating, through hard work and Agros' help, that they will rise above the poverty that has acted like a sea of mud drowning out their humanity.

While Tierra Nueva embodies Agros' hopes and plans, we are well aware of the serious challenges that face us. We know that every new group of people asking us to help them buy land is different. They have different stories that introduce new combinations of fear, anxiety, and hopelessness. For them to succeed, and for Agros to succeed, these are some of the significant obstacles we must overcome.

Poverty Mindset

In the earlier years, the people we helped in Guatemala and El Salvador had survived the brutal civil wars in their countries, but the personal tragedy and loss they experienced were hard to imagine even in one's worst nightmares. Today the trauma of experiencing and witnessing violence and death is psychologically and medically acknowledged and treated under the broad categorization of post-traumatic stress disorder. In the 1980s and 1990s all we could do was improvise each step along the way to help people climb out of the pit containing their demons from the past.

Today a new generation of rural poor are knocking at Agros' door. Many are too young to remember the horrors of the civil wars in their countries. What they know of the tragedies suffered by their families in the past comes through hearing stories from parents, grandparents, uncles and aunts. They are not haunted by memories and nightmares of atrocities seen and experienced first hand. No one is conscripting the men to serve as soldiers, taking them away from their homes to fight for or against the government. The women do not have to live in fear of armed bands of men coming into their villages and raping and pillaging and killing their husbands and children before their eyes.

The people we now serve in the post-civil war era in Central America must still overcome the mindset of extreme poverty. In Guatemala it is said that a man can fall *out* of his cornfield and break his leg, a wry commentary on how a poor Mayan farmer, not being able to afford land in the valleys, must grow his crops on the steep mountainsides. Terracing could save his meager topsoil and even make it safer for him to farm his land. But terracing requires thinking beyond the immediate and for a man with no money and a family with little to eat, longer term thinking is not just an unaffordable luxury; it is a totally alien concept.

This poverty mindset might further be explained by considering the American Thanksgiving table.

The traditional Thanksgiving dinner served in homes in the U.S. resembles a cornucopia of edible blessings – representing, from the times of the Puritan colonists, provisions from a gracious and merciful God. Family and friends gather around the table in expectant wonder as they behold the offerings. Besides heaping piles of turkey, how about some ham or chicken? Undecided between candied yams and mashed potatoes? That's okay. Go ahead and take both. Likewise when it comes to choosing between pumpkin or apple pie. Maybe add a slice of pecan pie too.

This annual feast is an apt metaphor for something we take for granted in the U.S. as much as the air we breathe. I do not mean our abundant material blessings, or the free exercise of speech, religion, and the other great freedoms we cherish.

I speak of making choices – at the dinner table and in everyday life.

Until my Agros travels opened my eyes to the extreme poverty of rural people in Central America, it had never occurred to me that the depth of poverty could be measured by the absence of choices.

From earliest childhood those of us in the developed world learn to choose constantly: the food we eat, clothes or shoes we put on, books we read, music we play or listen to, games we play. As we grow older we choose the classes we take in school and, for many of us, a field of study in college (if we choose to go to college) and a career path.

The poorest of the rural poor in Central America and elsewhere, whether they are young children or mature adults, are never faced with those kinds of choices. The daily choices we make are totally superfluous when you only have the clothes you wear today and every day, when you may not even own a single pair of shoes, and when your daily fare never changes: corn tortillas and beans (you hope), day in, day out.

Reading books, going to school, or playing sports? Out of the question. Even as a young child, every day of the week you work in the fields or walk miles to cut and haul firewood, or get the corn ground at the mill for the family dinner that night. Shopping at the mall? You might as well talk of life on Mars.

Lifelong poverty of this kind, unimaginable to us who live in industrial countries, chokes the hope out of men and women and kills the human spirit. No wonder the first time we meet the people in a new Agros project their eyes are downcast and they speak in a whisper.

Grinding poverty has made them feel less than human.

In helping the rural poor get on their feet we have learned we must work tirelessly on issues of human development in addition to economic self-sufficiency. Our challenge is not only to give them an economic hand-up but to help people who have never had choices in life learn to choose, and to choose wisely. In doing so our hope is that they can also break out of thinking only of daily survival and instead think of the next month, the next year. We must help them believe that what might have seemed impossible in the past is within their ability and reach. They have to believe that the very hard work they face is worth the effort.

Agros has found that a significant indicator of transformation in the lives of the poor is the emergence of choices when villagers own their own farmland and live in their own houses. As their children now go to school, parents can begin to hope and dream that those children might choose to become doctors, teachers, or agronomists some day. With new-found economic opportunity and access to literacy classes, the adults themselves might even dream of choices that were once unthinkable – starting a small business, raising a small flock of animals, or buying some more farmland.

The work is not now and never has been easy, nor do I expect working with the poor ever will be easy.

Soaring Land Prices

When we started Agros in the 1980s the word globalization was the kind of idea generated by egghead academics with too much time on their hands. Who could have imagined back then how the world would become so interconnected economically and electronically? The bright side of this picture means that our Agros villagers can grow snow peas and have their product exported to the UK and their coffee sought after by multiple U.S. roasters. On the not-so-bright side the U.S.-generated demand for crops that go into making alternative fuels has not just escalated the price of food but the price of arable land as well.

Thus we now find in some parts of Central America that agricultural land is selling for prices comparable to what one would pay in the U.S. This correlates into much greater up-front capital expenditures for Agros when we start a new village, and also means higher loan amounts the families will have to bear and repay.

Migration Effects

The tremendous migration of poor Central Americans to the U.S. has brought new challenges unknown 30 years earlier. It is no longer unusual in our villages that some of the men are not to be found, leaving women to care for the children and work the land by themselves. These women are not widows as one might have supposed during the civil war years. Ask enough questions and you eventually discover the men have made their way to the U.S. through the illegal migration pipeline. After finding work in the U.S. they usually begin sending money back to their families. Known as "remittances," these funds sent from hundreds of thousands of migrants who have made their way to the U.S. now constitute the largest single source of foreign currency earnings in all of the Central American countries, exceeding by far earnings from traditional exports.

I was in El Salvador in November 2001 and saw how the ripple effects of the 9/11 terrorist attacks had reached this tiny country in Central America. A banner headline on the front page of the major national daily newspaper reported a 60% drop in remittances in the prior month. El Salvador, with a population of only 6.5 million, received at that time over $1.4 billion annually in remittances. That amounted to more than $200 for every man, woman, and child in that country. Who knows what the actual number comes to for those who are actually receiving the money?

As in so many cases, there are positives and negatives to this phenomenon. A migrated husband's earnings in the U.S., even at common labor rates, is high enough so that the portion remitted might pay off a family's land debt sooner than otherwise possible. It might even finance the startup of small businesses for the families left behind. While Agros has not conducted any study of the sociological impact of absent husbands and fathers, there is no doubt the consequences of a prolonged absence can be devastating on the family. This is particularly so if the migrated man marries or takes on a relationship with another woman in the U.S. This can end with a man abandoning his family altogether.

Personnel and Culture

With headquarters in Seattle and operations and field staff in five countries, the task of finding the right people with the right heart and skills to fill key executive and managerial positions is not simple. For key U.S. positions some cross-cultural experience is a must to navigate the often-tricky channels of language and culture. One mistake can result in misunderstanding and offense that may consume inordinate time and effort to redress. For national staff I have earlier mentioned the difficulties of finding the people with the right skills who are motivated by helping the poor rather than filling their own pockets.

The culture and language barriers sometimes crop up in surprising ways as U.S. board and staff interact with counterparts in Central America and Mexico. In the early years in Guatemala we had difficulty conveying the North American concept of "accountability" to our Guatemalan board members. The difficulty starts with there not being a word in the Spanish vocabulary for accountability. What would appear the obvious translation, *contabilidad*, in fact is limited in its meaning to the English "accounting." We had many written and verbal communications on this issue, with much exasperation from the Guatemalans for our asking for something they believed they had fully given to us. We finally realized there was no equivalent word in Spanish. *Responsabilidad* – responsibility – came closest, but any English speaker can tell you it does not really convey the full meaning of people being held accountable for their commitments.

We have found cultural difficulties not just in the North American/Central American context. Just as often problems arise between staffers of different nationalities in Central America and Mexico. This makes it particularly difficult for our nationals with regional responsibilities. Someone in Guatemala or Mexico, the two largest countries in the isthmus, may react negatively when asked to do something by someone from Honduras or Nicaragua, two countries deemed to be far more backward and poor than either Mexico or Guatemala.

Our Agros International president from 2008-2011, Hans Theyer, is Chilean by birth. When the board hired Hans we thought that, being Latin American, he could easily relate to and be accepted by the nationals in the five countries. Imagine our surprise when his Chilean nationality proved a stumbling block to some key national staffers. As we later discovered, the fact that Chile is one of the more prosperous countries in South America meant Hans had one strike against him even before he got to the plate. They thought Hans could not really understand the problems of the rural poor in Central America and Mexico because he was a Chilean who had worked a number of years for Microsoft in the U.S.

Unexpected Challenges

Agros has seen the occasional "one-off" challenge as well. The most recent example in this category happened in Nicaragua in 2008 when a notorious drug lord who owned land adjacent to one of our villages decided he wanted to have the Agros village land as well. His henchmen began a "persuasion" campaign with the villagers, promising to pay off their land loans to Agros if they and their fellow villagers would let the boss-man have access and use of their land. When Agros' Nicaragua staff tried to intervene, the goons barred entry to the village, prominently displaying their assault rifles and other assorted weapons to make it very clear that our staff should stay far away if they valued their lives. The "lockdown" of the village also prevented the people from getting their tomato harvest to market.

After considerable deliberation on what courses of action were available to us we eventually negotiated a deal with Universidad Nacional Autónoma de Nicaragua – the largest state-run university in the country – whereby we deeded the property to that institution and they took over our role as overseers of the agricultural projects and land title issues. We could readily see that the university, as the most prominent and respected higher education institution in Nicaragua, had far more leverage and connections to deal with the drug lord than Agros ever would. The latest information I have indicates most of the families are still on the property and are doing fine.

Global Economics

Even as I write this, the U.S. and global economies have been mired since 2007 in the recession of a lifetime. Even the most optimistic economic forecasters do not predict any quick recovery. The fragility of the world economic system is such that stumbles in Europe or Asia can cause a quick drop of confidence in the U.S. and elsewhere. Gradual gains in climbing out of the downturn can be erased overnight.

Agros, like most U.S. nonprofit organizations, has suffered a corresponding drop in income as donors everywhere have had to engage in belt-tightening. Repeated budget cuts are felt throughout the system as lay-offs require remaining staff to take on far more than their own share of duties. Even so, we feel fortunate to be survivors of the Great Recession and are encouraged and determined to move forward after being forced to increase efficiencies in our operations.

❖ ❖ ❖

The list of challenges Agros faces is daunting. Working with the poor, as someone told me once, is not for the faint of heart. But my, what great rewards come your way when you persist at it. Sometimes, when things get tough and nothing seems to be going right, I think of the children in our villages – their smiles, their laughter, their play. I recall the feel of a child's hand in mine as we walk through a village. Children are a great barometer of whether our work in the villages is accomplishing our aims.

When we first meet the participating families in a new Agros village the children are shy and withdrawn, hiding behind their parents. There is no laughter. A spirit of oppression and fear is tangible.

As the reality of a new life, secure from the violence and deprivation of the past, begins to take hold on the families, the most noticeable difference is in the children. They come running and shouting to greet you when you arrive on a visit.[2] For the duration of your time in the village you are likely to have one child at each side, their small hands in yours, and several others in front and back so that you walk together in a swarm.

Early one morning in 2000, on the balcony of the "Waldorf" in Cotzal, my good friend Chris Canlis thought of the previous day's activities in one of our Ixil villages, and said something I have never forgotten:

> Skip, what Agros has done in these villages is to allow children to be children again.

I have often pondered Chris' remark. What an enormous tragedy it is when children, caught up in circumstances beyond their control or understanding, must witness or constantly be on the run from the horrors of war, or even in times of peace, must carry backbreaking loads of wood or work in the fields all day. What an enormous privilege it is, then, to have a small part in

---

[2] One of the great and unforgettable joys of my lifetime, is the shouts of "Esquip, Esquip" ("Eskeep") from children who see me emerging from a vehicle that has just arrived at their village. As they swarm around me my introvert nature falls away and I become, for those moments, a completely different person. This seldom happens anymore, because with the number of villages and countries today, I no longer return for multiple visits to the same two or three villages in the same country.

bringing tangible evidence of God's mercy and love to those who have suffered so greatly, so that men and women can regain their dignity, and children can indeed be children again.

11

ESSENTIALS

Organizations change over the years. Without change they become like clogged arteries in humans – arteries that calcify and fail to transport lifeblood to and from the heart. Yet even in the sometimes difficult and complex process of change, the best of organizations retain their distinctives and stay true to them. They hold on to fundamentals that gave them their reason for being in the first place, drew others to the cause, and fashioned an identity that separated them from the pack.

Here are what I consider eight essentials that have made up the heart and soul of Agros over the years. These are my distinctly personal views and they are stated as principles, not as inviolable law. Principles do not prescribe specific action; they invite thoughtful application. I have full confidence in the collective wisdom of present and future Agros board and staff to stay true to these principles yet bring needed change for the better.

1. Jesus

We take seriously Jesus' call to love and care for the poor. Our focus on following Jesus is not a summons to religiosity. Rather, it is a call to remember that Jesus' work of forgiveness and redemption opened the door for us to show redemptive love to others, and in particular to the poor. In this process we welcome all, regardless of faith, to join in the work. We do not make faith a prerequisite for the people we serve.

We do not proselytize because that is not our calling. On the other hand we recognize that Jesus' teaching on money, responsibility, generosity, and human relationships contains invaluable wisdom that we hope to pass on to Agros villagers. That need not be done in a proselytizing context.

The world of Christian faith is a vast one. Doctrines, creeds, catechisms and practice abound on a broad spectrum. One group's orthodoxy may be another group's heresy. The mission of Agros does not include defining the boundaries of orthodox faith, doctrine and practice. We have a straightforward calling to help the rural poor break their generational cycles of poverty through land ownership. Biblical justification for our work is plentiful; Jesus began and ended his ministry on earth speaking about the poor. We should not waste our time defending our calling or being defensive about why this calling does not include what others believe ought to be encompassed in our mission.

We have lost support within segments of the Christian community for not proclaiming the gospel of Jesus Christ overtly. Our website and promotional materials are regarded in some quarters as too secular. It is not an easy task to maintain an appropriate equilibrium between proudly stating our faith heritage and motivations while inviting men and women of good will to join us in the effort regardless of their faith. The Agros board and staff have spent a good amount of time and effort in coming up with a written Christian identity statement that reflects that equilibrium. As hard as we labored the finished product has never been quite satisfactory to one group or another.

As secular as some may regard our written description of Agros and its work, there is another segment that is repelled by any notion of Christian faith underlying our work. I once met with the CEO of a well-known philanthropic organization in

New York City. Our meeting was suggested and facilitated by someone who was a major donor to both that organization and to Agros. The chill I felt as I entered the CEO's office was palpable and had nothing to do with the winter weather outside. Once the handshake and usual courtesies were dispensed with he immediately bore in on Agros' Christian identity, utterly convinced that Agros only helped the poor in order to evangelize them. He made it very clear he felt that was highly unethical and outright devious. Nothing I said moved him from his entrenched predisposition. He had pronounced judgment before I ever walked into the room. Needless to say the meeting was not a long one.

2. Land Ownership

Non-governmental organizations abound whose mission is to serve the poor. Agros is the only one we know of that focuses on land ownership – acquired in a private, market transaction – to break the cycle of poverty for the rural poor.

I learned in my early trips to Guatemala in 1982 and 1983 that a poor farmer will never feel secure or self-sufficient unless the title to the land is in his own name, or he is in the process of paying for the land and will acquire title in the foreseeable future. The relationship of a farmer to the land is deeply rooted in centuries of tradition and culture. In certain parts of the world, including some tribal cultures of Africa, individual land ownership may be disdained in favor of tribal or communal ownership. But in Latin America individual ownership is the paramount goal.

In 2009 I participated in a land title ceremony at the Agros village of La Bendición in Guatemala. The first on the list of recipients that day was an elderly widow about 4'8" in height.

She came up to the stage where I presented her with her title deed. To my surprise she refused to accept it. Instead, she looked me straight in the eyes and, with a stern countenance, said something to me in her Ixil dialect. The village president translated for me:

Pres: *Don Esquip, ella le pide leerlo.* (Mr. Skip, she wants you to read it.)

Me: *¿Entero?* (The whole thing?)

Pres: *Si, favor leerlo entero.* (Yes, please read the whole thing.)

Anyone who has seen a Guatemalan title deed will understand the daunting task I faced. In the U.S., the equivalent statutory warranty deed is one printed page with two or three paragraphs of print. Sometimes the deed may go to two pages if there are unusual conditions or exceptions placed on the deed. In Guatemala, title deeds are four to five legal-sized pages of densely packed, single-spaced print containing what can only be described as the most flowery and redundant legalese one would ever want to read. The land is described in minute geographical detail and in metes and bounds, which takes up almost an entire page. Then there is a recited history of the land, detailed descriptions of the grantor (in this case Fundación Agros) and the legal status and domicile of the grantor, the name, title, gender, and domicile of the person signing on behalf of the grantor, then another detailed description of the grantee, the grantee's date of birth, place of birth, gender, marital status, and current domicile.

It must have taken me close to 15 minutes to read the title deed from first to last printed word. I did not want to rush the reading, believing that would be disrespectful. At several points the widow's full name was referred to, and out of the corner of my eye I noticed how she perked up every time I read it. I also noticed that while I read her deed all the villagers gathered there listened as intently as if I had been reading a holy proclamation from God. When I finally finished reading, I looked at the elderly *doña* and saw a smile come over her face. When I again presented to her the title deed, she accepted it with both hands, her face glowing.

That experience reinforced in me the awareness of the deep and almost spiritual relationship of the Ixil Indian to land. Land holds such a unique place in the psyche of the people that the title deed I read that day might as well have been sacred scripture. For the Ixil Indian, so deep is the distrust developed over centuries of abuse and oppression by the *ladino* that this widow would not believe the deed I presented to her really gave her ownership of her land unless I read every word on the deed, and those of her fellow villagers who understood Spanish confirmed for her that the deed really did confer title to the land in her name, and her name alone.

What if the document I read that day had been a lease? Or some form of permit or license to use the land for a defined period of time granted to her and the other villagers by the government of Guatemala or even by Agros? Would she and the other villagers have regarded the occasion with such reverential solemnity? The answer, to me, is painfully obvious. I suspect they would have listened to the reading with disdain and silent contempt if they had bothered to be there at all.

My most recent experiences only confirm this conviction. In January 2012 three of my law partners and a fellow Agros board member joined me in visiting the village of San José in the Matagalpa region of Nicaragua. This was an exploratory trip for our law firm to decide whether to commit to the "back-end" funding of this village of 28 families. The village was started in 2007 with funding provided by donor Carlene Gaudette on a five-year pledge. Now those five years had passed, her pledge had been fulfilled, and Agros staff was looking for other donors to help the villagers in the final stages as they came nearer to paying off their loans.

At a welcoming ceremony in the community building at San José that doubles as the school, the villagers told us about their progress on all fronts – agricultural and human development. One young villager, Mauricio, spoke for the entire village in explaining the progress of their productive projects in coffee, tomatoes, peppers, and other vegetables and fruits. Throughout his 10-minute presentation he repeatedly talked about approaching the final goal – paying off his loan so he could receive title to the land. He knew he was getting close to achieving his greatest dream in life – to become the *dueño* of his own land. He must have repeated this in almost the same words each time at least eight times in his short presentation. My partners, as they listened to the English translation of Mauricio's presentation, noticed it too and commented on that aspect of his talk.

I had visited San José in March 2011 with Carlene Gaudette, her husband and son, and other visitors from the Seattle area. We heard similar presentations from the villagers on their progress and heard of their growing pride in their achievements. In my memory, we did not hear any mention of getting their title deeds, much less anything resembling Mauricio's urgent cry for finishing strong and getting the title deed as my partners and I heard in January 2012. In the intervening 10 months the people of San José had progressed significantly enough to see the finish line. They were driving themselves hard down the stretch, eyes intent on the goal. The first five years had taken hard work – really hard work. They were in no mood to slacken their efforts now.

What would Mauricio have told us about the finish line, the final sprint to the tape, if the end result had not been ownership of his land? Would he have talked as passionately about renewing a lease, or getting another five or 10 years of leased rights to the land?

The San José villagers had in fact tried their hand at working on land cooperatively owned in the early days of the project. Agros staff had laid out parcels of individually farmed land and collectively farmed land. The thought was that certain crops would be farmed by all villagers and the financial returns would be shared equally. Nicaragua staffer Oscar Escoto shared this bit of history with me as we were touring the San José fields. He talked about the cooperative project as having been a complete failure. There was no consistency of effort from the families in doing the work on the cooperative land. It even created division among the people as those who worked their fair share resented those they viewed as slackers. Agros staff finally decided to terminate the cooperative project and divided up the land and distributed the parcels to the individual families. Not long after that was done the land began to yield wonderful harvests as each family worked hard to make the land productive.

In my remarks to the villagers at the gathering I spoke directly to Mauricio's passion about paying off his loan and getting his title. I encouraged him – and all the villagers – to continue their hard work because indeed they were nearing their cherished goal. I told them about Don Pedro in Futuro del Mañana and how he managed to pay off his loan in seven years, becoming the first Agros villager in the country of Nicaragua to receive his land title. I told them that in the five years since Don Pedro got his title, all the other villagers from Futuro had also received their titles. I assured them Agros would not abandon them in this quest and that we would walk alongside them until they had also achieved their dreams of receiving their land titles.

Mauricio was not the only one at San José who talked about getting the title deed. As we walked around and looked at a beautifully tended field of tomatoes that he had planted just eight days earlier, "Concho" spoke of the same dream. Three more strong cycles of tomato harvests would earn him enough to pay off his land completely. He knew about one man in El Edén who had already done so in the same way. Then we heard the same theme from one of the 10 women who participated in the village's hen project. One of my partners asked if her family now ate eggs and chicken meat as part of their diet. She seemed taken aback by the question and said that while her family did eat eggs every so often, her reason for working hard on raising her flock of chickens was not to produce eggs and chickens for their own consumption, but to sell the eggs and chickens to earn enough money to help her husband pay off the loan on the land.

In these times many grant-giving foundations and major donors look for NGOs that can "scale" their work to reach maximum beneficiaries per dollar spent. Thus the microfinance model has proliferated all over the developing world, and billions of dollars have poured into microfinance entities. The notion that a $50 loan can jump-start a poor family's dormant economic engine has been wildly popular. The movement has slowed down a bit, having encountered some speed bumps along the way created by the controversy over profit-seeking opportunists entering the field.

The Agros model based on land ownership by the poor may never scale in ways that other models of helping the poor might. Any model to address rural poverty that involves land ownership will always mean much higher cost per beneficiary and far more administrative and developmental complexity in executing the model. Other forms of land rights may be palatable to the rural poor in some parts of the world as an acceptable alternative to land ownership, but my experience tells me it will not work in Latin America or anywhere in the developing world where the rural poor harbor deep distrust of governments and the wealthy classes. Why should they trust the corrupt and dishonest who have taken away their land and enslaved them in a permanent state of poverty?

At the risk of foreclosing our opportunity to receive major grants from donors who place a premium on cost and efficiency, I believe Agros must not deviate from its focus on land and land ownership. That does not mean Agros should not be concerned about reducing costs where feasible or doing things efficiently and according to best business practices in the nonprofit world. Neither does it negate the work we have done in Mexico that has not required purchase of land. But if we were to lose our distinctive of helping the rural poor own their own farmland, we would lose our reason for existence.

3. Repayment

Closely tied to land ownership is the notion that the land must not be given to our Agros villagers gratis, as a handout. They must share a portion of the financial burden to acquire the land and the development process in bringing families together to build a healthy agricultural community.

Early on we realized it would be unrealistic to expect repayment of 100% of the costs of a village – land and all human and community development programs included. At some point we settled on a target for repayment of capital costs – land, housing, and irrigation systems. The precise items to be included in repayment are not critical and may vary from country to country, and even village to village. Nor do I regard 100% repayment of land costs or capital costs to be essential. The important principle here is that the villagers repay an amount that is significant – not token – that requires focused effort and hard work on their part.

The idea of a complete giveaway so that villagers are required to pay nothing back to Agros goes directly against the fundamental value of helping the poor regain their human dignity. Dignity does not come through handouts but by achieving something as significant as land ownership by the sweat of their labor. For the rural poor I have time and again observed first-hand how hard they are willing to work when given the opportunity to attain a worthwhile goal. For many generations their backbreaking toil has benefitted themselves minimally and their *patrón* maximally. The Agros model offers them a chance to convert their labor into ownership for themselves and their families.

I have also seen first hand how a man or woman's work ethic can be destroyed by a culture of giveaway, giving rise to the expectation of receiving something for nothing – a sense of entitlement at its worst. We have a strict rule in Agros that visitors to an Agros village – whether on service teams or vision teams – are not to give anything to villagers or even children other than items such as school supplies for the children or an occasional soccer ball for the village. When this rule has not been followed, the next time a group of visitors arrive, they will be beset by requests for gifts. Thus I have had children ask me for the watch off my wrist or the sunglasses off my face. Grown men have asked me for money. In one particularly troublesome instant an entire village asked that their land loans be forgiven – they had heard that another Agros village had the land given to them, and they were resentful that they were being required to pay for their land. They had, of course, been given bad information. But however that information had come to them it made for a difficult task to turn their thinking around so that they could accept the idea of repayment again.

Our experience with repayment has been spotty – we have many instances of delinquencies in scheduled payments. We constantly work to improve the repayment statistics, but no one should be surprised by higher delinquency rates than what a commercial lending institution in the U.S. would expect. Our land loans can amount to several thousand dollars; these are not microloans to be repaid in a year's time. For people who have never had access to credit, the decision to join an Agros village is a major step of faith and courage. We see many drop away who find the required loan repayment far too daunting a challenge.

Repayment rates are also adversely affected by drought (an all too often occurrence), pestilence, and natural disasters. The effects of a hurricane (think Mitch in 1998) can be devastating and can set back our Agros villagers not only for the current year, but for the ensuing year as well. Certainly there are villagers who have no other excuse than mismanagement of their income and poor decision-making that results in delinquency. We should look for best practices to deal with those situations.

In every Agros village we seem to find a handful of families who, regardless of circumstances, are able to come up with payments on time – or even ahead of time in some cases. They are motivated by the goal of attaining that title deed and do not allow anything – hurricanes and drought included – to stand in their way. We have to find ways to improve repayment rates by all villagers. At the same time, I believe that any repayment is better than none, and even a late payment is a remarkable turnaround for a family that has never been able to borrow money before and has never had any expectation of income that they could plan for or manage. Part of rising out of the depths of poverty is learning to deal with what money you have on hand or can anticipate, and setting aside the needed amounts to repay debt.

4. Private Initiative

When Juan Carlos Ortíz's message took me by storm in February 1982, I was resolved to see what we as individuals could do to bring about private land reform without resorting to governments or government money. I knew instinctively this called for my personal response as well – meaning that my own time and money had to be on the line. Two strong impulses undergirded the conviction to do things privately and personally: (1) the inability of governments in so many developing countries to enact meaningful land reform because of corruption and bureaucratic incompetence and inefficiency; and (2) the belief that we as individuals, particularly those of us who take Jesus' teaching seriously, have a biblical responsibility to help the widow, orphan, alien, and the poor. Too often we shirk that responsibility and instead expect governments to do what we are called on to do ourselves. Up to that time, other than the effort to help the ethnic Chinese Cambodian refugees in the Thai camps, I had no personal encounter with the poor. I realized that needed to change.

Early on I found myself willing to compromise this principle given the open door we had to collaborating with the Guatemalan government during the Ríos Montt presidency. I was enchanted by the notion that we could cut through red tape and corruption with a sympathetic government as our partner. In the U.S. there are countless examples of successful public-private joint ventures, particularly in the renewing development of blighted urban areas. But Guatemala in 1983 was a far cry from say, the City of Seattle, where glittering examples of such partnerships have borne rich fruit to sweeten the lives of those of us who live in the Pacific Northwest. The coup and the political consequences of Ríos Montt's ouster in September 1983 cured me of any inclination to seek governments as partners in the work. In the intervening years we have steered clear of the governments in the countries we work in.

In 2009, Agros International[1] did receive an award of $250,000 from the World Bank. They had singled out Agros as

---

[1] We changed the name of the Agros Foundation to Agros International in 2004.

one of a handful of NGOs having an effective model of combating the causes of global poverty. But other than that award from a quasi-governmental organization, we have not received any government funding.

In 2011 Agros International was invited by USAID to submit a grant proposal for $2 million for projects in Guatemala. The staff recommended to the board that Agros apply for the grant – the first time the organization would be asking for funding from USAID. The invitation came to us in July and we were required to submit our grant proposal within a period of two to three weeks. I suspect USAID was coming to the close of its fiscal year and wanted to expend funds that still remained in their coffers so the money would not revert to the U.S. Treasury. After much thoughtful discussion the board voted to proceed with the grant proposal. After expending considerable staff energy to prepare a thorough grant proposal, Agros was informed that our proposal had been denied.

I confess to being relieved. I have written earlier about USAID's very negative reputation in the 1980s. Not only was USAID ineffective in its expenditures of large sums of U.S. foreign aid money, but during that era the agency was viewed as an instrument of U.S. foreign policy. Getting money from USAID in those days tainted an organization with a highly undesirable political association. In Central America back then, few people made any distinction between USAID and the CIA.

Perhaps today there is less stigma in accepting USAID money. Certainly there are no more guerrilla wars in Central America and Mexico or old cold war animosities and prejudices. Nevertheless in these countries there still lingers a deeply rooted anti-American sentiment aimed more at the U.S. government and its foreign policy than at American citizens individually. USAID is still regarded as tied inextricably to U.S. foreign policy. How can it be viewed otherwise when it is organizationally joined to the hip with the State Department?

USAID today has an improved reputation abroad, but there are still detractors who do not believe the agency is either smart or effective in its deployment of millions of American taxpayer money to foreign countries. To its credit, USAID recognizes its own limitations and has increasingly funded humanitarian and development projects through NGO channels.

One thing about USAID has not changed from the 1980s: getting involved with their money still means stepping into a quagmire of red tape and bureaucracy with endless forms to fill out and reports to write.

I recognize there is no biblical prohibition against using government money to help the poor. I confess that in my theology, governments will stand to account before God for their treatment of the widow, orphan, alien, and the poor.

I wonder though, if we should apply for and succeed in obtaining major USAID funding, how will that success affect our donors' perceptions of Agros? Will donors think that USAID money obviates the need for them to give generously as they have in the past, or for them to be personally involved with the rural poor we serve?

To what extent will Agros lose its soul in getting USAID money? I have never heard of an NGO settling for just one grant. The common pattern is for organizations to become increasingly dependent on the large infusions of USAID cash so that the proportion of funds from private donors diminishes as the NGO earns its place at the USAID trough.

5. Loving the Poor

At Agros we talk of loving the poor. I use that phrase myself in conversations. I do so deliberately to distinguish this core value from a major theme heard today across the world – solving global poverty. Governments, politicians, major charitable foundations, rock stars and celebrities of all stripes have jumped on the bandwagon to do away with global poverty. Debt relief and other grand ideas are advanced as rational solutions.

I do not speak against such efforts and am heartened that global poverty is a subject on the front pages of newspapers rather than on the back pages, or ignored altogether. But there lies a great chasm between looking on the poor as a global problem to solve and looking on the poor by loving one poor family (or group of families) at a time.

Global poverty as a concept is so overwhelmingly daunting that an individual may feel helpless to participate personally in the solution. We can easily fall into the mode of thinking that big governments and big people (think Bono and Bill Gates) will take care of the problem, usually by throwing enormous amounts of money at it, and therefore there is nothing a person can do individually, except maybe participate in a rally or two advocating global debt relief. My concern is that the activist caught up in solving the problem of global poverty over a lifetime may forget to help the poor today. Solving global poverty may sometimes resemble comforting a crying newborn babe with all the best of tender care and singing, but ignoring its immediate need: to be fed, and fed right now.

At Agros we do not have enormous amounts of money to tackle global poverty, but we can mobilize individuals and groups of individuals to love the poor by helping a village-full of families turn their lives around and break the cycle of poverty that they and their forebears have endured. We can anticipate with fair certainty that this will happen within 10 years of the startup of a new Agros village.

The Agros way of loving the poor means, additionally, taking the time to build a relationship with them. Our language overuses the term "relationship" today so that it can mean very different things to different people. As we apply the term at Agros, trust is a huge component of relationship. Trust means doing what you say you will do and being good to your word. The rural poor in Central America have suffered through 400 years of lies and broken promises. A relationship without trust is meaningless. A relationship built on trust can blossom into friendship.

If there is a "secret sauce" to Agros' work, it is this. If we were to look at the poor as a problem to solve, we would look for the most cost effective and quickest way to a solution. The Agros model will never be known for low costs per beneficiary and quick results. When a man or woman has known nothing but abject poverty for a lifetime it is not money or even a title deed alone that will lift that person out of poverty and overcome the mindset that goes with poverty and oppression. The human spirit itself must be lifted up and encouraged – and that takes time.

I love French provincial cuisine and have dabbled in it over the years. At the heart of great French cuisine is the right sauce. Some elite restaurants may claim to have a secret sauce, but most recipes for great sauces are well known. The best sauces are a labor of love. To prepare a proper beef bourguignon is really a two-day affair – shopping for fresh ingredients on one day and doing the preparation and actual cooking on the next. The rich blend of herbs, spices, roué, broth, and wine that makes up the bourguignon sauce develops slowly, over a period of hours over the stove. There is no microwave shortcut.

Developing friendships with the rural poor in Central America, like the best French sauces, takes time and patience. I am not a culinary expert so I cannot explain to you how those separate ingredients slowly cooked over hours break down as individual elements to make up the delicious smelling and tasting whole that makes up a beef bourguignon sauce.

Nor am I a psychologist so I cannot explain why our efforts on behalf of the poor take on such greater effect when we become friends with the poor; when we recognize them by name, and they do the same when they see us; when the relationships stretch over years of visits, conversations, laughs, and labor.

The early years in Guatemala were my schooling on building trust in relationships, in particular with Alfred Kaltschmitt and the Elliotts. My first trip raised their interest, curiosity, and no little skepticism. My second trip two months later told them this Chinese guy from Seattle might be serious after all. My third trip shortly afterwards erased their doubts, and friendships began to take root. Subsequent trips nurtured the friendship into full bloom.

The rural poor in Central America have seen and met "poverty tourists" as described in an earlier chapter – short-term visitors who travel to the rural areas for a few days, who then leave and are never heard from again.

Our Agros villagers have a finely tuned sense of skepticism when they first meet a group from the U.S. They wonder if these people are just another set of gawkers and well-wishers. In their poverty they do not meet people genuinely interested in who they are or what they have to say. When I visit a new village for the first time, a few of the men will generally ask me (just before I leave) when I am coming back to see them again. Even as I tell them I will be back in the near future or pin down a time period of 12 months, for example, I can see in their eyes they don't really believe me. Their skepticism is a defense mechanism developed over generations of disappointments and broken promises from people like me. It is only when I make good on my promise and greet them on my return that the smiles appear on their faces, their eyes take on a softer look, and their handshake or *abrazo* is no longer a token gesture. By the third visit, we are friends.

This is why Agros has tried to pair a particular church, a group of families, or a company with one village in a relationship that will stretch out over at least five years, sometimes longer. As the supporting group sends service teams to the village once or twice each year, year after year, the villagers come to know that these people from North America mean what they say and do what they say.

Friendship with our Agros villagers, I have found, must be a two-way street. It is not just our caring for them; it must flow the other way as well. This is a lesson that I experienced through an extraordinary event that happened on a visit in November 2001 to the Agros village San Diego Tenango in El Salvador.

When we first reached the village we saw that the whole community, young and old, had gathered to greet us, and I anticipated a typically heartfelt welcome. But this welcoming ceremony took a very different turn. Immediately we were asked about the events of 9/11, and our hosts expressed how horrified they were when they first heard the news and how they had prayed for the U.S. and for all their Agros friends in the U.S.

They gathered around us, and the village elder proceeded to lead everyone in 10 minutes of the most intense and heartfelt prayer I have ever experienced. They cried out to God, expressing sorrow over those who had died in the 9/11 attacks and imploring His mercy and protection over the American people and the 10 visitors who had just arrived.

The people of San Diego Tenango had suffered more than we could imagine from the long civil war in El Salvador. A number of them had lost family members in that war. They had all been displaced by the intense fighting and had fled as refugees to Honduras. The village church bell was made out of an emptied artillery shell, a grim reminder of the violence they had experienced for 12 long years.

I wondered at how those who had suffered so directly and for so long from political violence could pour out such compassion and kindness on us. None of the visitors had lost any family or friends in the 9/11 attacks.

That day I came to understand more clearly than ever that part of being human and living with dignity is caring for and giving to others. When we first work with the poor we might mistakenly think they have nothing to give to us. But these years of interacting with our villagers have made me marvel at how God has particularly gifted the poor with extraordinary generosity, both materially and spiritually. The more they have suffered, it seems, the more they are able to give freely of their possessions and of their love and concern.

Many of us can recall being served meals by Agros villagers with meat, potatoes, and vegetables – veritable feasts compared to their own meager fare of corn and beans. Some who can hardly afford to feed and clothe their families have given us gifts – woven bags or wall hangings made by their own hands.[2]

That day in San Diego Tenango I witnessed a generosity of spirit that left me humbled and awed. I also came to understand better that giving to others is another sign of recovered humanity and restored dignity.

6. Apolitical

The mission of Agros must not be hijacked by those who, even with good intentions, seek to promote a political agenda.

The early trips in 1982 and 1983 opened my eyes to the extremely complex political maelstrom that was Guatemala. Crosscurrents flowed and ebbed from every which direction – cold war hostilities between the U.S. and USSR, historical political enmities in Guatemala, racial oppression of the

---

[2] The most meaningful gift I received from Agros villagers was a beautiful, hand-made coat presented to me by the villagers at a title ceremony in the Xetzé village in Chajul, Guatemala. Deep red in color and with intricate sewn patterns, it was made in the style of coats worn by Ixil village elders on special occasions. It resembles a sophisticated "smoking" jacket, and substitutes wonderfully for a tuxedo coat. For me, it is a priceless gift because of the history and meaning sewn into that coat.

indigenous peoples who made up 60% of the population, dozens of indigenous languages and dialects, profound economic and social injustices, religious strife, and a culture of violence. Add to the mix endemic corruption, and you had a situation where it was often difficult to sort out the good guys from the bad guys.

I cannot count the times when, back in the U.S., I was asked to speak out against U.S. foreign policy in Central America at rallies or panel discussions. People assumed that since I was concerned for the poor I must sympathize with the guerrillas in Guatemala and El Salvador, and the Sandinistas in Nicaragua. I was asked more than once by activist friends how I could remain silent when what they described as the Reagan administration's outrageous actions in Central America were supporting oppressive military regimes in Central America. My answer — that I had been called to find a way to buy land for the poor, not to advocate highly charged political issues — was unsatisfactory to those friends. I found it a futile exercise to explain to them the complexities of the political situation in Central America, and that all was not what it appeared on the surface and in the newspaper headlines. They didn't want to hear about complexities. To them it was all obviously black and white with no shades of grey at all.

Later political developments underscored the complexities. Efraín Ríos Montt, for example, dubbed by the left-leaning press as the Butcher of Central America for the alleged massacres of Guatemala Indian peoples, founded a political party (*Frente Revolucionario Guatemalteco*) after the civil war ended in 1996. He then ran for president and his party presented a slate of candidates for the Guatemalan congress. The FRG's strongest support came from the Ixil region – from the very people among whom Ríos Montt was alleged to have committed horrible massacres. I have never read any explanation in the major news sources, including the *New York Times*, for his overwhelming popularity among the Ixil Indian people. His supporters have always claimed that the press got it wrong and were more interested in advocacy for the guerrillas than in checking their facts.

I told people many times that if I ever got killed in Guatemala for doing the work of Agros, the bullet in my head might just as well have come from a guerrilla weapon as a Guatemalan army weapon. That was an even less satisfactory response for the anti-U.S. foreign policy activists.

Out of my experiences and observations from the early years came the conviction that whatever work we did, we needed to stay apolitical. No matter my personal political persuasions, this work of getting land into the hands of the poor – an explosively political action in itself in a country like Guatemala – must never get enmeshed in the confusion of the dominant political currents. We would need to work quietly and stay away from any association with either government or anti-government movements either in Guatemala or in the U.S.

Some years back the Agros board invited a guest speaker to a board retreat. Our guest strongly urged us to speak out as an organization on justice issues. He believed that it was our Christian duty to engage in political advocacy for the poor. The board politely declined. Our work in countries where the rural poor have suffered so much by way of political violence and oppression is by its very nature political. Each Agros village is a powerful political statement in itself that the poor have a right to live with honor and dignity. There is more eloquence and political meaning in a family receiving the deed to their land in one of our village title ceremonies than anything we could possibly say. The Agros work is complex enough without our getting muddled in our efforts by throwing in activist-type political involvement.

We also need to beware of allowing ourselves to use the kind of language that not so subtly places us in one political camp or another. I have gently reminded Agros staff about the need to be thoughtful about the things we write and say to others, especially with the proliferation today of social media channels.

One written communication generated by an Agros staff member told the story of one of the families in an Agros village in Guatemala. Our staff person wrote about the interview with the father, who had found an undetonated bomb which he described as a bomb "your country dropped on us" during the civil war years. He clearly meant the bomb had been dropped by the U.S. The story had a wonderfully redemptive tone to it, contrasting the poverty of life during the violent past with the family's new life lifted out of poverty with Agros' help.

But I pointed out to the staff person that while we should be grateful the family came to no harm during a violent civil war, it might have been better to omit the description of who the father thought had dropped the bomb. For one thing, there is no historical evidence the U.S. ever deployed aircraft or helicopters in the Guatemalan civil war. More importantly, the mention of U.S. culpability in the civil wars of the region during that era was an unneeded distraction from the essence of that communication: the stark contrast between the family's life before and after their involvement with Agros.

The staff person was apologetic and open to correction. On reflection, I think what she wrote about who dropped the bomb was simply a conditioned response to the news media portrayal of those years of revolutionary struggles in Central America. The U.S. was cast in a great deal of press coverage as the villain in the story and the people of Guatemala, including our village family, as the hapless victims. Whatever the truth of U.S. involvement, that particular bit of history came off as an unneeded political jab.

On another occasion a key Agros staff person posted on his Facebook wall a link to a UK tabloid newspaper article ridiculing the Republican party in the U.S. as being made up of mindless, ignorant, and bigoted masses. I knew this staff person to be a particularly thoughtful and deep-thinking type. I also knew he was decidedly liberal and Democratic in his politics. I pointed out to him that his posting was unrepresentative of him as a thinking person, and the article represented the worst of journalism today in its blatant stereotyping. I pointed out how his Facebook post could potentially damage Agros donor relations because of his visibility in the organization. I am sure a representative sampling of our donor base would have disclosed at least as many inclined to support Republicans as Democrats in their political preferences. To endorse the UK news piece and its particularly ugly portrait of all Republicans was an insult, even if unintended, to a good portion of our donor base, regardless of whether those donors saw the posting on Facebook or not. To his credit the staff person not only deleted the post, but explained why he deleted it.

I have no quarrel with active involvement by Agros staff in politics, liberal or conservative. I do not believe they must leave their politics at the door when they go to work. But the world of social media is not a private world, and even the loss of a $10 donor for the wrong reason is a shame and detracts from our service to the poor.

This is where we must remind ourselves of our central value of following in the footsteps of Jesus. Regardless of claims otherwise, Jesus will never and can never be put into a box labeled with one brand of political belief or other. Agros should not be put in that box, either.

7. Unconventional thinking

Call it pride, call it snobbishness, call it stupidity. I have a streak in me that strongly reacts against going with the crowd. Even if that large mass of very good people were headed in the exact correct direction, I'd rather find out for myself what the right direction was even if it meant bumping my head into walls and trees and other obstacles in my chosen path. This can mean something as trivial as refusing to speak current jargon and lingo. More substantively, this aversion to bandwagons translates into the way we think about Agros, describe Agros, and how we do our work.

Conventional thinking would have steered us away from our focus on land and land ownership. It is far too complex and so much more costly to concentrate on land ownership. Conventional thinking would have kept us out of the Ixil Triangle and maybe even Guatemala in the 1980s. Surely it was far too dangerous and risky to venture into the heart of where the civil war violence was at its most intense. Why not help the poor near the more populated cities or on the coast? Why not start in Costa Rica and Panama where there are no civil wars raging? Aren't there plenty of poor people in countries around the world where there aren't bullets flying and mortar shells being lobbed between armies and guerrillas?

The Agros DNA from its earliest days took on far more than its share of risk-taking characteristics. I do not speak of wanton disregard for safety or deliberate invitation of unknown perils. In deciding to start working in the Ixcán, soon followed by the Ixil Triangle, regions in Guatemala where the war and violence were most intense, we did so based on the knowledge that these were also the areas of greatest need. These were also regions other NGOs bypassed because of the risks. And how could I forget my encounter with the story of Jeremiah buying land from his cousin on the eve of Jerusalem's devastation by Nebuchadnezzar's armies? That bit of inspiration chased from my mind any thought that Agros must operate on conventional wisdom and spilled over into other aspects of my life and work as well.

Conventional wisdom would have steered us in the early days of Agros into a public relations campaign to maximize our exposure through news stories, arranged interviews, direct mail, and speaking engagements. We had plenty of proposals from public relations and marketing consultants that proposed that kind of strategy. How about benefit concerts with headliner artists? We've got a great press strategy for you, Skip. Within a year the world will know about Agros.

That approach was out of the question to me. It would have been imprudent and wholly lacking in wisdom during our early days to go in that direction. For one thing, we were still in the pilot stages and I'm not sure we knew what we were doing yet, or that we had a business and operational model that actually worked. For another, we would have been casting a bright light on our efforts and inviting not just donor attention, but also the notice of the wrong crowd linked to bad guys on either side in the conflict in Guatemala.

In my gut there was also this nagging feeling that the "see what great work we're doing" approach inherently conflicted with Jesus' admonitions about publicly proclaiming our supposed good works and righteousness. To this day I describe Agros' public relations effort as more of a word-of-mouth, friend-telling-friend type of approach – relationship fundraising. Like our work model it takes far more time and effort. Our donor base is very small when you consider how long we've been around. But our work has generated significant passion and commitment among our donors. This is particularly true of donors who have visited an Agros village and seen the people and their lives. The work and the changed lives of the people speak for themselves far more persuasively than any promotional campaign.

It was pointed out to me recently that listing unconventional thinking as an Agros essential presents a contradiction in terms. How can someone think unconventionally when constrained by the boundaries of "essentials" prescribed by someone else? Does not a list of essentials establish and define a prevailing convention from which one must not deviate? Valid question, but the answer is to remind again that these are principles, not laws. There is ample room for unconventional thinking in applying the principles I suggest as constituting the heart and soul of Agros.

8. Volunteer spirit

The great joy I have heard expressed by many Agros supporters is that they have a direct connection to the poor and have developed friendships with people in the village they support. These have come about through countless service team trips, when women and men work side by side with Agros villagers. They might dig trenches to lay water lines, carry cinder blocks for building homes from where the truck dumps them to the home sites, swing hammers and saw boards in building of homes or community structures, plant or harvest crops. Or the village ladies might teach North American women how to make tortillas or how to wind an elaborate headdress around their heads. Sometimes there are soccer games where men, women and children all join in the fray. All participants on these teams cover their own costs. Even those with little or no means to make such a trip have found employers, churches, or friends who are willing to help them pay their own way.

I should clarify that it does not take traveling to Central America to get caught up in the volunteer spirit of helping Agros and the people we serve. Many of our ardent supporters, whether for personal or financial reasons, have never made any trips. Their support is just as essential to Agros as the support from those who are able to travel there.

At our headquarter offices in Seattle, people like Joan Selvig and Kathy Riper have given new meaning to the word "volunteer." There is no work too menial for these helping angels. At fundraising events such as our annual Tierras de Vida dinners, volunteers swarm over the premises getting everything ready and doing the little, often unnoticed things that help to make the experience memorable for attending guests. The event itself is the tip of the iceberg – think of all the hours spent during a year of planning and preparing.

Over the years, board members have devoted countless hours to committee and board meetings and conference calls – even stepping in to fill a role vacated by a departing staff person. They have joined in trips to our five countries on service teams and accompanied friends and potential donors on vision trips. Board service comes with the understanding that all expenses incurred in such travel come out of their own pockets so that those dollars are not taken away from supporting the families in the villages.

The spirit of volunteerism is strong at Agros. The value of volunteers' service and encouragement cannot be measured in dollar amounts, but anyone who understands Agros knows the incalculable contribution they make. We cannot afford to lose that spirit. As Agros grows, staff is inevitably hired to cover specific areas of responsibility and greater professionalism is needed throughout the organization. Sometimes this results in volunteers being squeezed out of the picture. That would be a sad day for Agros. So much of the vibrancy of the organization emanates from the women and men for whom involvement with Agros has worked itself into the fabric of their lives. They care deeply about the people Agros serves and do not hesitate to give of their time or money for those people.

As of this writing Agros has about 100 professional staff people employed in the five countries and in the U.S. There will always be plenty of room in the boat for volunteers – and oars for them to pull on.

12

AGROS TOMORROW

In meetings held in my Seattle office in 1995 the combined U.S. and Guatemala boards engaged in a process of dreaming about the future and casting a vision for what Agros might look like a quarter century later in the year 2020. We agreed that we should dare to dream big and aim far beyond what we thought was attainable. Anything short of that would not be a dream, but a goal.

At the end of that process we agreed to work toward a dream of 1,000 Agros villages by the year 2020. Considering that in 1995 we had only four villages in process, this was as close to an impossible dream as we could have come up with. And yet we wanted to believe Jesus' exhortation that with faith the size of a mustard seed we could move mountains. 1,000 villages in 25 years – that would certainly be like moving a mountain or two.

Mimi Barrueto, wife of board member Richard Barrueto, on hearing about the joint boards' dreaming exercise and final consensus, came up with a play on words in Spanish that captured our very audacious dream. The Spanish word for thousand is *mil*. Combine *mil* with Agros, and you get *milagros* – the Spanish word for miracles. 1,000 Agros villages, one thousand miracles. In addition, she pointed out that 20-20 is the standard for perfect vision. 1,000 Agros villages in year 2020. Perfect vision. Miracles. The word play was not just clever, but inspirational.

In the late 1990s we felt we had learned enough from our work in Guatemala to begin growing aggressively as an organization. We felt prepared to take on the enormous task of achieving 1,000 villages by the year 2020. There was nothing magical about the number. I do not think any one of us believed we were under any compulsion to achieve that dream, or that our inability to reach that mark by 2020 would make our work a total failure.

Around 2007, after almost nine years of aggressive growth, going from about $400,000 in annual revenues to over $4 million, the Agros board agreed we should stop talking about the 1,000 villages dream. We were finding out the difficulties and challenges in working with the very poor and realized that being driven by a specific number of villages would not do justice to the relationship-heavy model of creating new communities and helping break the cycle of poverty.

At the same time we still felt confident in the Agros model and desired that the model could be taken to new countries and new continents – South America, India, and Africa in particular. By this time we were receiving regular invitations from a number of countries pleading with us to take the model to this country or that, and promising help on the ground if we did. Thus in 2006 we settled on an expansion model to take Agros around the world that relied not on building the Agros organization worldwide, but by giving the model away to other like-minded NGOs in partnership with us.

It took us years in each of our five countries to develop the relationships necessary to begin an Agros village and to build the national staff and infrastructure to sustain in-country operations. How long would it take to try to build a new organization in India or in African countries like Uganda, Burundi, Rwanda? Going from Guatemala to El Salvador and Nicaragua was not a huge cultural reach. Language and culture, after all, did not differ significantly from country to country in Central America. But the Asian subcontinent and Africa? How much time and money would it take?

The answer came easily: far too much money and more time than we could imagine even with our most optimistic projections for financial and organizational growth. What if, we asked ourselves, we were to find like-minded NGOs already established with their own organizations and networks of people in India or Africa, and offer to give them the model, along with technical assistance to start new villages? We might even help them raise the funds to buy the land. There was already a precedent of sorts for doing this: Agros' first project in El Salvador was done in partnership with Habitat for Humanity. The housing component of the El Milagro village was handled by the Salvadoran branch of HFH. We relied heavily on HFH's connections and networks to get started in El Salvador. Some variation of the HFH partnership in El Salvador could be the model for the future to take Agros into countries and continents where it might otherwise have been prohibitively expensive for us to accomplish on our own.

We have considered holding a by-invitation-only symposium in Guatemala, bringing together NGOs who would be likely partners for expanding into India and Africa. We might even raise funds to finance the travel expenses of representatives of those organizations to attend the meetings. Some amount of time would be devoted to touring the Agros villages in Guatemala at various stages of development, from startup to graduation and self-sustenance. Potential pilot projects could be considered in different countries and a process developed for determining where to begin the collaboration.

Donors with particular interest in funding new Agros villages in India and Africa could also be invited to participate in the discussions of where, when and how to do the first pilot projects in different countries.

2020 seems just around the corner now. Plans for expansion have been sitting on the shelf since the recession began. As we look ahead now, having survived the worst of the downturn, those plans can be taken off the shelf, dusted off, and tweaked.

At this point, for Agros to expand into India and Africa by year 2020 would be the fulfillment of a personal dream. The 1,000-village notion might never happen. That is not what is important. To see generational poverty broken in those other parts of the world and the poorest of the poor rural farmers in those countries lifted up from their ash heaps to seats of self-sufficiency and dignity – that is a dream worth waiting for.

Who knows? Perhaps some day I might stand at that same airline counter in Guatemala City again and have that same conversation I had almost 30 years ago with the airline agent.

Agent: Mr. Li, this is very interesting.
Me: Why so?
Agent: Because you just handed me an American passport that says you were born in India. You're talking to me in Spanish, but you look Chinese. What are you, really?

I imagine myself in that conversation actually taking the time to give a real answer, not just a flippant or clever retort:

What am I? You cannot imagine how hard it is for me to answer that question.

All my life I have felt like I did not quite belong. Born in India, but I would never be at home there. Chinese, but I'm far too westernized – too much a "foreigner" in my thinking – to belong among real Chinese. I speak Spanish, and like to imagine I have Latin blood in me, but let's face it, they see me as *chinito*, and not one of them. American passport? I got that through marrying my wife Cyd. I'll never forget how the immigration examiner did everything he could to trip me up in my citizenship test. He really didn't want me to pass. So I am American, and yet I'm not.

I sometimes feel like a man who goes to see a stage play on Broadway, and five minutes before curtain time he's summoned backstage by the director and told to take the lead role in the play. "No," I protest. "I'm not an actor, I don't know the lines, and there are so many really good actors in the audience. Ask them please." But the director insists and tells me something I can hardly believe: "Go on. Don't worry. Just follow my cues from the wings." I go out on the stage and discover the director is right.

But there is not a moment during the entire production when I don't feel like an impostor up on that stage.

Let me put it another way. I sometimes imagine that I have been invited to go look at a large, wall-size tapestry – a tapestry being woven to tell the story of my life. When I first enter the studio all I see is a confused image of utter chaos. Strands of fabric long and short come out of nowhere and proceed in no apparent logical pattern. Colors jar my senses by their visual dissonance. Threads crisscross here and there. The woven sum of this random mess amounts to nothing but nonsensical patterns. I wonder if this confused jumble is really a representation of my life.

And then I think to myself, "Well, yes." That confused jumble is how I have often felt during my life. But my goodness, does the weaver have to be so brutally honest about the mess I've made?

But then the weaver takes my hand and leads me to look at the tapestry from the other side of the room. I'm stunned. I realize I had been looking at the backside of the tapestry. Here on this side confusion and chaos have been transformed into a stunning work of beauty in progress.

I think, "That's not me. The backside is a better representation, not this beauty I see. This front side must represent someone else's life, not mine." But then I look closely and I see familiar faces. My family. Close friends. Professional colleagues. Then I see something that breaks my heart – images of men, women, and children engaged in backbreaking toil in fields for long days, going to sleep at night with hunger pangs that will not go away. But the weaver directs me to look a little further at some other images. These are the same men, women, and children – and I recognize now that they are my friends from Agros villages! They look so different now. They look human. Their faces seem to brim with hope.

I can hardly look any more. It is overwhelming. Is this really my life? How could it be? How could so much blessing come to someone like me who deserved so little? I get that impostor feeling again – no, this cannot be me. The immigration examiner was right. I am a fake. I don't deserve any of this.

But one look from the weaver and I know I've got it all wrong. Again. This is not about the fake me, the arrogant 16-year old me. Or even the mature me of today. This isn't about me at all. This is about the weaver and what he has chosen to make. This is about the people he put around me, who all figure into those beautiful images.

This is his tapestry.

So that, sir, is who I am.

Others will write the story from here on. And when the weaver has finished their tapestry, may they be as overwhelmed with thanksgiving and joy as I am.

Gloria a Dios.

ACKNOWLEDGMENTS

My family. Cyd, for throwing her complete and unquestioning support behind what must have seemed like a crazy idea, and for bearing with my absence during so many trips. It seemed each time I left for Guatemala or elsewhere on this quixotic quest, something at home would go wrong and put her to the test – clogged plumbing, leaking roof, sick child or some other crisis. How do I begin to describe the difference it made when I could embark on, and for 30 years follow, this grand adventure with a real peace of mind knowing she and I were as one in the effort? My children, for loving their father even though he was gone so much as they were growing up. What a joy when each one came with me on trips, visiting the villages and seeing first hand a way of life in a different universe from theirs.

My partners at Ellis, Li & McKinstry PLLC. For understanding, accepting, and supporting the Agros dream through all these years. How many billable hours were lost to our common financial good, not only on my countless trips, but to board meetings and other time spent in the Agros cause? Or during the times when I worked so often out of the Agros office in the University District of Seattle, running the organization and handling client matters at the same time? And most recently, for their generosity in committing to fund the last portion of the needed financial support for the people in the San José village in Nicaragua to achieve their dreams of getting their land titles.

The Agros family. Board, staff, volunteers, donors, in the U.S. and in all our countries – for their tireless work and sacrificial generosity that combine to make Agros what it is today. Unsung heroes dot the Agros landscape but are woven into the Agros tapestry, their contributions ranging, among a myriad of other tasks, from swinging hammers to cleaning toilets to digging ditches; board members who have given of themselves in so many ways and made countless trips at their own expense. Particular thanks to those who have served as chairmen of the board over the years: Richard Barrueto, Joel Van Ornum, Del Wisdom, Richal Smith, Don Valencia, Kay Schroedl, Susan Moulton, and Bruce Andrews. I know the extra time and effort it took. Special thanks too are owed to Agros staff in the five countries and U.S., now headed by fellow Seattle lawyer Don Manning as the newly chosen president, for persevering and continuing to work tirelessly through budget cuts of recent years.

Alfred Kaltschmitt. A very special note of deep appreciation from *el chinito* – you have become like a true brother to me over these 30 years. What a great adventure we have shared! What stories we have to tell. I am grateful we both survived your maniacal driving during those long road trips to and from the Ixil Triangle. Your heart for the poor and your positive spirit have encouraged me immeasurably.

Our Agros villagers. What a privilege to have worked with men, women, and children in our Agros villages, beginning with the friends at Buen Samaritano in 1984. They have taught me so much over the years about hardship, suffering, faith, joy; about life. Walking with them for these years has transformed me and enriched my life beyond measure. There are many who have passed on since I first met them; there are others I have never met; still others in the villages that I have not seen for perhaps two decades. I may not remember every one of them, but they will forever be part of me and who I am. Perhaps, some day we will meet in heaven – where, as Don Raimundo taught the Ixil people, there will be no tears, no hunger, no cold, and no more suffering.

Hans and Maria Fernanda Theyer, Paul and Susan Moulton. For conspiring with Cyd to find the key to unlocking the mental inertia that had trapped this book in my brain, unwritten. Three years ago they gave me a collective kick in the pants (lovingly) that finally got me going.

My editor and readers. What an extraordinary delight to have my own son Peter Li to act as my principal editor for this book. I had a choice of editors, but in the final analysis chose Peter because of his intellectual acuity, his advanced critical reading skills, his thorough understanding of my mind and heart, and his sometimes painfully honest critique of my writing. For 10+ years when I wrote op-ed columns for the *Seattle Post-Intelligencer*, I always ran my draft column past Peter before submitting it to the *PI* editors. He never failed to point out where my writing showed arrogance or ignorance, contradiction or presumption, or just plain bad grammar. I have readers to thank as well – who took the time and effort to get through a rather rough manuscript and offer key critical insights: Cyd, Daniel Ichinaga, Chris Canlis, Jeff Vancil, Ryan Thomas and Lindsay Schuette. Don't blame Peter or any of the readers for the faults in the book. Those are mine, and mine alone.

INDEX

ABOUT THE AUTHOR

Chi-Dooh Li lives in Seattle. He and his wife Cyd have four children and four grandchildren. Nicknamed "Skip" early in his life, he is a partner in the law firm of Ellis, Li & McKinstry PLLC in downtown Seattle. His lifelong passions are backpacking in the Alpine Lakes region of Washington's Cascade Mountains, opera, baseball, soccer, great literature, and *New York Times* crossword puzzles.

Made in the USA
Lexington, KY
19 October 2012